Warren, Jarrell, and Lowell

Warren
Jarrell
&Lowell

COLLABORATION
IN THE RESHAPING
OF AMERICAN POETRY

Joan Romano Shifflett

Louisiana State University Press
Baton Rouge

Published by Louisiana State University Press
Copyright © 2020 by Louisiana State University Press
All rights reserved

Designer: Michelle A. Neustrom
Typeface: MillerText

Portions of chapter 5 first appeared, in different form, in "The Relatable Robert Lowell," *Literary Matters* 10.1 (Fall 2017), and are reprinted with permission of the editor. Portions of chapter 7 first appeared, in different form, in "'Reckoning' with America's Past: Robert Penn Warren's Later Poetry," *rWp: An Annual of Robert Penn Warren Studies,* ed. Mark D. Miller (Bowling Green, KY: The Center for Robert Penn Warren Studies and Western Kentucky University, 2012), 63–82, and are reprinted by permission of the publishers.

Library of Congress Cataloging-in-Publication Data

Names: Shifflett, Joan Romano, author.

Title: Warren, Jarrell, and Lowell : collaboration in the reshaping of American poetry / Joan Romano Shifflett.

Description: Baton Rouge : Louisiana State University Press, 2020. | Includes bibliographical references and index.

Identifiers: LCCN 2019050577 (print) | LCCN 2019050578 (ebook) | ISBN 978-0-8071-7217-9 (cloth) | ISBN 978-0-8071-7381-7 (pdf) | ISBN 978-0-8071-7382-4 (epub)

Subjects: LCSH: American poetry—20th century—History and criticism. | Warren, Robert Penn, 1905–1989—Criticism and interpretation. | Warren, Robert Penn, 1905–1989—Friends and associates. | Jarrell, Randall, 1914–1965—Criticism and interpretation. | Jarrell, Randall, 1914–1965—Friends and associates. | Lowell, Robert, 1917–1977—Criticism and interpretation. | Lowell, Robert, 1917–1977—Friends and associates.

Classification: LCC PS323.5 .S55 2020 (print) | LCC PS323.5 (ebook) | DDC 811/.5209—dc23

LC record available at https://lccn.loc.gov/2019050577

LC ebook record available at https://lccn.loc.gov/2019050578

The paper in this book meets the guidelines for permanence and durability of the Committee on Production Guidelines for Book Longevity of the Council on Library Resources. ∞

To Nathan, my Renaissance man,
and our cherished daughters, Juliana Belle and Lucia Lyn

CONTENTS

Photographs follow page 90.

PREFACE

This project, in the making for over a decade, began with a fortunate "coincidence." I recall first reading Robert Lowell's "The Quaker Graveyard in Nantucket" as a freshman in college. There was something about those lines—about that "brackish reach of shoal off Madaket"—that struck me, took hold, and then took root. In the way that all students of poetry who resign their lives to the mission of unpacking carefully rendered verse can understand, I was gripped by the pulsing muscularity of that poem, the way it tasted of (ancient) seawater in my mouth. I was equally taken by the depth and ripple effect of meaning generated by Lowell's allusions to *Moby-Dick*, to Greek myth, to the Bible. How did he fit all of this—the sounds, the textures, the layers of philosophical thought—into one poem? And, I pondered—but later, as a graduate student—how did that same man accomplish the same feat years later in a free verse poem like "Waking in the Blue"? Entirely separate from my long-lasting fascination with Lowell's verse, I similarly fell in love with Robert Penn Warren's poetry. I was set on fire by *Audubon: A Vision*, with Warren's earthy voice that rang with authenticity but also posed critical metaphysical questions about identity, time, and the power of story. It would be years until I realized that my unique appreciation for both poets was far more than a coincidence, but in the beginning, the work of these accomplished poets was enough to convince me to devote my career to examining movements and patterns in twentieth-century American poetry.

From that early love came the motivation to complete a sustained and comprehensive study of both poets, which led to my discovery that Warren and Lowell had an enormous impact on each other's work, far more than has previously been documented. Furthermore, there was a third, lesser-known poet who was equally instrumental in this sphere of influence: Randall Jarrell. Within studies of twentieth-century American literature, there is a general awareness that Warren (1905–89), Jarrell (1914–65), and Lowell (1917–77) knew one another well; some critics have even studied them in tandem. After all, Warren taught Jarrell at Vanderbilt University and Lowell at Louisiana State University in the 1930s, and Jarrell and Lowell formed a lasting friendship while studying and rooming together at Kenyon College during that decade. Though various works have explored these writers' careers within sundry contexts, no sustained examination of their relationships with one another exists. My project demonstrates how the men of this trio quickly became equals, colleagues, confidants, and invaluable lifelong critics of one another's work.

According to a common view of American literature, Warren—the former Agrarian southerner and coauthor of New Critical standards such as *Understanding Poetry* and *Understanding Fiction*—is traditionally grouped with John Crowe Ransom, Allen Tate, and Cleanth Brooks. Jarrell, somewhat forgotten and often neglected in literary matters save his criticism, does not appear to deserve a spot alongside Warren and Lowell as a major literary figure in American poetry. Lowell, the aristocratic Bostonian and "father" of the Confessional movement, seems least likely of all to be linked in literary history to Warren and Jarrell. However, there is a serious need to reconsider these limited views that preclude a full understanding of how these poets changed American poetry.

Despite the fact that these three artists enjoyed and benefited professionally from lifelong, well-documented relationships with one another, previous histories have discouraged scholars from investigating the significance of these connections. The traditional understanding of American poetry at mid-twentieth century holds that after the dominance of high modernism and the New Critical mode for thirty years, younger poets looked to figures such as William Carlos Williams and Charles Olson in order to break free from their predecessors to create what is now defined as postmodern poetry. In addition to this "breakthrough narrative," midcentury poets commonly are grouped in relation to the five major schools of contemporary verse: Black Mountain, New York School, Beat, Confessional, and Deep Image. As with most established patterns in literary history, there is utility in categorizing broad literary movements, but it is also reductive in nature. Some of America's important poets, including Elizabeth Bishop, Howard Nemerov, Karl Shapiro, Louis Simpson, and Richard Wilbur—as well as lesser-known female and multicultural writers—are excluded from these categories. More important for this book, much of the poetry that Warren, Jarrell, and Lowell were creating in the 1950s and 1960s does not align with any one of these schools. For instance, though Lowell's poetry is considered the model for Confessional poets, that label contributes to narrow and sometimes inaccurate representations of Lowell's career.

Essentially, the previously unexplored connections among these three poets, and the innovative poetry they encouraged one another to create, serve as a case study for an alternative view to the current understanding of American literary history. My methodology for this book was to focus both on literary history and aesthetics, thereby developing a historical narrative that includes close readings of primary texts within a variety of social, literary, and historical contexts. Exploring the parallel literary development of Warren, Jarrell, and Lowell through this lens offers a new understanding of the changes their poetry underwent at midcentury. Their relationships with one another served as a catalyst for a simultaneous shift in which they transcend formalism and high modernism with a new poetic mode that, while partly reflective of these traditions, draws on innovative stylistic choices to engage in an authentic exploration of selfhood within the contexts of the postmodern world. Ultimately, having closely scrutinized the personal exchanges and creative output of all three poets—while also considering current criticism on these authors, relevant historical and aesthetic issues, unpublished archival findings, and the established views of formalism, high modernism, and the New Criticism—I hope to have provided a better sense of where these authors fit into literary history and, more specifically, into the landscape of American poetry.

This project joins a host of recent critical works—including Ernest Suarez's "Writing the South," *Cambridge History of American Poetry* (2015); Natasha Trethewey's final lecture as U.S. poet laureate, "'The World of Action and Liability': On Saying What Happens" (2014); Robert H. Brinkmeyer Jr.'s *The Fourth Ghost* (2009); Adam Kirsch's *The Wounded Surgeon* (2005); Steven Gould Axelrod's "Lowell's Postmodernity" (2003); Anthony Szczesiul's *Racial Politics and Robert Penn Warren's Poetry* (2002); and Stephen Burt's *Randall Jarrell and His Age* (2002)—that fray the edges of hard-drawn boundaries that have become generally accepted truths about American literature. The inherent value of identifying significant trends and movements goes without saying; however, the purpose of this study is to suggest a need to widen and reevaluate current views of American poetry in the second half of the twentieth-century. The connections among Warren, Jarrell, and Lowell serve as just one example of significant literary relationships that have hitherto been ignored. The question is: how many more of these significant connections are currently being neglected due to the inadequate labels that classify American poets? What do these omissions say about the way literary history has been written? This book aims to more fully grasp the complexities and origins of contemporary poetry and forge a better understanding of American verse traditions.

ACKNOWLEDGMENTS

It is with immense gratitude that I acknowledge the following people for their guidance and encouragement toward the completion of this book. I would like to thank Charlotte Beck of Maryville College and Glen Johnson and Ernest Suarez at the Catholic University of America, who helped to shape this project from its earliest stages. A special thanks to Ernest, whose expertise and unwavering support was essential for the conceptualization and completion of this project, and to Anca Nemoianu, whose wise advice and unfailing sense of humor got me to this point. Thanks also to the fine scholars of the Robert Penn Warren Circle, particularly John Burt, William Bedford Clark, Victor Strandberg, Mark Miller, Jim Perkins, Randy Hendricks, Randy Runyon, Aimee Berger, Kyle Taylor, Joseph Boyne, Ryan Wilson, Noah Jampol, and Christopher Suarez. I would also like to thank the publication and editing team at Louisiana State University Press, especially James W. Long, acquisitions editor, and also the anonymous reader who read my manuscript with an attentive and insightful eye. Thanks also for the valuable assistance and the permission to reproduce photographs from the Western Kentucky University Center for Robert Penn Warren Studies, the Henry W. and Albert A. Berg Collection, and the Greenslade Special Collections and Archives at Kenyon College. Thanks, also, to *Literary Matters* and *Robert Penn Warren Studies* for the permission to reprint sections of previously published articles.

Special thanks to my support system in Annapolis, including those in the United States Naval Academy Academic Center (especially Bruce Bukowski), Writing Center, and English Department, as well as my Navy Gals, "Inner Ring," and Fairwinds Crew—particular thanks to Jack Ryan, my invaluable reading and writing buddy. Thanks also to my students, who have given me far more than I could ever give to them. I would also like to thank Victoria and Robin Ortiz, for their ever-present enthusiasm and motivation, and Marilyn, Joseph, Christian, Anastasia, Gemma, Carmella, Nina, and Rocco Romano, my pillars of love and joy. A final thanks to Nathan Shifflett—my husband, my best friend—and to our beloved daughters, Juliana and Lucia. Here's to a lifetime of supporting each other's hopes, dreams, and imaginations. Thank you.

Warren, Jarrell, and Lowell

1

Fugitive Roots &
Blossoming Friendships

Robert Penn Warren, Randall Jarrell, and Robert Lowell came from strikingly different backgrounds but were brought together by literary study. Warren was born on April 24, 1905, in Guthrie, Kentucky, to Anna Ruth Penn and Robert Franklin Warren, a teacher and bank clerk, respectively.[1] Later Warren would recall fond memories of Guthrie, with its "fine rolling farmland breaking here and there into barrens, but with nice woodlands and plenty of water, a country well adapted to the proper pursuits of boyhood" ("Self Interview" 2). In addition to recollections of target shooting and other childhood adventures with his friend Kent Greenfield, Warren also remembers "some very vile children" who bullied him for being "bookish." It is no mystery why Warren would come to love books, with a father and grandfather, Grandpa Penn, who were passionate for poetry and a mother who taught school in their own home (Blotner 18, 24, 26).

Warren's natural intelligence and love of learning allowed him to achieve academic success and ensure graduation from Guthrie High School by the spring of 1920. At this point, Warren had dreams of entering the United States Naval Academy and took an extra year at Clarksville High School as a "special student" while biding his time to fulfill the sixteen-year-old age requirement for Annapolis. One year later, having passed all necessary written and physical exams for admission, Warren received his acceptance letter to the Naval Academy. To the detriment of Warren's military officer aspirations—and the unforeseen good fortune of American letters—an accident changed Warren's fate. While playing in the yard, his younger brother hurled a "baseball-sized" chunk of unburnt coal that landed on Warren's left eye, knocking him unconscious. This incident would mar him, both physically and emotionally, for the rest of his life, and it forced him to fall back on his alternative plan to enter Vanderbilt University in 1921 (Blotner 27–30).

Born on May 6, 1914, just nine years after Warren, Randall Jackson Jarrell took a markedly different path to Vanderbilt. Jarrell's biographer William H. Pritchard notes: "Jarrell's childhood, divided between Tennessee and California . . . [is] an appropriately doubly rooted beginning for a person who throughout his life could never be identified with or understood in terms of a single locale" (11). Whereas Warren's childhood was marked by the rolling farmland of Kentucky—tales of which would often surface in his writing—Jarrell was born in Nashville, Tennessee, but moved just one year later to Los Angeles, California, with his parents, Owen and Anna Campbell Jarrell. Owen, son of a working-class family from Shelbyville, Tennessee, earned modest wages in L.A. as a photographer's assistant. Anna, daughter of a wealthy Nashville family, was accustomed to a more lavish lifestyle. Though Owen later moved the family to Long Beach to start his own portrait studio, the marriage was already strained, and a divorce was imminent.

In 1924, when Jarrell was ten years old, his parents separated, and he returned to Nashville with his mother and younger brother. After two years, Jarrell returned to California to live with his grandparents and great-grandmother in Hollywood. Once he finished school a year later, in June 1927, he was deeply saddened to return to his mother's home in Nashville, where he remained through high school and part of college. Like Warren, Jarrell's literary interests developed early in high school; he was active in journalism, the drama club, and the school's magazine. Despite his scholarly inclinations, upon graduation his mother's prosperous brother, Howell Campbell, sent Jarrell to a commercial school in Nashville in hopes that he would eventually join the ranks of Campbell's successful candy company. After one year filled with illness and discontent, in the fall of 1932, Jarrell persuaded his uncle to send him to Vanderbilt University, where Warren had recently accepted a position as assistant professor (Pritchard, *Randall Jarrell* 19–23).[2]

Robert Trail Spence Lowell IV, born March 1, 1917 in Boston, Massachusetts, has the most sensational life story and most dramatic path to Vanderbilt out of this influential literary trio. Part of New England aristocratic society, Lowell's mother, Charlotte, a Boston Winslow, was in the direct line of the *Mayflower* Winslows; her father, Arthur Winslow, was a self-made millionaire. Lowell's father, Bob Lowell, was progeny of the Somerset "Lowles," who arrived in the United States in 1639, therefore making the list of Massachusetts's first families. In addition to this prominent heritage, Lowell also had two poets in the family, James Russell and Amy Lowell. Though Lowell did not think very highly of this family legacy, naming James Russell "a poet pedestalled for oblivion" and Amy "a scandal," he later learned that these names could open doors for him ("Conversation with Hamilton" 276).

Since Bob Lowell was a career naval commander, the family moved several times during Lowell's early years. Throughout these relocations, Lowell's primary school attendance, though always at fine private schools, was interrupted. He jumped from the Brimmer School in Boston to the Potomac School in Washington, D.C., back to the Brimmer School, and then to the Rivers School in Boston for three years. In 1930, a thirteen-year-old Lowell began his studies at St. Mark's in Southborough, Massachusetts, a prestigious boarding school that his father and great-grandfather had attended. Lowell's nickname, Cal, bestowed upon him by his classmates but maintained for a lifetime, stood for Caliban and "for good measure the mad emperor, Caligula"; this clever young man, capable of manipulating the other boys, was also physically powerful and full of vigor, "ready to take on anyone and everyone" (Mariani 41, 43).

Similar to Warren and Jarrell, Lowell's literary pursuits started early. In the fall of 1934, Lowell's senior year at St. Mark's, he began studying poetry under Richard Ghormley Eberhart and became the associate editor of *Vindex*, the school's literary magazine. At seventeen, he had written his first poem, thereby discovering a new outlet for his boundless energy. Before entering Harvard in September 1935, a choice dictated by his parents, Lowell and his close friend Frank Parker spent the first of two consecutive summers in Nantucket, reading, writing poetry, and sharpening their intellectual focus. Though Lowell was able to expand his poetic knowledge under the tutelage of Harvard's James Laughlin, he was largely unhappy with his collegiate experience. Despite his distaste for Harvard, it was ultimately his parents' disapproval over his engagement to Anne Dick that drove Lowell to the South. His father's insistent meddling in their relationship led to a violent confrontation between father and son, in which Lowell knocked his father to the ground with a punch. Merrill Moore, a fringe member of the Fugitives, a group of poets and literary scholars based at Vanderbilt, also happened to be Lowell's psychiatrist. After the incident between Lowell and his father, Moore drew on connections to Allen Tate and John Crowe Ransom in order to arrange an escape for Lowell—from his parents, from Harvard, and from Anne Dick and the engagement (Mariani 46–59). This plan landed Lowell in a tent on Allen Tate's lawn in the summer of 1937; soon after, he began attending Ransom's classes at Vanderbilt.[3]

FUGITIVE BEGINNINGS

While Vanderbilt University served as the initial magnet for these three writers, it was the men of Vanderbilt, John Crowe Ransom (1888–1974) and John Orley Allen Tate (1899–1979), who provided the figurative glue. Both Warren and Lowell would come to see Ransom as a "father figure" and Tate as "a combination of older brother and tutor."[4] Though Jarrell was less forthcoming in crediting any influences on his work, Adam Kirsch acknowledges that Ransom "was [Jarrell's] mentor in college and graduate school" (155). Furthermore, Charlotte Beck notes that after Warren introduced Tate and Jarrell, "a close friendship began . . . which flourished for a few years." Jarrell did, after all, dedicate his first book of poetry to Tate.[5]

  While John Crowe Ransom and Allen Tate had a strong hand in laying a foundation for the future careers of all three poets, Vanderbilt and the English Department did little more than to provide a foil. In fact, the English Department's chair, Edwin Mims, known for being "old-fashioned," was ultimately responsible for driving Tate, Warren, and Ransom—and Jarrell and Lowell along with them—away from Vanderbilt (Conkin 4). Before this exodus, however, the campus provided fertile ground for the Fugitives, a group whose members continued to nurture, shape, and bring recognition to the poetry of Warren, Jarrell, and Lowell long after their time in Tennessee.

  The history of the Fugitives is well-known at this point, from their initial meetings in 1915 at the home of Sidney Hirsch to their literary and political endeavors during their most active period, 1922 to 1925, and the literary world is replete with analyses and commentary on their well-respected literary magazine, *The Fugitive: A Journal of Poetry*.[6] Furthermore, Warren's involvement with the Fugitives as an undergraduate at Vanderbilt has already been narrated in detail.[7] For the purposes of this study, however, it is necessary to highlight the crucial role the Fugitives played in the artistic development of these three authors. It was clear from the start that the Fugitives never tried to fuse their beliefs into a unified poetic school; one of the only common principles all Fugitive members agreed upon was "a hierarchical view of literature in which poetry was at the pinnacle" (Meyers, *Manic Power* 31). Despite the fact that all three authors published extensively in other genres—Warren even winning the Pulitzer Prize for his novel *All the King's Men* in 1947—it is arguable that each writer upheld this hierarchy throughout his career. Furthermore, the connection among the Fugitives "provided each poet a critical but appreciative audience" and served as the driving force to keep these poets actively writing (Conkin 17). What Warren, and later Jarrell and Lowell, learned from the Fugitives they would continue to practice with each other for the rest of their poem-producing lives: namely, the priceless value of genuine camaraderie and honest criticism among peers.

In addition to the less tangible lessons of the Fugitives, Ransom and Tate had a measurable impact on the content and style of Warren's, Jarrell's, and Lowell's early verse. Though these three writers would come to modify, amend, and even transform the aesthetics of their mentors, evidence of a common foundation can be detected in their work for the rest of their careers. Before discussing how they eventually distanced themselves and their work from Ransom and Tate, it is necessary to understand their starting point, beginning with ideology. Though the Fugitives never agreed upon a set theory of aesthetics, they did share mutual skepticism of the effects of industrialization on modern society. Some of these early concerns inspired the main tenets of the Southern Agrarians, of which Ransom, Tate, and Warren were included. Even in this shared concern, however, there are distinctions among Ransom and Tate that are reflected in their poetry.

For Tate, industrialization meant the dehumanizing transformation of man into a nonthinking automaton, a fear voiced by other major poets of the early twentieth century, including T. S. Eliot, Ezra Pound, and Wallace Stevens, to name a few. In a contemporary twist on Matthew Arnold's *Culture and Anarchy* (1869), Tate believed poetry could rescue man from alienation and return him to faith in brotherhood among men, to a fuller sense of self, and to a restored connection to the divine. This theory underpins both Eliot's *The Waste Land* and Tate's "Ode to the Confederate Dead," in which Tate laments the fallen Confederate soldiers, executors of great action, while acknowledging the simultaneous deterioration of their dead bodies in the graveyard with the degeneration of a paralyzed modern society, "we who count our days and bow / Our heads with a commemorial woe" (62–63):

The brute curiosity of an angel's stare
Turns you, like them, to stone,
Transforms the heaving air
Till plunged to a heavier world below
You shift your sea-space blindly
Heaving, turning like the blind crab.
. . . .
Turn your eyes to the immoderate past,
Turn to the inscrutable infantry rising
. . . .
What shall we say who have knowledge
Carried to the heart? Shall we take the act
To the grave? Shall we, more hopeful, set up the grave
In the house? The ravenous grave? (19–24, 44–45, 84–87)

The isolation of Tate's narrator and his frustration with the resulting inaction of his contemporary fellow man is reminiscent of Eliot's "The Hollow Men" (1925), with modernized victims who "whisper together," "quiet and meaningless," as "Shape without form, shade without colour, / Paralysed force, gesture without motion" (ll. 6–7, 11–12). Both Tate's and Eliot's poems serve as a wake-up call for a postwar generation that needed to heal and reunite, to rediscover community and God in an increasingly industrialized, and therefore mechanized, society.

Though Ransom also viewed poetry as a potent force for shaping culture, his poems do not depict the same desperate, grand-scale attempt to "save" man from modern times. Warren recalls a face-to-face interaction in which Ransom was "politely declining" a position among those contemporary poets who vehemently spurned the ills of modernity. Warren observes: "[Ransom] was not writing about modern man, but about man. If modern man came in as a case in point (as modern man most surely did), it was under that rubric" ("Notes" 305–306). While Eliot, Tate, and other modernists were breaking tradition and experimenting with aesthetic forms partly in an attempt to restore humanity—and vitality—to modern society, Ransom chose to handle universal themes within the boundaries of traditional forms and local subject matter. With form illuminating content, these respective ideas underpin Tate's high modernist and Ransom's formalist aesthetics and thereby exemplify the contrast between the two authors.

Though Ransom wouldn't publish *The New Criticism* until 1941, the carefully constructed, flawlessly metered poems of his second and third volumes of poetry, *Chills and Fever* (1924) and *Two Gentlemen in Bonds* (1927), seem crafted purposely to invite the close analysis his theory of art would demand. Paralleling a similar ideology in England voiced by critics such as Eliot, William Empson, and I. A. Richards, Ransom's formalist approach increased in popularity, and therefore so, too, did his influence on writers from the 1920s through the 1950s. With the perspective that the work of art is an object in itself, Ransom often infused irony, sometimes through a playful mocking of his own traditional forms, in order to achieve a unique detached tone. This effect is illustrated in "Bells for John Whiteside's Daughter," an elegy in five quatrains that describes the funeral of a young girl. His use of irony in the first quatrain is typical. It begins: "There was such speed in her little body, / And such lightness in her footfall." The ballad form was originally created to accompany dances, and the repetition of *l*'s in *little*, *lightness*, and *footfall* adds to the musical, whimsical quality of these lines. After observing the balladic meter and charmingly old-fashioned language of these first two lines, the reader comes to expect a quaint tale about youth marked by movement and vigor.

The next two lines turn the reader's expectations upside down: "It is no wonder her brown study / Astonishes us all" (3–4). The irony in Ransom's choice of the ballad form is clear from this point onward; a stark contrast to the ballad's characteristic jubilant dance, Ransom instead employs this form for a dead young girl's elegy. Ransom's skillful diction contributes to the ironic effect. In contrast to the lighthearted *l*'s of the first two lines, lines 3 and 4 are laden with hard, heavy consonants, weighing the reader down along with the reality of death. While the light, quick words of the first two lines create a skipping effect, the sounds of won*der* and *br*own and the four-syllable word *Astonishes* succeed in slowing the reader down. Even the near-rhyme of *body* and *study* is purposefully awkward, drawing attention to the shocking image of her small corpse inside the coffin. Such detailed attention to technique and word choice exemplifies one of Ransom's principal theories on aesthetics: that form and content are inextricably linked.

As is evident in "Bells for John Whiteside's Daughter," Ransom favored harmony in poetry over the disjointed incongruity of modernism. While modernists like Eliot and Tate often create emphasis with jarring juxtapositions, the balanced contrasts and opposing tensions exemplified in "Bells" are what enabled him to achieve such power at unexpected moments in his poetry. The main tension within this poem is created by the contrast of movement versus stillness—more precisely, the "astonishment" created when something that should be moving is suddenly still. Quatrains 2 through 4 relate the narrator's wistful memory of the "little Lady" alive and well, playing in a field of geese. Unlike the active youngster with her "tireless heart" that "made them rise," the geese are comparatively "lazy," "sleepy," engaged in "apple-dreams."

Readers are jarred from this idyllic pastoral scene when "now go the bells" in the fifth quatrain. Anyone who has heard bells tolling from a tower knows that the ensuing silence is ever more noticeable once they cease. So, the mourners are "ready," they have braced themselves for the funeral, yet they are "sternly stopped" upon seeing the corpse. Ransom's precise, concrete diction is exemplified in these final lines:

> In one house we are sternly stopped
> To say we are vexed at her brown study,
> Lying so primly propped.

No word other than *vexed* could more perfectly express not only the grief and sorrow of these mourners but also their anger, deep disturbance, and perhaps physical discomfort caused by seeing the epitome of youth "lying so primly propped." In a commentary on this poem, Warren admires "the tension between the irony and the tenderness, between the impulse to withdraw and the impulse to approach" ("Notes" 313). It is easy to understand why a sixteen-year-old Warren sitting in Ransom's composition class during his freshman year would want to emulate the success of his mentor.

WARREN'S FORMATIVE FOUNDATION

While at Vanderbilt, Warren contributed poems to *Driftwood Flames,* a book of poems dedicated to Ransom; the *American Poetry Magazine; Voices;* and the *Double Dealer;* and he also published over a dozen poems in the *Fugitive.* Though several of these poems show promise, this period was most valuable for the intense years of apprenticeship Warren enjoyed under Ransom and Tate. Within these early poems, Ransom's influence is apparent in Warren's tight rhyme schemes, regularly metered lines, and general adherence to classicist principles; one may also note the occasional echoes of Ransom's themes and content. For example, in December 1924, the year "Bells for John Whiteside's Daughter" was published in *Chills and Fever*, Warren published "Admonition to Those Who Mourn" in the *Fugitive*. Warren's traditional poem, composed of four quatrains with alternating rhyming lines and regular meter, is an elegy of sorts that begins: "Now is the hour to rhyme a song for death"; note the familiar combination of melody with mortality. In a quatrain particularly reminiscent of Ransom's "Bells," Warren writes:

> From adequate oblivion unto tears
> The house is empty now, the portals broken,
> The tenant thief has fled; no one there hears
> The bells that once so silverly had spoken. (4–7)

Ransom's bell metaphor, which so effectively embodies the contrast of movement versus stillness in "Bells," is echoed here in Warren's early work.

Another parallel may be seen in Warren's poem "Vision," published in *American Poetry Magazine*. Warren upsets readers' expectations by juxtaposing a playful traditional form with a shockingly dark tone, just like Ransom in "Bells." Warren's poem of three quatrains has an anapestic meter with alternating rhyming lines that creates a singsong effect: "I shall build me a house where the larkspur blooms / In a narrow glade in an alder wood" (1–2). The bouncing rhythm of this poem does not prepare the reader for the dismal final quatrain, which begins, "I shall burn my house with the rising dawn" (9). Though this quatrain is metrically similar to the rest of the poem, its solemn content is shocking when juxtaposed to the deceptively uplifting, lighthearted meter, reminiscent of Ransom's first line in "Bells." Rather than the masterful balance of irony and tone in Ransom's work, however, Warren's poem reads like a boyhood folk song, but already Warren was experimenting with how to achieve irony within the confines of traditional forms.

As Warren matured as a poet, he developed the insightful human sympathy that is characteristic of Ransom. In presenting "Notes on the Poetry of John Crowe Ransom at His Eightieth Birthday," Warren observes that Pound and Eliot address many of the same issues as Ransom, but "they set the issues on a world stage, and the issues become aspects of their major theme of the crisis of culture. This expansiveness is precisely the opposite of the reductiveness of [Ransom], for whom the great issues are most poignantly or forcefully dramatized in the local and small" (310). Some of Warren's finest works follow Ransom's model that he so admired, from early poems such as "Kentucky Mountain Farm," published in Warren's first volume, *Thirty-Six Poems* (1936), to later masterpieces such as *Audubon: A Vision* (1969). "Kentucky Mountain Farm," indicative of Warren's early naturalistic view of the universe, depicts the local "little stubborn people of the hill" struggling to survive amid this "rocky place" where the "hills are weary" and "the rocks are stricken." Like Ransom, Warren keeps his focus small, allowing the local hawk and sycamore, that "same old tree," to speak for the greater world.[8]

Another poetic quality that Warren initially imitated from Ransom but continued to develop on his own is his concrete diction. John M. Bradbury posits that, like Ransom, Warren's "thinking is directly figurative and his language . . . is concrete, earthy, and vivid" (78). Warren's skill with language, which increasingly pairs the abstract and earthy together as his style develops, is revealed in early lines like this, which allow the reader to clearly visualize a corpse being swept along a riverbed:

> Wind, down the eastern gap, will lie
> Level along the snow, beating the cedar,
> lull the drowsy head that it blows over
> startle a cold and crystalline dream forever.
>
> The hound's black paw will print the grass in May,
> And sycamores rise down a dark ravine,
> Where a creek in flood, sucking the rock and clay,
> Will tumble the laurel, the sycamore away.
> Think how a body, naked and lean
> white as the splintered sycamore, would go
> and turning, hushed in the end. ("Kentucky Mountain Farm:
>   III. History Among the Rocks," 3–13)

Warren may have learned the aesthetic implications of such imagery from Ransom, but he arguably possessed an inherent ability to capture vibrant scenes with vivid language.

Though Warren respected Ransom and benefited much from his example, he recalls harboring an "imperfect rebellion" against Ransom's poetry when he was "nineteen to twenty-five years old"—not only because Ransom opposed the high modernism that caught Warren on fire during his college years or because Ransom's polished poetry was a "painful reproach" to Warren's own early stabs at greatness but also because of a resentment rooted "against the cast of the author's mind which made such graceful gestures, enunciated such deep truths, and exercised such fascinating authority" ("Notes" 303–4). With a rawer, more corporeal voice, Warren would achieve all of this and more by the end of his literary career, though it was those early yearnings fueled by his mentor that encouraged him to attain such success.

Perhaps even more than Ransom's, Tate's mentorship was invaluable during Warren's apprentice years. In January 1923, Warren moved in with Tate and Ridley Wills. When Tate first introduced Warren to Eliot's poetry, he recalled coming home to discover that Warren had painted scenes from *The Waste Land* on their dorm room walls, "the rat creeping softly through the vegetation and the typist putting a record on the gramophone" (Bradbury, *Fugitives* 74). Though Warren acquired knowledge of traditional forms and balanced poems from Ransom, he learned innovation and experimentation from Tate and Eliot, and when Ransom publicly berated the very poem that inspired Warren's dorm room murals, Warren's loyalty to Tate was strengthened.

In the July 1923 issue of the *New York Evening Post Literary Review,* Ransom published a cutting review—cruelly titled "Waste Lands"—of Eliot's new poem, which he faulted for "its extreme disconnection." Ransom continued: "I do not know how many parts the poem is supposed to have, to me there are something like fifty parts which offer no bridges" and, furthermore, "[there is] a frequent want of grammatical joints and marks of punctuation; as if it were the function of art to break down the usual singleness of the artistic image, and to attack the integrity of the individual fragments" (825). Perhaps Ransom did not realize that the "flaws" he so sharply criticized in Eliot's work would become marking characteristics of the rising high modernism; perhaps it did not affect his position. In addition to the disjointed form, Tate, and other authors of that time period, chose to emulate Eliot's juxtaposition of "many tongues," "the fragments . . . in many metres," and "above all," in Ransom's words, the "emotions kept raw and bleeding, like sores we continue to pick" (826). When Tate responded to the *Review* in a sharp public letter that condemned Ransom's myopic opinions, he not only became a new champion for high modernism, but he also firmly established himself as the primary mentor for the first publications of Warren, Jarrell, and Lowell alike.

Tate's first volume of poems, *Mr. Pope and Other Poems* (1928), demonstrates the influence of Eliot alongside small echoes of Ransom. Like Eliot's, Tate's poems are heavily allusive from both history and personal experience. In "Ode to the Confederate Dead," Tate references Zeno and Parmenides, Greek philosophers of the fifth century BCE, and "Shiloh, Antietam, Malvern Hill, and Bull Run," famous battles of the Civil War, alongside "the hound bitch," "tangle of willows," "screech-owl," and "mulberry bush" that leapt onto the page directly from Tate's hometown in Winchester, Kentucky (48, 55, 68, 69, 88). Some of the more technical devices, such as the abrupt juxtaposition of words and scenes that lack logical transitions, the deployment of the *objective correlative,* and the density and complexity in language and images are also echoes of Eliot.

Conkin notes that Tate's earliest poems "were often so packed and dense that even he had difficulty explaining their meaning" (18). By 1928, Tate's Eliotic images and metaphors were more mature and effective, yet he still occasionally chose to unpack them for readers so that nothing would be lost in his carefully constructed layers of metaphor. For example, Tate explains the "blind crab" metaphor in "Ode to the Confederate Dead" as a "figure [that] has mobility but no direction, energy but, from the human point of view, no purposeful world to use it in. . . . The crab is the first intimation of the nature of the moral conflict upon which the drama of the poem develops: the cut-off-ness of the modern 'intellectual man' from the world" ("Narcissus as Narcissus" [1938], qtd. in Ellman and O'Clair 626). In reading Tate's lines and his explanation, one is instantly reminded of Eliot's "pair of ragged claws / Scuttling across the floors of silent seas" (73–74), which also symbolizes the alienated "modern intellectual" narrator of "The Love Song of J. Alfred Prufrock." Not entirely free from Ransom's influence, however, the elements of irony—the title of "Ode" itself, for example, since the poem is more of a devastating commentary on modern times than a traditional ode—are as much from Ransom as they are from Eliot.

More so than Tate, who generally favored Eliot's high modernism over Ransom's formalism, the early poems of Warren, Jarrell, and Lowell appear to have been crafted according to a blend of Ransom's and Tate's aesthetic principles. The result is a confused mixture that often results in poems that combine Ransom's traditional forms with Tate's dense language and intricate metaphors. Only after Warren, Jarrell, and Lowell developed their mature poetic styles in the forties and fifties were they able to draw from Ransom's and Tate's influence while avoiding the stilted, contrived qualities that characterized their early attempts at this amalgamation. Of course, there were many early influences on these authors in addition to Ransom and Tate. Warren and Lowell similarly emulated John Milton and the Metaphysical poets, while Jarrell and Lowell equally esteemed Charles Baudelaire and Arthur Rimbaud. Warren was further influenced by Thomas Hardy and A. E. Housman, Jarrell by W. H. Auden, and Lowell by Hart Crane, yet the foundation personally laid by Ransom and Tate during those early years in university classrooms, literary magazine meetings, and social gatherings would prove to have the sturdiest and most lasting footing.

By the January 1928 publication of *Fugitives: An Anthology,* Warren's poems were still confined to mostly traditional forms that Ransom championed, such as couplets, quatrains, and sonnets; however, within his more formal constructions, there are traces of Eliot and the high modernism that Tate encouraged Warren to appreciate. Just as Tate's "blind crab" resembles Eliot's "pair of ragged claws," Warren also chooses to echo Eliot's "Prufrock" in the final two lines of his poem "Midnight." Warren's narrator questions in desperation: "Am I doomed to stand thus ever, / Hesitating on the stair?" which mirrors Prufrock's neurotic, self-doubting lines:

> And indeed there will be time
> To wonder, "Do I dare?" and, "Do I dare?"
> Time to turn back and descend the stair,
> With a bald spot in the middle of my hair. (37–40)

In addition to tonal and contextual similarities, Warren's "Midnight" also contains the historical allusions and loaded images that both Warren and Tate admired in Eliot's technique. Warren's poem reads:

> Have you forgot the green Egyptian moon
> That leered into the casement where
> You sat, wiping bloody fingers through your hair?
> . . . .

I perceive you are thinking
of leprous mists above the muddy Nile
And you, a leper, howling among the tombs. (12–14, 17–19)

Warren's language, though sometimes mottled by clumsy diction in his earliest works, would never be as opaque or impenetrable as Tate's; therefore, his "Egyptian moon" and "howling" "leper" carry a directness that was all his own. It is this natural penchant for clarity that marked his distinction, and later Jarrell's and Lowell's, from their high modernist mentor, Allen Tate.

After graduating summa cum laude from Vanderbilt in 1925, Warren entered the University of California at Berkeley as a graduate student and teaching assistant. There he met Emma "Cinina" Brescia, whom he secretly wed in the summer of 1929, and completed his master's degree in 1927.[9] Soon after beginning graduate work at Yale University in the fall of 1927, Warren was selected as a Rhodes Scholar and entered New College at Oxford in October 1928, completing his B. Litt. degree in the spring of 1930. After a brief assistant professorship at Southwestern College, Warren returned to Vanderbilt as an acting assistant professor in the fall of 1931, a year before Jarrell enrolled as an undergraduate. By this time, Warren had already completed a prestigious education, published a successful biography,[10] contributed dozens of poems to reputable literary magazines, and earned a place of respect among the most important literary figures of the time (Blotner 1997; Clark 2001). Yet none of this, nor the equally impressive accolades of Ransom and Tate, was enough to intimidate young Jarrell, arriving on the literary scene.

JARRELL TAKES VANDY BY STORM

In the fall of 1932, Jarrell began his bachelor of arts degree at Vanderbilt, where he studied directly under Ransom and Warren, and was soon introduced to Tate. Jarrell was conspicuous among his peers from his induction into academia; his first year at Vanderbilt began with Ransom's course in Advanced Composition. Ransom recalls: "Nobody could ignore Randall, in those years when I was seeing him daily. He was an insistent and almost overbearing talker," an *"enfant terrible"* (*Randall Jarrell, 1914–1965* 155; Pritchard 23). Despite Jarrell's overwhelming presence, Ransom and Jarrell developed a relationship grounded in healthy debates over literary aesthetics. Lowell would recall: "[Jarrell] knew everything, except Ransom's closed provincial world of Greek, Latin, Aristotle, and Oxford" ("John Crowe Ransom" 24). While Ransom opened this world to Jarrell, the precocious pupil continued to assert himself against his elder mentor in matters from Shakespeare to modernism.

Like Ransom, Warren came quickly to recognize and appreciate Jarrell's keen mind. After finishing Ransom's course in the fall, it was obvious that, even as a freshman, Jarrell belonged in the top section of Warren's sophomore survey course, a "Beowulf-to-Hardy sort" (Travisano 138; Pritchard 23). Warren shared anecdotes of that fateful semester, with Jarrell frightening the other students, "not out of malice but with the cruel innocence of a baby" (Blotner 123). Warren, only twenty-six years old and at the start of his teaching career, had to pull Jarrell aside to suggest that "perhaps [Jarrell] could help the other students rather than 'terrorize' them." Jarrell was entirely unaware of "how intimidating his classroom presence was" and vowed to change his ways. From this humorous, yet telling, introduction to one another, a trusting friendship blossomed and grew. Warren and Jarrell often made trips to the home of Bernard Breyer for his warm hospitality and, as Warren named them, "jolly Jewish dinners" (Pritchard 27). Jarrell also visited the Warrens' home outside Nashville, sometimes alone and often with his first love, Amy Breyer. Warren remembers: "[Jarrell] would come out to my little whitewashed house and talk poetry and philosophy and brutally criticize my poems. I would listen carefully. He was often right" (qtd. in Blotner 123). It is this sort of honesty and receptiveness that typified their lifetime literary relationship.

Only a few years ahead of Lowell, Jarrell was already making waves in the poetry community, particularly with Tate and Warren. In May 1934, Tate was asked to assemble a poetry supplement for the *American Review*. Along with poetry from Ransom, Warren, Louis MacNeice, John Peale Bishop, and Mark Van Doren, Tate included five of Jarrell's poems. Already attentive to his former pupil's poetic achievements, Warren wrote to his colleague Cleanth Brooks on May 20, 1934: "What did you think of the poetry issue of the *American Review?* Jarrell is pretty hot, isn't he? He is a sophomore now, the most precocious fellow I ever knew: has read everything, writes polished critical prose, is on the tennis team, and is a damned good fellow besides. I know him extremely well and like him extremely" (Clark, *Selected Letters,* 1:244). Warren's personal and artistic estimation of Jarrell would only increase over the years, but it was already favorable in light of Jarrell's early poems. Though only a limited number of those poems are included in Jarrell's *Selected Poems* (1955), Warren must have appreciated the potential within them.

Like Warren's, Jarrell's early poetry reveals the influence of both Ransom and Tate; first and foremost, his work contains a similar treatment of common topics. Though never to be a father himself,[11] Jarrell's poems on children would become almost as widely recognized as his war poems. It is likely that he was originally drawn to these characters during his apprenticeship with Ransom. Bradbury observes, "Ransom's characters are exhibited to us for the most part in the precarious stage of innocence or of experience still unabsorbed" (33). By similarly depicting young characters in this impressionable state, Jarrell is able to produce irony that rivals Ransom's carefully crafted lines.

Lighter in tone than "Bells for John Whiteside's Daughter," Ransom writes on death from a child's perspective in "Janet Waking," a poem with seven tight quatrains and an unfaltering *abba* rhyme scheme. Warren admired Ransom's poem of "the pastoral tradition," with "the irony of wisdom out of innocence" and "the shock of truth out of a presumed naiveté" ("Notes" 310). Young Janet, an innocent farm girl, wakes in anticipation of seeing her dear hen "Chucky," only to go "Running across the world upon the grass" to find him dead (10). Ransom is at his best here with cleverly ironic lines such as "It was a transmogrifying bee / Came droning down on Chucky's old bald head" (13–14); and "Now the poor comb stood up straight / But Chucky did not" (18–19). Though adult readers are able to laugh through Janet's exaggerated crisis, the last stanza is curiously powerful and touching.

Janet is "weeping fast as she had breath" (25), while she begs her family to revive her pet. The last two lines describe this young girl who "would not be instructed in how deep / Was the forgetful kingdom of death." With a child's disbelief and lack of understanding, she is unwilling to accept the depth of such heartrending loss, yet in a universal sense, this denial reflects how most adults process the loss of a loved one. The choice of a child narrator allows Ransom to create a realistic yet still effectively detached and objective demonstration of true human emotion. Sister Bernetta Quinn highlights this common trend among Warren's and Jarrell's poetry, observing that it "has no American superior in its celebration of childhood, standing in wonder before the 'brave new world'" (40). The technique of using a child narrator is far from exclusive to Ransom, though Warren and Jarrell, along with Lowell, succeeded in applying Ransom's same mixture of childhood, irony, and universal wisdom within in their poetry.

Early in his career, Jarrell was already making great strides with child narrators in poems such as "The Christmas Roses," which is a first-person lament from a young girl suffering in her hospital bed. This poem, published in Jarrell's first book, *Blood for a Stranger* (1942), is excluded from his *Selected Poems* (1955), possibly due to the empty sentimentality in lines such as:

> And now I'm dying and you have your wish.
> Dying, dying; and I have the only wish
> That I had strength or hope enough to keep,
> To die. (30–33)

Aside from this heavy-handed attempt at capturing emotion, there are clever lines that achieve a similar effect as Ransom's "Janet Waking." Jarrell's lines read:

> but yesterday I cried
> I looked so white.
> I looked like paper.
> Whiter. I dreamt about the pole, and bears,
> And I see snow and sheets and my two nurses and the chart. (11–15)

Like Ransom's "Janet Waking," Jarrell's ironic tone generates both humor and genuine sympathy.

As the young female narrator builds on the description of her white face, Jarrell's line breaks add to the humorous effect. One can easily imagine a dramatization of this scene: girl looks in mirror, "I looked so white"; girl's eyes dart to "the chart," "I looked like paper"; girl's eyes glance back and forth from her face in the mirror to the chart until she determines, "Whiter." In the next line, she reports that she is dreaming "about the pole, and bears"; the extra comma after *pole* forces the reader to consider the pole and the bears separately, as the girl has done. Her innocence is emphasized in this mistake, as she most likely misheard or misremembered tales told to her about *polar bears,* not "pole, and bears," perhaps even from the nurses present in the scene. The humor in these lines is paired with sorrow when subsequent lines remind readers that the white paper and the pole and bears are part of the context an inexperienced girl must rely upon in order to make sense of her illness.

In addition to similar content and narration techniques, Jarrell's early work, for the most part, adheres to Ransom's traditional forms. Jarrell, however, distinguishes himself from Ransom by choosing ordinary language over erudite and by infusing spontaneity into his poetry, as is exemplified in "The Christmas Roses." Jarrell respected and learned a great deal from Ransom in the 1930s, but he was ultimately drawn more to Tate, though even this attraction only lasted into the early 1940s. The reason for Jarrell's mixed feelings for Ransom may be understood by examining Ransom's review of *Five Young American Poets* (1940).[12] On the one hand, Ransom praises Jarrell's verse by arguing: "I think Jarrell is quite the most brilliant of the five. . . . He has an angel's velocity and range with language, and drops dazzling textures of meaning" ("Constellation" 15). One may argue the "range" and "textures" are the very characteristics that may be attributed to Ransom's tutelage.

On the other hand, Ransom's review also reveals that he was aware, and somewhat critical, of Jarrell's divergence from his own poetic practice. Ransom took issue with Jarrell over his bit of introductory prose entitled "A Note on Poetry," in which Jarrell states, "'Modern' poetry is, essentially, an extension of romanticism. . . . It is the end product of romanticism, all past and no future" (48). In 1940, Jarrell was already announcing the death of modernism, an argument he would elaborate upon in "The End of the Line," published on February 21, 1942, in the *Nation*. Ransom, who found fault with the radical experimentation of modernist poets like Eliot, gently scolds Jarrell for daring to consider what comes next: "In the prose conclusion, as in the poetic sequel, Jarrell forbids us to say yet that he is a post-modernist. But probably he will be. It is self-consciousness which stops the young poets from their own graces; too much thinking about all the technical possibilities at once, as well as too much attention to changes in the fashion" (16). By paying "too much attention to changes in the fashion," Jarrell was distancing himself early from the teachings of his formalist mentor. Jarrell therefore chose to embrace Tate's more progressive approach to poetry, enough to dedicate *Blood for a Stranger* (1942) in his honor, but Tate's unwillingness to look past high modernism would ultimately sever that literary relationship for Jarrell as well.

LOWELL: THE LAST LINK IN THE CHAIN

Unlike the limited window of Tate's influence on Jarrell, Lowell was Tate's devoted protégé until the late 1950s, when Lowell's loosening of form and innovation in content ultimately drew disapproval from the once forward-thinking Tate, thus causing a parting of ways. Like Jarrell, however, Lowell also owed much to the early teachings of Ransom. Jeffrey Meyers summarizes: "Lowell and Jarrell came together as pupils of John Crowe Ransom: they absorbed the same lessons and shared the same goals. Their education provided the ideals and context for their literary work"—ideals and context that would persist throughout their careers (*Manic Power* 31).

By the time Lowell arrived in Nashville, in the summer of 1937, the Vanderbilt crew was already dissipating. After having his troublesome left eye removed on February 7, 1934, Warren was dealt another difficult blow. Edwin Mims, always an obstacle for Ransom, Tate, and Warren, had given Warren's classes to Edd Winfield Parks, forcing Warren to leave the place where he had found encouragement, support, and unrivaled intellectual stimulation (Blotner 137–38). A measure of their friendship, in Mary Jarrell's edition of Jarrell's letters, she notes that when Warren left Nashville, "Jarrell keenly felt the loss" (2).[13] Without a renewal of his contract for the fall 1934 term, Warren relied on his Rhodes scholarship connections to secure a teaching position at Louisiana State University, where he would eventually teach Lowell (Clark, *Selected Letters*, 1:2, 7).

Before graduate work with Warren, however, Lowell had an opportunity to undergo the same intensive Ransom-Tate conditioning as Warren and Jarrell during his remaining undergraduate years. Merrill Moore played an instrumental role in facilitating Lowell's move to the South by establishing connections between the young poet with Ransom and Tate. Lowell had already decided to transfer from Harvard to Vanderbilt, and so in the spring of 1937, he paid Tate a visit at his home, Benfolly, near Clarksville, Tennessee, and attended some of Ransom's lectures at Vanderbilt (Beck, *Fugitive Legacy* 102). Lowell returned that summer with Ford Madox Ford, whom he had impressed at a Boston cocktail party, to attend two writers' conferences in July and August.

Lowell's Benfolly days are famously colored with eventful twists. As Beck notes in *The Fugitive Legacy*, the tale of Lowell's visits to the home of Allen and Caroline Gordon Tate has been told from many perspectives, including

Lowell's, with varying details and degrees of truth (102). Lowell dramatically relates his arrival that spring: "My head was full of Miltonic, vaguely piratical ambitions. My only anchor was a suitcase, heavy with bad poetry. I was brought to earth by my bumper mashing the Tates' frail agrarian mailbox post. . . . I had crashed the civilization of the South" ("Visiting the Tates" 58). His summer sojourn was also marked by an unusual beginning. The Tates already had a full house, so when Lowell "offered" himself "as a guest," they replied that there was no room for him unless he pitched a tent on the lawn. Missing the irony, perhaps purposely, Lowell relates: "A few days later, I returned from Nashville with an olive Sears, Roebuck umbrella tent. I stayed for three months" (60).

Returning to Beck's summation of the situation, the details about the mailbox and tent are relatively unimportant; what is significant is that "[Lowell] was actually invited in and allowed to form a bond with Tate and his circle" (Beck, *Fugitive Legacy* 102). Lowell would never officially enroll at Vanderbilt because of another disappointing choice by the institution's administration. In May 1937, Ransom was offered a better salary by Kenyon College in Gambier, Ohio. Despite the grand efforts by his loyal followers to keep him—Tate, who wrote a public letter to the chancellor of Vanderbilt in the *Nashville Tennessean,* and Jarrell, who led a student petition—Vanderbilt refused to match the offer, thereby chasing Ransom away like Warren. Ransom, however, took Lowell and Peter Taylor to Gambier as students and Jarrell—almost finished with his master's degree—to become an English instructor along with him at Kenyon College (Doreski 47).[14] Thomas Travisano relates the instant bond between Lowell and Jarrell: "These young poets, one in his early twenties, one not yet out of his teens, formed an instant and lasting friendship when they met as John Crowe Ransom's protégés that autumn at Kenyon College" (27).

Lowell quickly became a devotee of Ransom's work; in particular, he voiced his admiration for "the unusual structural clarity, the rightness of tone and rhythm, the brisk and effective ingenuity, the rhetorical fireworks of exposition, description, and dialogue; but even more: the sticking to concrete human subjects—the hardest; and a balance, temperament" ("John Crowe Ransom" 19). Praise for these particular elements is echoed in letters between Jarrell and Lowell, included in critiques on what was lacking or how this or that poem excelled. In fact, Ransom's presence loomed over every bit of their experience at Kenyon College, not just in literature lessons. In September 1937, Lowell and Jarrell roomed together in the attic of Ransom's on-campus house. The following year, they moved into the "Old" Douglass House, "home of eggheads and longhairs," where each man "identified himself as a budding writer and a 'Ransom man'" (Mariani 69, 73). The early college camaraderie between Jarrell and Lowell led to a lifetime of friendship, honest criticism, and mutual influence on one another's work.

In addition to the important role Ransom played in Lowell's burgeoning career, Tate's enormous impact cannot be overlooked; William Doreski fully explores this significant connection in *The Years of Our Friendship: Robert Lowell and Allen Tate* (1990). Unlike Warren, who began developing his own poetic voice from the start, and Jarrell, who seemed suspicious and cynical of literary imitation of any kind (or at least of admitting to it), Lowell experimented with everything from heroic couplets and sonnets to blank verse and free verse, often emulating this writer or that, in an attempt to find his poetic voice.[15] Paul Mariani notes that Lowell tried imitations of Spenser, Milton, Keats, Wordsworth, and William Carlos Williams, and "a world-weariness derived from Eliot, Laforgue, and surrealism" (51). Ultimately, however, in the 1930s Lowell favored the hard, classical poetry espoused by Ransom and the high modernist techniques of Tate, his heaviest influence drawn from Tate. Lowell later explained: "When I began to publish, I wrote literally under the rooftree of Allen Tate. When I imitated him, I believed I was imitating the muse of poetry" ("After Enjoying," *Robert Lowell: Collected Poems* 992). The poetry of that "muse," as demonstrated earlier, is highly allusive, dense in language and tangled metaphors, and—somewhat to its detriment—self-conscious and transparent in its artifice. Even within these parameters, Lowell's early poetry takes on a life of its own, with muscular lines that burst off the page with vigor and vitality.

Tate, the "muse" who had an equal esteem for young Lowell, is almost entirely responsible for Lowell's successful entrance into the literary world. Not only did Tate convince a publisher to accept Lowell's first book of poems, *Land of Unlikeness* (1944), but he also wrote an introduction, in which he proclaimed: "There is no other poetry today quite like this. T. S. Eliot's recent prediction that we should soon see a return to formal and even intricate metres and stanzas was coming true, before he made it, in the verse of Robert Lowell." Tate's introduction names Lowell as "the true heir, in both form and content, to Fugitive modernism with all its political implications."[16] The expectations were set high for the young poet, and he did not disappoint. As

Tate explains in his introduction, Lowell's book has two kinds of poems: the first, a heavily religious brand of poetry with "Christian symbolism" that is "intellectualized and frequently given a savage satirical direction"; and the second, poems "richer in immediate experience" with "the references being personal and historical" ("Introduction" 859). Lowell had converted to Catholicism in March 1941, and these poems were fueled by a mixture of religious fervor and the effects of widespread fear caused by the heightening situation in World War II.

Like Tate, Lowell questioned the fate of modern man in his poetry. *Savage* is an appropriate word to describe Lowell's tone in the religious poems as he draws on Christian myth in order to pass caustic, ironic judgment on modern society (Kirsch 5). "The Boston Nativity," for example, is a poem written from the perspective of a parent who is forced to endure "unchristian carollings" of Christmas after losing a child. The narrator complains:

> Progress can't pay
> For burial. The Town Hall
> Shall be his box and pall. (10–12)

And Lowell howls that

> If Baby asks for gifts at birth,
>   Santa will hang
> Bones of democracy
> Upon the Christmas Tree. (21–24)

In a contemptuous harangue addressed to his "dead baby's clay," and also to the baby Jesus of the nativity scene, the narrator commands mockingly: "So, child, unclasp your fists, / And clap for Freedom and Democracy" (25–26). The faithless narrator, critical of political promises, is a personification of the mood Lowell imbibed from American society in the early 1940s.

"Christ for Sale," another poem that draws on religious symbolism, is a similarly graphic condemnation of mankind (specifically of New Yorkers, in this case), "the lunchers" who "stop to spit into Christ's eye" (17). Lowell does not save grotesque descriptions for sinners in order to highlight the comparative glory of Christ; instead, he references Jesus in equally repulsive language to create an ironic effect (Kirsch 5). The narrator questions,

"Dirty Saint Francis, where is Jesus' blood[?]"; states, "These drippings of the Lamb are Heaven's crime"; and offers, "Us still our Savior's mangled mouth may kiss" (8, 10, 13). By the last line of the poem, "O Lamb of God, your loitering carrion will die," the threatening violence seems just as much directed to Christ as to the filthy sinners the narrator detests. Lowell's later poems, though also prophetic in nature, eliminate this self-righteous, lofty tone. While crafting *Lord Weary's Castle* (1946), largely a revised version of *Land of Unlikeness*, Lowell chose to omit "Christ for Sale" and most of his other religious poems while keeping the more secular verses from Tate's second category, those poems richer in immediate experience.

Tate's influence is more easily recognizable in this second category of poems, from similarities in literary technique, as in Lowell's "A Suicidal Nightmare," to a common preoccupation with personal and learned history, as in "Scenes from the Historic Comedy." "A Suicidal Nightmare" is composed of three tightly constructed sestets with an irregular rhyme scheme. The first six lines reveal Tate's influence; Lowell's lines are loaded with surprising juxtapositions, such as the "maimed man" unexpectedly "stooping" amid this tiger's "jungle-bed." Another characteristic of Tate's poetry that contributes to its density is a tendency to favor unusual pairings of adjectives with nouns that force the reader to stop and consider their meaning, such as "casual sacrament," "Ambitious November," "uncomfortable angels," "blind crab," "immitigable pines," "crazy hemlocks," and "insane green" in "Ode to the Confederate Dead." In "Nightmare," Lowell adopts this technique, with adjectives that breed curiosity in the reader, almost to the point of distraction: "gutless heart," "grinning sphinx," and in the rest of the poem, "catapulting fur," "wooly lava," and "memory's inflated bag." Tate's technique may also be identified in Warren's early poetry; for example, "To a Face in the Crowd," originally published in June 1925, contains "lascivious grass," "arrogant bones," "lean gulls of your heart," and "taciturn tall stone." Later in their careers, Lowell and Warren maintain an intellectual complexity in their language but shed the overwhelming adjectives.

Lowell's "Scenes from the Historic Comedy" resembles Tate more in content than form; Lowell adopted a fixation on history from Tate, a preoccupation that was equally shared by Warren and Jarrell. Doreski suggests that "Lowell learned much about the formal aspects of verse from Frost, Eliot, and Ransom, but the historical sense . . . derives from Tate" (20). In addition to multiple historical references to "Apollo," "Narcissus," "Babel," "The

Lignum Vitae," "Jacob's Well," and "Allah," among others, "Scenes" also exemplifies the large-scale dramatization of modernity's cultural crisis found in Tate's "Ode" and Eliot's *The Waste Land.*

Ultimately, Lowell's poems of Tate's second secular category contain a hint of the brilliance Lowell would later achieve as he moved constantly toward generating a more authentic portrayal of human life. For example, "Death from Cancer" contains the lines:

> Grandfather Winslow, look, the swanboats coast
> That island in the Public Gardens, where
> The bread-stuffed ducks are brooding. (11–13)

While the diction and structure of these lines maintain a classical form, the content is drawn from Lowell's own memories, infusing the lines with a sense of realness. Together Lowell, Jarrell, and Warren shifted from the classicism and contrived artificiality of Ransom and Tate, respectively, to the immediacy and authenticity that characterized the simultaneous change in their poetry at midcentury.

WARREN, JARRELL & LOWELL: CREATING LIFELONG BONDS IN THE 1930S & EARLY 1940S

The 1930s mark the years of apprenticeship and early friendship among Warren, Jarrell, and Lowell. As noted, these three poets were already forming literary relationships that were outside of the Ransom and Tate axis of influence. The friendship between Jarrell and Lowell as roommates and the teacher-student relationship between Warren and Jarrell formed the original ties, but these men also established regular habits of correspondence with one another—which mostly centered on writing. Mary Jarrell notes that after Warren left for Louisiana State University in 1934, Jarrell's "letters to Warren were basically about his own writing, or Warren's" (2). These letters were inspired by Warren's appointment in 1935 as the managing editor of the *Southern Review.* In the words of William Bedford Clark, the *Southern Review* was "at the center of [Warren's] working life." Warren was "determined to establish and maintain the stature of the quarterly even as he systematically nurtured the talent of a younger generation of writers that included . . . Randall Jarrell" (Clark, *Selected Letters,* 2:49). The "nurturing" that Clark describes took shape in Warren's willingness to solicit and publish Jarrell's early work—only, however, after first providing constructive criticism on his writing.

Before publishing the first issue of the *Southern Review* in 1935, Warren wrote to Jarrell that he was unhappy with "the last two stanzas of [Jarrell's] Asphaltine poem," especially with phrases he labeled "arbitrary and a trifle hysterical." Pritchard notes that "Jarrell changed the offending phrases" before the publication went to print (36). Beck also acknowledges that Jarrell's early work was influenced by Warren: "The impact which Warren had upon Jarrell's career in the beginning was . . . considerable" ("Jarrell and Warren" 83). This impact was not one-sided; Jarrell influenced Warren in return. A letter from Jarrell to Warren in February 1937 exemplifies the kind of give-and-take that characterizes their literary relationship: "I've written twenty or thirty poems since summer, some of which I send. (For you to read and comment on, saying that they make you cry or the top of your head come off or something similar.) Send me your long one. I see a lot of Mr. Ransom, who is well and wise but not writing poetry" (M. Jarrell 7). Jarrell's witty, relaxed tone demonstrates the ease of their friendship; Jarrell's desire for Warren's work, in return, marks a sense of equality among the colleagues; and Jarrell's subtle dig made at Ransom's expense reflects their mutual trust and gives the impression that they are both affectionately critical of their one-time mentor. In response to the last element, Beck notes: "These acts of rebellion [against their Fugitive family] . . . generated the creative energy that characterizes Bloom's anxiety of influence. It is evident, therefore, that the poets of the Fugitive legacy succeeded, not *in spite of* but *because of* those exercises in letting go" (*Fugitive Legacy* 72). For Warren, Jarrell, and Lowell, a large part of "letting go" meant moving forward together.

In line with eschewing elements of Jarrell's Fugitive roots, J. A. Bryant Jr. acknowledges that "Jarrell's natural inclination to go his own way was discernible to acquaintances long before his Vanderbilt days" (5). It is for this reason that his lasting connections with Warren and Lowell are particularly significant. There are a few others—Hannah Arendt, Elizabeth Bishop, and Peter Taylor among them—with whom Jarrell maintained lifelong literary relationships but arguably no others who parallel Jarrell's poetic trajectory as closely as Warren and Lowell. One can trace multiple influences in Jarrell's poetry, including W. H. Auden, Robert Frost, William Carlos Williams, Marcel Proust, Rainer Maria Rilke, and Johann Wolfgang von Goethe and the philosophies of Sigmund Freud and Carl Jung. Yet other than his early fascination with Auden, it is rare to identify instances in which any one of these figures overpowers Jarrell's own voice. Neither Warren nor Lowell overshadows Jarrell's own writing style, but their influence is apparent within the entire body of his work, just as his influence is evident in theirs.

The final piece of this triad's puzzle, the Lowell and Warren connection, falls into place in the early 1940s. Jarrell accepted a teaching position at the University of Texas at Austin in 1939 and continued there until 1942, when he entered the U.S. Army Air Force, thereby leaving Lowell to his graduate studies at LSU under Warren's tutelage. Beck observes, "Warren functioned best in one-to-one relationships with such writers as Jesse Stuart, Randall Jarrell, Robert Lowell, and Peter Taylor" (*Fugitive Legacy* 7). The friendly, honest, closely attentive relationship that Warren developed with Jarrell at Vanderbilt had been recreated at LSU with Lowell, his dazzling new pupil.

On June 9, 1940, Lowell graduated summa cum laude, Phi Beta Kappa, and class valedictorian from Kenyon College. Ransom used his connections with Cleanth Brooks and Warren to secure a junior fellowship for Lowell and a typing job for his new wife, Jean Stafford, at the *Southern Review* (Mariani 88).[17] Before Lowell began at LSU in the fall, he wrote with heady anticipation to his friend Robie Macauley, "Brooks and Warren / Brooksandwarren are excellent, especially Warren" (S. Hamilton 31). This eagerness was warranted; Doreski argues that Warren was "another former Fugitive who, like Tate and Ransom, haunted Lowell's career" (50). *Haunted* is arguably an odd word choice to describe the mutually beneficial literary relationship that developed between the two men, but Doreski is accurate in emphasizing this significant link.

Like the Vanderbilt connections that developed as much in Fugitive meetings as in the classroom, Warren and Lowell strengthened their bond at social gatherings and over the production of the influential literary magazine. As soon as Lowell and his wife were settled in Baton Rouge, in the home the Warrens had just vacated, they reported to the offices of the *Southern Review*, which was then in its fifth year and under the editorial control of Warren, Brooks, and Albert Erskine. At an important time for American poetry, the *Review* was "preparing for a major offensive in the New Critics' campaign to convert the academic world to their kind of criticism: the close critical analysis of Modernist texts" (Mariani 89). Ransom was doing his part in Ohio at the *Kenyon Review* by preparing a piece on "Literature and the

Professors" that was also scheduled for the fall. Though Lowell did not take on editorial duties as Warren had done for the *Fugitive,* his close proximity to such important work had an effect on him. In fact, his wife, Jean Stafford, also a budding writer, was reportedly jealous because while her secretarial job drained her time and creative energy, her husband "rather than she . . . received the benefit of Warren's advice and influence" (Blotner 192).

The classical conservatism and high modernist tendencies that were characteristic of Lowell's first two books of poetry were certainly indicative of Ransom's and Tate's respective influence, but Warren's instruction initially encouraged Lowell in this direction as well. These were the years in which Warren and Brooks were developing *Understanding Poetry* and championing the New Criticism, both in the classroom and in every issue of the *Southern Review.* In addition to the scope of aesthetic form, Warren also had more pointed influence on the content of Lowell's early work.

Beck, Blotner, and Mariani all refer to Warren's anecdote about getting to know Lowell. In Warren's words, "Cal Lowell took graduate work with me and then Cal and I locked up the doors several days a week at twelve o'clock and had a sandwich and a quick Coke and then we read Dante for two hours."[18] At this point, Warren knew just enough to read Dante in the original Italian, and Lowell was in the process of learning the language. Allusions to Dante's *Divine Comedy* would forevermore make appearances in the poems of both writers. Lowell edited the original epigraph from "Napoleon Crosses the Beresina" in *Land of Unlikeness*—"And wheresoever you see Eagles, look for the bodies"—to quote Dante's *Purgatorio* in *Lord Weary's Castle:* "There will the eagles be gathered together."[19] Lowell also borrows Dantean imagery for this poem in lines such as "Ascend the tombstone steppes to Russia" and "the snow / Blazes its carrion-miles to Purgatory" (7, 13–14).

Warren's extracurricular Dante readings with Lowell similarly informed his poetry. For example, *Rumor Verified: Poems, 1979–1980* (1981) begins with a quotation from Dante's *Inferno* that translates to

I beheld through a round opening
Some of the beauteous things that Heaven doth bear;
Thence we came forth to rebehold the stars.[20]

Furthermore, this book is noticeably loaded with Dantean imagery, such as the opening poem, "Mediterranean Basin," which contains "the dwindling aperture," "Eyes starward fixed," and the "Chalky, steel-hard, or glass-slick" cliff "That you crawl up." Moreover, *Rumor Verified* is underpinned by the main theme of Dante's *Inferno*. Only after Dante has witnessed a realistic portrayal of the past, horrors included, is he able to emerge from hell and behold the stars with new vision. While the narrators of Warren's poems do not end up in heaven, they are often awakened to a more enlightened understanding of themselves and of the world after confronting the past—all echoes of Dante.

Aside from the lingering influence of Dante's poetry, Warren's seminar on sixteenth-century Elizabethan literature further shaped the content of Lowell's early work. Warren's course focused on "tyrants" such as Cesare Borgia, Huey Long, and Machiavelli (Beck, *Fugitive Legacy* 109). With these figures and their respective power dynamics in mind, Lowell wrote poems for *Land of Unlikeness* such as "Cistercians in Germany," a political poem that condemns the "tyrants" of World War II. The following lines by Lowell reveal disgust for those in power and sympathy for their religious victims:

> Rank upon rank the cast-out Christians file
> Unter den Linden to the Wilhelmsplatz,
> . . . .
> And what a muster of scarred hirelings and scared sheep
> To cheapen and popularize the price of blood! (11–12, 16–17)

In addition to the similar theme, Lowell's lines also seem to reflect Warren's poem "Terror" in tone and diction.[21] Warren's poem reads:

> Not picnics or pageants or the improbable
> Powers of air whose tongues exclaim dominion
> And gull the great man to follow his terrible
> Star, suffice; . . .
>
> Blood splashed on the terrorless intellect creates
> Corrosive fizzle like the spattered lime,
> And its enseamed stew but satiates
> Itself, in that lewd and faceless pantomime.
> You know, by radio, how hotly the world repeats,

When the brute crowd roars or the blunt boot-heels resound
In the Piazza or the Wilhelmplatz. (1–4, 51–57)

A similar theme is also present in Lowell's "Napoleon Crosses the Beresina" and other, more secular poems in *Lord Weary's Castle*.

A more unexpected outcome, Warren's seminar was also partly responsible for Lowell's conversion to Catholicism on March 29, 1941. Warren asked Father Maurice Schexnayder, the college chaplain for Catholic students on campus, to lecture to his class on the Reformation. Father Schexnayder's talk "so impressed Cal that day that he followed him out into the hall afterwards and asked for instruction in Catholicism" (Mariani 92). Lowell's conversion, short-lived though it was, had one of the greatest effects on his work and on his life. Long after he left the church, in 1948, simultaneously divorcing his first wife, religious symbolism and Catholic teachings remained a large influence on his poetry. While of course there were additional factors that motivated Lowell toward this conversion, it was, indirectly, a result of Warren's seminar that the descendant of Puritan, Unitarian, and Episcopalian clergy became Catholic (93).

With the development of mutual esteem and respect for one another during this time at LSU, Warren and Lowell would maintain a friendship and a heightened awareness of one another's poetry for the next twenty-five years.[22] In an interview with David Farrell, Warren admitted his disturbance by and subsequent distance from Lowell because of Lowell's public battle with manic depression in later years (92). While it is true that their more intimate meetings became less frequent in the late sixties, both poets continued to write to one another and critique each other's poems for the rest of their lives.[23] With bonds established among Warren, Jarrell, and Lowell in these early years, it was time to change American poetry.

Creating a New Aesthetic, Together

With their literary relationships established and constantly deepening, the 1940s brought professional maturity and success for Warren, Jarrell, and Lowell. Though Warren published *Thirty-Six Poems* and received a Guggenheim Fellowship by 1940, Jarrell and Lowell quickly made up for lost time with their literary achievements over the following ten years. In addition to earning a Guggenheim Fellowship in 1946, Jarrell's poetic publications were numerous: *The Rage for the Lost Penny* (1940), *Blood for a Stranger* (1942), *Little Friend, Little Friend* (1945), and *Losses* (1948). Jarrell was also already establishing himself as a valuable, insightful literary critic and serving as editor for the *Nation*. Lowell, also awarded a Guggenheim Fellowship (1947), became well respected in this decade for *Land of Unlikeness* (1944) and *Lord Weary's Castle* (1946), for which he received the Pulitzer Prize in Poetry. Warren, not to be outdone, received another Guggenheim Fellowship in 1947 and earned praise for *Eleven Poems on the Same Theme* (1942) and *Selected Poems, 1923–1943* (1944). More notable for his fiction than the other two,[1] in 1947 Warren was awarded the Pulitzer Prize for Fiction for *All the King's Men* (1946) and also contributed other successful novels and influential critical publications, including *Understanding Poetry* (1938) and *Modern Rhetoric* (1949), to the world of letters. As final evidence that these three poets had "made it" in the literary world, Warren was named consultant in poetry to the Library of Congress in 1944 and Lowell in 1947; Jarrell would later serve in this honorable position in 1956–58. Amid growing success and relocations around the country—at times, the globe—Warren, Jarrell, and Lowell maintained frequent communication and attention to one another's work. In fact, their correspondence throughout the 1940s reveals a growing reliance on one another's honest critiques, both good and bad, both in person and in writing, as they yearned for, experimented with, and ultimately created a new aesthetic mode that would influence American poetry at midcentury and beyond.

In the 1940s, the tradition of high modernism that had dominated the poetic scene since the early 1920s began its gradual decline. Though the more experimental Black Mountain poets, New York School poets, Beat poets, Confessional poets, and Deep Image poets would not reach their height until the 1950s and later, some poets—including Warren, Jarrell, and Lowell—were already searching for a new poetic style. William Carlos Williams, for example, in 1948 declared "the poem as a field of action" and proposed "sweeping changes from top to bottom of the poetic structure." His aspiration stemmed from the fact that he was "*through* with the iambic pentameter as presently conceived" (Williams 51). Convinced that traditional forms were limiting, Williams claimed: "Forcing twentieth-century America into a sonnet—gosh, how I hate sonnets—is like putting a crab into a square box. You've got to cut his legs off to make him fit" (qtd. in Wagner, *Interviews* 30). Furthermore, Charles Olson's "Projective Verse" (1950) expanded Williams's theory by arguing for "projective or OPEN VERSE," which is "opposed to inherited line, stanza, overall-all form, ... the 'old' base of the non-projective" (174). Years before these artists called for radical changes to the conventions of poetic structure, however, Jarrell revealed his budding search for a new aesthetic in a letter to Allen Tate in the fall of 1941.

Though he had recently produced many poems, Jarrell complained, "I have the impression that I'm at a sort of dead end." William Pritchard assumes that Jarrell's "dead end" stems purely from his "lack of a subject" (93). No scholar would deny that Jarrell's time in the military from October 1942 to February 1946 had provided him with the life experience and fresh subject matter necessary for success in *Little Friend, Little Friend* (1945) and *Losses* (1948), but in addition to the need for new material, Jarrell was also feeling stymied by the aesthetic forms of his predecessors. Soon after his letter to Tate, and in an elaboration of his introduction to *Five Young American Poets* (1940), he voiced his frustration in the *Nation*, claiming that modernist poetry was merely "the culminating point of romanticism, ... the end of the line" ("End of the Line" 81).[2] Within his article, Jarrell announces his yearning for what would come *after* modernism, a motivation that would drive him, along with Warren and Lowell, to redefine their poetic styles.

During and directly after World War II, artists felt moved to create new methods of expression for their changing world. Thomas Travisano posits that World War II provided a "dynamic arena in which to test and bring to life a conception of [new] poetic structures" (176), and David Perkins refers to the "new human consciousness" that was being formed within poets by "contemporary history and technology" during this time (332). Poets were forced to ask, "How do we write poetry after the horror of concentration camps, Dresden, and Hiroshima?" Fortunately for the legacy of American poetry, finding answers to this question resulted in vigorous post–World War II poetic production. As Jarrell wrote to Amy Breyer de Blasio, his first love, shortly after enlisting in the army: "To write what you can about the world makes it almost bearable" (M. Jarrell 65). A notable trend for Jarrell and many other poets finding their artistic voices in the second half of the century, salutary writing was often stripped of the tightly constructed lyrics, erudite language, classical references, dense allusions, and ideal of impersonality that was largely characteristic of the last twenty-five years in American poetry. The formalist and modernist traditions suddenly felt inadequate and, ultimately, inauthentic for many artists who were striving to make the modern world more "bearable."

In particular, the post–World War II poems of Warren, Jarrell, and Lowell breathe new life with more flexible poetic forms that are better suited for their highly charged content of current political issues and events in American history. The way Warren looks to poetry to "fulfill its function of bringing us face to face with our nature and our fate" reveals a trend among these three poets who were all using art to voice their concerns for America in the modern world ("Use of the Past" 31). Though most obvious for Jarrell in light of his military experience and war poems, there is evidence within correspondence, interviews, and works—both poems and prose—that all three poets were affected by the palpable sense of impending doom that partly defines the post–World War II era. Warren reports in *Democracy and Poetry*, "The experts tell us: somebody may, really, drop the big bomb; the air may really get unbreatheable" (44). Furthermore, after reading Jarrell's apocalyptic poem "Jerome," its first line warning, "Each day brings its toad, each night its dragon," Lowell wrote to Elizabeth Bishop, insisting that one of the "great facts which had emerged since World War II [was] our *probable* total nuclear extinction." Furthermore, Lowell observed that Jarrell was "nuts on the subject" but agreed that "he was right" and laments the country's "growing reliance on the Bomb" and the resulting "crass commercial vulgarity of our country," a common topic for all three writers (S. Hamilton 341).

An important part of this defining period for American poetry, Warren, Jarrell, and Lowell distanced themselves from their early mentors without completely rejecting them. Their shared goal—frequently articulated and encouraged by Jarrell—to define and capture a new sense of authenticity in their poems after World War II, became a recurring theme of their correspondence and literary reviews as they continued to encourage one another on this path. In an echo of Jarrell's "dead end" confession to Tate, Lowell wrote to Peter Taylor after publishing *Mills of the Kavanaughs:* "It's hell finding a new style or rather finding that your old style won't say any of the things that you want to" (S. Hamilton 196). Also swept up in the search for a new aesthetic, Warren commented on his poem "The Ballad of Billie Potts," published in 1943: "I was trying to get back, make a tie between modernism and balladry and make them both stack up to a kind of view of American history *and* a kind of interplay of styles" (qtd. in Blotner 210). Though Warren would not publish another new poem for ten years, this quotation reveals that he was also hankering for something stylistically fresh.

It was clear that all three poets craved a change in their poetic styles in the 1940s; the next challenge was how to achieve it. With friendships strong, correspondences frequent, and critical attention to one another's work constant throughout this decade, the poetry of Warren, Jarrell, and Lowell shifted in similar ways, both in content and style, by no coincidence. Ultimately, Warren, Jarrell, and Lowell purposefully amended the formalist and modernist aesthetics taught by their Fugitive mentors in order to create poetry that engaged in an authentic exploration of selfhood within the contexts of the postmodern world. In terms of content, the authors began to mine their autobiographies for concrete details and to address political matters more frequently; furthermore, each poet began drawing more heavily from American and local history and less from classical antiquity (though this did not disappear).

As for poetic style, there were five major changes. First, there was an overall loosening of forms and a reduction in strictly metered poetry, which resulted in greater use of free verse, blank verse, varied rhythms and line lengths, and less regular rhyme schemes.[3] Second, the effort to create more realistic characters resulted in more narrative and less lyrical poems. In an attempt to capture everyday speech, the three writers increased their use of realistic dialogue, vernacular, and colloquialisms. Third, the authors favored less ornate language in order to create more conversational diction, without sacrificing philosophical complexity. The more accessible verse, marked by a less formal tone and the use of the inclusive *you*, led to a style that, in many ways, engages the reader's involvement directly. As Warren explains in "Pure and Impure Poetry" (1943), "A good poem involves the participation of the reader; it must . . . make the reader into 'an active creative being'" (25), and these aesthetic changes do just that.

As early as 1942, Jarrell articulated two more of their style changes in a lecture: "We think of the structure of poetry too much in static terms. . . . But the poem is completely temporal, about as static as an explosion; there are no things in a poem, only processes" ("Levels and Opposites" 389).[4] Partly, this argument provides a method for reading poetry that opposes the New Critical technique: a poem should not be methodically dissected in a predictable step-by-step formula, mined for a checklist of irony, ambiguity, and tension, for instance; instead, it should be approached in a more flexible manner that allows for, as Jarrell puts it, the "extremely complicated systems of thoughts, perceptions, and emotions, which have extremely complicated non-logical structures," to be appreciated and understood (392). Moreover, aside from serving as a subtle critique of the New Criticism, this lecture provides insight into the kind of poetry Jarrell was creating—more accurately, hoping to create—in the mid-1940s. Jarrell's lecture emphasizes "the importance of process, of dramatizing the mind in action, . . . of polivocality and multiple points of view" (Travisano 173). These elements, which are now commonly understood as defining characteristics of postmodernism, describe the last two stylistic changes within the post–World War II work of Warren, Jarrell, and Lowell: the fourth, their tendency to depict the narrator's mind as it processes emotions, images, and experiences; and the fifth, their occasional implementation of multiple voices as a narrative mode.

Jarrell's call for "dramatizing the mind in action"—though somewhat reminiscent of nineteenth-century "automatic" writing and the modernist stream-of-consciousness mode—more significantly foreshadows Olson's theories on projective verse, in which poetry must "put into itself certain laws and possibilities of the breath, of the breathing of the man who writes as well as of his listening." Jarrell's emphasis on the "processes" of a poem also prefigures Olson's insistence that the poet capture "the process of the thing," and Jarrell's advice to heed the "complicated systems of . . . perceptions" in poetry foretells Olson's command: "In any given poem always, always one perception must must must MOVE, INSTANTER, ON ANOTHER!" ("Projective Verse" 174–75). Through this method of dramatizing the mind's continuous perceptions, the poet often succeeds in depicting a narrator's realistic self-exploration.

In Warren's "The Child Next Door," for example, the narrator watches two children, one "beautiful like a saint," the other a "defective," "monstrous other." The narrator cynically views the handicapped girl as she smiles, thinking: "I come, and her triptych beauty and joy stir hate / —Is it hate?—in my heart" (9–10). The line break gives the reader a moment to absorb the impact of the word *hate* before the narrator himself questions if this is a fitting description of his current emotion. In a similar move, Jarrell's "A Conversation with the Devil" contains two voices, those of the narrator and the devil, both working through individual thought processes. At one point, the Devil thinks through the plural versus the singular form of *man*, while the narrator attempts to identify the source of the Devil's voice: "*Mortal men, man! mortal men!* So says my heart / Or else my belly—some poor empty part" (11–12). As in Warren's poem, the line break allows the initial impression (heart) to sink in before the narrator questions his own observation (belly) in the next line. This structure resembles an act of real-time revision by the poet; the narrator increasingly grasps the truth, or improves his understanding, as the poem (and the poet's perception) moves forward.

Lowell often replicates this method in creating his post–World War II imagery. In "My Last Afternoon with Uncle Devereux Winslow," for example, the narrator observes: "What were those sunflowers? Pumpkins floating shoulder-high?" (I.37). Though he correctly identifies the objects as sunflowers, he revises his description to reflect what he is seeing more accurately. Ultimately, this technique allows the poets to portray the world before them more effectively. Their fifth, and final, movement toward contemporary verse—the pointed presentation of multiple voices—achieves the same effect. As will be explored in detail within this book, whether in Warren's *Brother to Dragons* (1953), Jarrell's war poems, or Lowell's biographical poems in part 3 of *Life Studies*, the additional voices present a fuller picture of the historical situation or personal experience or individual at hand.

THE GRADUAL TRANSITION

Contrary to this orderly overview, these changes did not occur instantaneously. Even after the poets recognized a shared desire to capture authenticity in their writing, there were fits and starts for all three of them as they struggled to achieve this effect in poetry. The series of aesthetic shifts they adopted was not fully realized until the 1950s: for Jarrell in *The Seven-League Crutches* (1951), for Warren in *Brother to Dragons* (1953) and *Promises, Poems, 1954–1956* (1957), and for Lowell in *Life Studies* (1959). However, their works from the 1940s contain early intimations of these stylistic changes, as each poet published a transition work (my label) that foreshadows future success amid lingering weaknesses: for Warren, *Selected Poems, 1923–1943* (1944); for Jarrell, *Losses* (1948); and for Lowell, *Mills of the Kavanaughs* (1951). Through this period of experimentation, their correspondence reveals reciprocal support and encouragement toward these shared aesthetic changes. Charlotte Beck is one of the few critics to recognize the full impact of the literary relationship between Warren and Jarrell during this time: "The impact which Warren had upon Jarrell's career in the beginning was . . . considerable; and the manner in which their poetry evolved in parallel directions constitutes a slight but remarkable chapter in the literary history of America in this century." However, Beck pairs this wise observation with a corollary: "Evidence of poetic cross-fertilization is scarce, for neither wrote widely on the other's poetry in his role as critic" ("Fugitive Fugitives" 83). Though Warren and Jarrell may not have published as frequently on one another's work as, say, Lowell and Jarrell, their letters from the 1940s reveal a mutual awareness of and encouragement toward one another's literary advancements, specifically when those advancements meant achieving similar effects in poetry.

When Warren's *Eleven Poems on the Same Theme* was published on April 4, 1942, Jarrell was wild for the poems and wanted to express his appreciation publicly. In August 1942, he wrote to Tate: "I've taken great pleasure in reading Red's late poems, which are wonderful. . . . I am writing around to magazines trying to get Red's poems to review, if it is not too late; I should love to say what I think of them"(M. Jarrell 62–63). Still under the poems' spell three months later, Jarrell wrote to Edmund Wilson: "Have you read Robert Penn Warren's poems, the ones in a New Directions book named *Eleven Poems on the Same Theme?* Several of them are awfully good,

I think" (68). In yet another letter to James Laughlin, Jarrell expresses his displeasure at the failed pursuit he had mentioned to Tate: "Thanks for the qualified praise about my reviews. I've generally been unlucky enough to be given the bad books and deprived of the good: for instance, if I'd been given Warren's book I'd have praised it very much" (75). Jarrell was quite right about the special quality of these poems, some of which—"Bearded Oaks," "Original Sin: A Short Story," and "Terror"—are still included among Warren's finest poems.

Though Warren's slim volume is still characterized by Ransom's highly technical, formal style, it contains Warren's first genuine meditations on selfhood, a theme that would dominate his later work. Ransom taught Warren to ask larger metaphysical questions, but Warren's poems in the 1940s take a more personal approach. "Original Sin," for example, details a "short story" of man's reckoning with the stain on his soul, "Nodding, its great head rattling like a gourd, / . . . It acts like the old hound that used to snuffle your door and moan" (lines 1, 5). Warren's attempt to emulate Tate's style also still surfaces, notably in his occasional distractingly dense, clumsily turgid lines such as:

> Never met you in the lyric arsenical meadows
> When children call and your heart goes stone in the bosom;
> the orchard anguish never, nor ovoid horror. (26–28)

Aside from these weaknesses, or growing pains, there are also moments of the profound human sympathy that would come to mark Warren's greatest verse, such as these lines from "Bearded Oaks":

> All our debate is voiceless here,
> As all our rage, the rage of stone;
> If hope is hopeless, then fearless fear,
> And history is thus undone.
> . . . .
> We live in time so little time
> And we learn all so painfully,
> That we may spare this hour's term
> To practice for eternity. (25–28, 37–40)

A pair of lovers devote themselves to a quiet meditation, even fantasy, on the state of death. More than just an echo of the carpe diem theme in Andrew Marvell's "To His Coy Mistress," however, these lovers acknowledge that to escape Time, even in a temporary and imaginary underwater realm, renders all emotions—from "hope" to "fear"—meaningless. This poem, locked into ten quatrains of iambic tetrameter, bound by a naturalistic sensibility, lacks the hope that abounds in Warren's post-decade-long poetic hiatus, but its highly meditative quality and capacity to capture human emotion foreshadows the prowess of Warren's mature poetry.

Jarrell's volume *Blood for a Stranger,* published in September 1942, just five months after Warren's *Eleven Poems,* also has a markedly different tone than his earliest works. Pritchard observes, "We hear for the first time the distinctive note of a human voice in Jarrell's poetry" (76). Similar to Warren's thoughtful contemplations, Jarrell's narrator in "90 North" proclaims:

> I reached my North and it had meaning.
> Here at the actual pole of my existence,
> Where all that I have done is meaningless,
> Where I die or live by accident alone— (22–25)

Even this relatively strong quatrain is lacking in authentic human emotion compared to what Jarrell later captures, but it is significant to note how both Warren and Jarrell slowly moved away from static, heavy-handed rhetoric toward a more realistically human reflection on the self. In a ripple effect of sorts, it was after reading Jarrell's *Blood for a Stranger* that Lowell returned to writing poems, though only after a brief stint in jail as a conscientious objector to World War II (Mariani 101).

World War II played a great role in all three writers' lives, though somewhat more personally for Jarrell and Lowell. In October 1942, Jarrell chose to enlist in the U.S. Army. His original goal of becoming a ferry pilot or flight instructor in the army air corps changed when he failed the flight part of the program; instead, he became a training navigator at army airfields in Texas, Illinois, and Arizona (Pritchard 99; Bryant 2). Though Jarrell never saw active duty, these years (1942–46) brought valuable life experience and worldly sophistication to his poetry, as in his widely anthologized "The Death of the Ball Turret Gunner" (1945), in which he embodies life's fragility and the horror of war in just five hard-hitting lines. In the words of Stephen Burt,

"Barrels of printer's ink have been used on this poem," and for good reason; the violence and dehumanization that make this poem memorable present a microcosm for what those feared at war and at home: "children" dying in the skies and on the front lines, a numberless herd (94).

Far from those front lines, Lowell imbibed his wartime knowledge from a jail cell. He volunteered for the army and the navy, only to be rejected for "physical disabilities." By 1943, however, he was so opposed to "Roosevelt's insistence on unconditional surrender of the enemy" and to Roosevelt's and Churchill's "*de facto* policy of bombing civilian populations" that he decided to draft a letter—published and sent to President Franklin D. Roosevelt—of refusal to serve in the armed forces, in which he denounces the war's objectives (Mariani 106).[5] On October 13, 1943, Lowell was sentenced to one year and a day in jail for objecting to the war, an event he later memorialized in his poem "Memories of West Street and Lepke." Because of its reference in this popular poem, Lowell's role as a conscientious objector to World War II is often recounted as a fundamental part of his public persona.[6]

While serving jail time as a "fire-breathing Catholic C.O.," Lowell performed moderate manual labor, such as mopping floors, while intermittently working on his poetry proofs. Lowell presents a less than torturous account of his time in jail: "I slept among eighty men, a foot apart, and grew congenial with other idealist felons, who had homemade faiths. I was thankful to find jail gentler than boarding school or college—an adult fraternity" ("Conversation with Ian Hamilton" 279; Mariani 106; Meyers, *Manic Power* 39). After being released on March 15, 1944, having served five months of his sentence, he had stores of material to draw upon for poetic inspiration (Doreski 66). With new, provocative material at their fingertips, these were fertile years for Jarrell and Lowell, who were publishing new works in the *Sewanee Review*,[7] drafting volumes of poetry, and writing frequent letters to each other that centered on their newly energized poetic production, such as this short note from Jarrell to Lowell: "I've written two poem and finished my Spinoza ['The Place of Death']. One of them ['A Camp in the Prussian Forest'] is in the summer number [of the *Nation*] that the 'Indian Killer' [Lowell's 'At the Indian Killer's Grave'] is in. . . . Anytime you want to come down we can give you a lovely room looking out over a lot of trees, with a brand new desk to write poems on, and the same old me to try them out on" (M. Jarrell 168).

All three authors' letters to one other are telling, but sometimes it is their letters *about* each other that reveal a fuller truth. In October 1944, Jarrell wrote a letter to Amy Breyer de Blasio including almost two full pages of ruminations on Warren's most recent publications, *At Heaven's Gate* (1943) and *Selected Poems, 1923-1943* (1944). Toward the close of this letter, Jarrell explains why he didn't publish on *Selected Poems:* "Aren't the best poems wonderful, though? They certainly make most other poets look sick and trivial. I'd certainly love to write an article about them—but it would be embarrassing and impossible, so I've just written a little of it in this private form." This confession demonstrates Jarrell's admiration for Warren's most recent work; however, the rest of the letter reveals his personal dissatisfaction with Warren for the way he presents the world as "so purely Original Sin, horror, loathing, morbidness, final evil, that to somebody who knows Red it is plain he manages his life by pushing all the evil in it out into the poems" (M. Jarrell 117). In other words, Jarrell, the close friend and ever-insightful critic, notices how Warren's personal turmoil—namely, his unhappy marriage to his first wife, Cinina—negatively affected his earlier work.[8] In the long run, Jarrell is right. Warren had a ten-year poetic dry spell after *Selected Poems* during which he ended his difficult first marriage, found happiness with his second wife, Eleanor Clark, discovered joy by fathering two children, and eventually experienced a revival of poetic creativity that lasted almost until his death nearly forty years later.[9]

Aside from Jarrell's private reaction to Warren's *Selected Poems*, his direct response to Warren proves that he was aware of and impressed by Warren's stylistic changes in this transitional work. He wrote to Warren in 1945 that the newly published *Selected Poems* is "the best book of poetry anybody's published in seven or eight years—I thought it decidedly better than [T. S. Eliot's] *Four Quartets*, for instance" (Beck, *Fugitive Legacy* 87). Jarrell, a bluntly honest critic, and also one known for his subjective appraisals, praises Warren by purposely naming his success greater than Eliot's. Beck notes, "Both Jarrell and Warren had, in effect, loosened ties with the past and deliberately set out to forge new allegiances and new poetic styles" (*Fugitive Legacy* 87). Jarrell acknowledges Warren's departure from modernism and offers approbation for the successful result, just as he would do for Lowell.

Out of the three new poems in Warren's *Selected Poems, 1923-1943*, "The Ballad of Billie Potts" is most indicative of Warren's shifting style.[10] Truly an "interplay of styles," as Warren called it, this narrative poem shifts between bawdy, singsong balladic lines—

Big Billie Potts was big and stout
In the land between the rivers.
His shoulders were wide and his gut stuck out
Like a croker of nubbins and his holler and shout (1–4)

—and philosophical meditations on selfhood that are set off by parentheses:

(There is always another country and always another place.
There is always another name and another face.
. . . .
As you lean with the implacable thirst of self
As you lean to the image which is yourself.) (214–15, 219–20)

Experimentation with these two voices, the balladic folktale and the philosophical narrator, foreshadows Warren's technique in the long verse play *Brother to Dragons,* in which he uses multiple narrative voices to tell a story from various points of view. By 1953, Warren would trade in clumsy narrative lines in "Billie Potts" such as:

The name and the face are you.
The name and the face are always new.
And they are you.
Are new (236–39)

for the ever-observant R.P.W. character, who tells the truth in idiomatic speech.

Aside from favoring the narrative over the lyrical mode, the loosening of form in "Billie Potts" also foreshadows Warren's later work; the "tie between modernism and balladry" takes shape with varying rhythms, an irregular rhyme scheme, and sections of inconsistent length. Though these stylistic changes are reminiscent of the experimentation in modernism, Warren's style differs in that it simultaneously achieves the unity and harmony espoused by Ransom—instead of the purposeful discordance of Tate and Eliot—along with a dramatic quality that marks Warren's originality. "Billie Potts" contains some of the realistic dialogue that brings Warren's later characters to life: "'Durn if'n hit ain't Joe Drew!' / 'I reckin hit's me,' says Joe and gives a spit, 'But whupped if'n I figger how you knows hit'" (266–68). One

final characteristic here that foretells Warren's later work is how the narrator speaks directly to readers, inviting their participation in self-reflection:
"Think of yourself at dawn: Which are you? What?" Notably, this is one of
the only lines of all 513 that stands alone as its own stanza. Warren would
increasingly set off lines in this manner in order to draw attention to their
particular significance. In this poem about a family of robbers, with a father
who, after failing to recognize his son through eyes blinded by greed, acci-
dentally "set the hatchet in his [son's] head" with the help of his scheming
wife, the question "Which are you?" causes readers to question their own
morals (368, 144).

Much like Lowell and Warren, in 1945 Jarrell also presents a realistic
depiction of Americans and America, with all their faults, flaws, and fears.
He was deeply affected by what he observed firsthand during his time in the
military and was therefore inspired to depict these observations in his art.
Though he never actually saw combat, he did witness the "great machine"
of the military. In September 1945, he wrote to Lowell: "I *am* going to write
about Nagasaki. I'm going to write a lot about the war, articles and stories
too." Three months later, he reiterated to Lowell: "After I'm out I'm going to
write—besides a great many army poems about the war—some historical poems" (M. Jarrell 132, 151). In uttering these early ambitions, Jarrell was fore-
telling a shift in content for all three authors, who would turn to writing more
political poems from the close of World War II to the end of their careers.

This shift in content, as well as a changing aesthetic form, can be easily
recognized in Jarrell's *Little Friend, Little Friend* (1945), which most critics
agree serves as the starting point of what would become Jarrell's mature
poetic voice. For the purpose of comparison, one can examine a sample of
the emptier, forced verses of Jarrell's earlier years, in which the emotions
presented do not seem justified, such as in these lines from "Eine Kleine
Nachtmusik" (1940):

> My daemon shifts, impatient, laughs at me
> As I sit crying, lonely, out of luck,
> Asks like a grey mouse: Am what? Why?
> Thinks little of my loss, is careless if I die.
> . . . .
>   "Pity me!
> I too was happy. And I too have lost

The little I could make my own, my life, my love—
Speak for me!" May they be plain to me! (3–6, 23–26)

Rather than evoke sympathy from the reader, the frantic, desperate tone of this poem seems unmerited. The laughing "daemon" and the crying narrator are static characters, leaving the reader with nothing more than excessive, inexplicable demonstrations of sentimentality punctuated by an abundance of exclamation points and question marks.

Little Friend, Little Friend, however, demonstrates Jarrell's growth. Lowell argued that this book "contains some of the best poems on modern war, better, I think, and far more professional than those of Wilfred Owen" ("Wild Dogmatism" 27). One of Lowell's former students recalls what Lowell declared while teaching Jarrell's poems in class: "[Jarrell] found himself as a poet by writing about war" (Partridge 310). These poems also identify Jarrell's movement toward his new poetic style. Pritchard notes, "Jarrell's perception . . . of what had happened to him and his fellow human beings comes sharply to life" (129). No longer as dryly satiric or ironically detached, Jarrell follows the advice he had prescribed for Lowell by "start[ing] from a real point of departure in contemporary real life" (M. Jarrell 139). Beck notes this change: "Like Warren's fiction, Jarrell's war poems were intimately concerned with real events. . . . [They] uniquely capture the voices of war's victims" ("Fugitive Fugitives" 88). One may recognize these real events and real voices in lines from Jarrell's "Soldier [T.P.]":

When the runner's whistle lights the last miles of darkness
And the soldier stumbles into the hard green clothes
. . . .
And stands for his hour there in the cold green lines
That are always waiting for something, or waiting;
There wakes in the cropped dusty head, one supposes,
In the blistered hands, in the soft uneasy eyes,
The smell of the ages where no one is dying. (1–2, 6–10)

Gone are the stilted, contrived lines of Jarrell's earliest work and the awkward, accidental humor created by botched attempts at serious irony; Jarrell was learning how to "start from a real point of departure" and portray realistic events in concrete terms.

Another example of Jarrell's artistic development is the poem "Losses," originally published in 1944 and later collected in its title collection in 1948. The first line strips death equally of its mystery, horror, and glory: "It was not dying: everybody died." Warren later echoed Jarrell in the first line of "Harvard '61: Battle Fatigue" in order to achieve the same effect: "I didn't mind dying—it wasn't that at all." With an even, matter-of-fact tone throughout, Jarrell's narrator describes the "losses" of war, from those in training who "blazed up on the lines we never saw" to soldiers who died in battle for whom "It wasn't different: but if we died / It was not an accident but a mistake" (9, 18–19). The tangible details and conversational tone of Jarrell's newer poems succeed in evoking a real emotional response from the reader, as in these lines from "Losses":

> We died on the wrong page of the almanac,
> Scattered on mountains fifty miles away;
> Diving on haystacks, fighting with a friend,
> We blazed up on the lines we never saw.
> We died like aunts or pets or foreigners. (6–10)

The clever, unconventional metaphors that so uniquely characterize Jarrell's poignant literary reviews were finally making their way into his poetry, as in "We died like aunts or pets or foreigners." The repetition of the conjunction *or* serves to diminish the significance of these living creatures to an even more pitiful degree by highlighting that they are all interchangeable, which is fitting for the dying soldiers in the poem.

The last seven lines of the poem also demonstrate how Jarrell is able to manipulate ordinary language skillfully in order to explore complex, philosophical matters:

> We read our mail and counted up our missions—
> In bombers named for girls, we burned
> The cities we had learned about in school—
> Till our lives wore out; our bodies lay among
> The people we had killed and never seen.
> When we lasted long enough they gave us medals;
> When we died they said, "Our casualties were low." (21–27)

For example, in the three lines: "We read our mail . . ." to "learned about in school," Jarrell juxtaposes the innocence (boys who read mail, gave nicknames, and studied geography) and guilt (men who dropped bombs and burned cities) that universally characterizes the duality of soldiers during wartime. The last few lines continue in a philosophical vein, as Jarrell subtly reveals his cynicism for America. Here Jarrell is pointing to the commodification and mechanization of human beings that resulted from industrialism (enduring ideas of the modernists) and, more recently, atomic warfare. Soldiers are no longer seen as human; they are replaceable parts that earn meaningless awards for merely lasting past their warranties. The new style and content of this poem serves as a fairly accurate representation of the poems in *Little Friend, Little Friend* and *Losses*. To quote Warren's definition of a good wartime writer, Jarrell "presented the pathos and endurance . . . of the individual caught and mangled in the great anonymous mechanism of a modern war fought for reasons that the individual could not understand" (Warren, "Ernest Hemingway" 164). Warren wrote these words about Hemingway, but they are just as fitting for Jarrell.

Also experimenting with new content and forms, in July 1944, Lowell sent an expanded and heavily revised version of *Land of Unlikeness* to Jarrell, who was currently stationed at Davis-Monthan Landing Field in Tucson, Arizona. The series of letters between Lowell and Jarrell that followed this manuscript and preceded the publication of *Lord Weary's Castle* is an exemplary instance of Jarrell's capacity for intellectual generosity and poetic insight. Beck acknowledges, "Not since the Pound excision of Eliot's *Waste Land* had there been such a fruitful collaboration between equals" (*Fugitive Legacy* 112). The multiple-paged letters written with care and the extensive handwritten notes that Jarrell produced on Lowell's manuscript serve as evidence for the crucial role he played in the success of Lowell's second book.

After *Unlikeness* was published, Jarrell wrote a glowing review in the *Partisan Review* commending Lowell, a "traditional poet," for how "his world, his rhetoric, and his beliefs are joined in an iron unity of temperament" ("Poetry in War and Peace" 132), a quality that Ransom would have similarly praised. Looking toward the future, Jarrell prophesied: "At his best Mr. Lowell is a serious, objective, and extraordinarily accomplished poet. He is a promising poet in this specific sense: some of the best poems of the next years ought to be written by him" (134). As if fueled by his own prediction,

Jarrell assumed an integral role in Lowell's next publication. He instructed Lowell on large-scale decisions—which poems should remain, which should be omitted, and which should make a reappearance from *Unlikeness*—as well as small-scale changes in structural form, diction, tone, and punctuation; he advised, for example, "I'd use a dash here instead of a comma," in the last two lines of "Colloquy in Black Rock." Adam Kirsch mistakenly credits Lowell for the "sureness" of his "revisions" from *Unlikeness* to *Lord Weary's Castle*. For Kirsch, the fact that "[Lowell] discarded all the weakest and most confused poems in the book—makes clear that he himself understood the problems with his early work" (5). Contrary to this assertion, however, the letters and unpublished manuscript draft reveal that Jarrell was the one supremely aware of Lowell's poetic strengths and weaknesses; Lowell was thankfully wise and humble enough to take Jarrell's good advice.

Bruce Michelson carefully details most of Jarrell's suggestions to Lowell, those in letters and manuscript margins, and traces Lowell's subsequent changes in the article "Randall Jarrell and Robert Lowell: The Making of *Lord Weary's Castle*" (1985). Providing a litany of all modifications here would be redundant; however, identifying the major trends of this exchange will provide insight into the core of this study. Michelson concludes from his close analysis, "Together Jarrell and Lowell set American verse on a new course after the war; these letters show how they managed to do it" (403–4). Indeed, the letters, reviews, critiques, and conversations among Jarrell and Lowell—and Warren—played a very large role in their post–World War II poetic change and resulting influence on American poetry.

Like any well-intentioned critic, Jarrell began his commentary on Lowell's manuscript with praise in his August 1945 letter: "I had rather read your poems than anybody else in the world who is writing now. . . . You are the only writer I feel much in common with (when I read your poems I not only wish that I had written them but feel that mine in some queer sense are related to them—i.e., if I didn't write the way I do I might or would like to write the way you do; your poems about the war are the only ones I like except my own—both of them have the same core of sorrow and horror and so on) and the only good friend of my own age I have" (M. Jarrell 127–28).

This letter reveals the tenderness and respect Jarrell has for Lowell while also demonstrating Jarrell's awareness of the inherent "same core" present in their poetry. Deeper than the surface "sorrow and horror," the core of both of their poems reflects their common beginnings. They are, in fact, related to each other through their "upbringing" by Ransom, Tate, and Warren. Jarrell echoes Ransom when he reprimands Lowell for "not putting enough about *people* in the poems—they are more about the actions of you, God, the sea, and cemeteries than they are about the 'actions of men'" (139). Capturing the essence of the "actions of men" is a skill that Jarrell surely admired in Ransom but also noticed in the more recent poems by Warren that he so highly praised. Jarrell's second admonition, to avoid "being too harsh and *severe*," would also please Ransom, the champion of balance, harmony, and refinement.

The rest of Jarrell's advice in the letter, however, encourages Lowell to depart from their poetic mentors: "Your worst tendency is to do too-mannered, mechanical, wonderfully contrived, exercise poems; but these you don't do much when you feel enough about the subject or start from a real point of departure in contemporary real life" (M. Jarrell 139). Jarrell called for Lowell to increase the authenticity in his portrayal of the world and to leave behind the more formal, lofty, self-conscious poetry of Ransom and Tate. Not a coincidence, this is exactly what Jarrell had just achieved in *Little Friend, Little Friend.*

Jarrell's marginal comments on Lowell's manuscript reiterate this advice for achieving authenticity. These are the last lines of Lowell's "At a Bible House" draft:

> "I must move
> Down, down, and neither good
> Nor evil, hopes nor fears
> Compassion nor desire
> Will mar the dowered, adored
> All-moment." Come, O Lord:
> Arm with bow, shafts and fire.

Jarrell drew a dark circle around the last three lines and wrote, "I don't think the end is nearly up to the rest of the poem; it seems elevated and general and rather arbitrarily said by the poet—the rest seems particular, real" (Houghton Library, MS Am 1905, 2079–80). In response to Jarrell's suggestion, Lowell changed the lines to:

> It is all
> A moment. The trees

Grow earthward: neither good
Nor evil, hopes nor fears,
Repulsion nor desire,
Earth, water, air or fire
Will serve to stay the fall.

Replacing the awkward, archaic "dowered, adored / All-moment" with the more conversational, "It is all / A moment" eliminates the unfavorable "elevated" tone; the addition of "The trees" that "Grow earthward" literally roots the image to the ground. Also, calling on the elements of "Earth, water, air or fire" makes tangible the otherwise "arbitrary" call to the Lord, with his "bow, shafts and fire."

In a similar attempt to only keep what is "real" and energetic, Jarrell advises Lowell to remove the last lines of his "Forest Hills Cemetery" draft: "I think you ought to leave out this stanza, which is *very* flat and scrappy compared to the other two, more like an afterthought" (Houghton Library, MS Am 1905). Essentially, Jarrell instructed Lowell to increase the authenticity in his portrayal of the world while leaving behind the more formal, self-conscious poetry of their mentors. Jarrell lavished the same level of attention to detail on all of Lowell's poems, resulting in a Pulitzer Prize–winning book of poetry that confirmed Lowell's role as a leading poet in those days.

Jarrell's landmark review of *Lord Weary's Castle*, "From the Kingdom of Necessity," published in the *Nation* in January 1947, identifies a trend that would continue to mark Lowell's poetic career (likewise for Jarrell and Warren): "Anyone who compares Mr. Lowell's earlier and later poems will see this movement from constriction to liberation as his work's ruling principle of growth" (22). Jarrell also spends time extolling the very elements of Lowell's new poems that he had a hand in shaping. He praises Lowell's ability to discover "powerful, homely, grotesque, but exactly appropriate particulars for his poems" and the "flowing ease of a few passages, the . . . colloquial ease of others" (24, 25). Jarrell had announced the death of modernism in 1940 and again in 1942. By molding Lowell's poetry and consequently publicly praising the elements he most heavily favored, Jarrell was personally determining "what came next," for what he identified in Lowell's new poems as "a unique fusion of modernist and traditional poetry," "a post- or anti-modernist poetry, and as such is certain to be influential" (Mariani 148;

and Jarrell, "From the Kingdom" 24). It is significant that the answer to "What comes next?" according to Jarrell, is not a complete abandonment of formalism and modernism but, rather, an altered version of both.

In this highly influential review, Jarrell goes on to describe in Lowell's poetry what he and Warren would similarly achieve in their post–World War II works: "Inside its elaborate stanzas the poem is put together like a mosaic: the shifts of movement, the varied pauses, the alternation in the length of sentences, and the counterpoint lines and sentences are the outer form of a subject matter that has been given a dramatic, dialectical internal organization; and it is hard to exaggerate the strength and life, the constant richness and surprise of metaphor and sound and motion, of the language itself" ("From the Kingdom" 24). As Warren, Jarrell, and Lowell began to experiment with new ways of bringing "strength and life" to their poetry, they distanced themselves from their earliest mentors without completely rejecting them. What unites these three authors is how they learned the rules before breaking them, how they stood on the shoulders of giants while experimenting with new ways to achieve "sound and motion" in poetry.

Warren echoed Jarrell's praise for Lowell in a letter to the poet on December 3, 1946, that expresses his admiration for *Lord Weary's Castle:* "Your book [*Lord Weary's Castle*] has given the Warren household a great deal of pleasure. . . . It is real poetry, very strong and original, and doesn't bear the slightest resemblance to most of the stuff which is passing as poetry. There is nobody around any better than you are" (qtd. in Beck, *Fugitive Legacy* 116). Confirming Warren's statement, Doreski claims that by this point "Lowell had grown independent of Tate—and also of Eliot, Crane, Ransom, Williams, Frost, and all his other early influences" (81). Frost's influence was far from over, but Doreski is correct to acknowledge that Lowell was already forging a path of his own, one that was paved by Jarrell and also followed by Warren.

In addition to the personal note Warren sent to Lowell, Warren's appreciation is evident in an interview of Lowell he conducted with Cleanth Brooks. Warren requests that Lowell read "some of the Warren Winslow elegy," which refers to "The Quaker Graveyard in Nantucket," a poem about Lowell's cousin, whose body was never recovered after his naval ship sank in the New York harbor during World War II (*Robert Lowell: Collected Poems* 1008).[11] In response to Warren's request, Lowell chooses section 2, an eighteen-line rhymed segment in iambic pentameter. After reading aloud,

Lowell acknowledges Allen Tate's influence on the lines, stating, "I feel it's like [Tate's] poetry and yet unlike it, and I've never quite known how." Warren immediately agrees with Lowell, identifying his divergence from their common mentor: "Your rhythm is entirely different from his. . . . It has a different feel to it. It'd be very hard to prove it by a graph but no one could miss that difference" ("Robert Lowell" 39). Despite the traditional form of these lines, Warren notices how Lowell's unique rhythm somehow overwhelms the conventional syllable count. Even if Warren does not put this "difference" into words, it is significant that he thought, or at least wanted to claim, that Lowell's poetry was different than that of their shared mentor.

Next in the interview, Warren specifically requests the third section, "one of the best," which is noteworthy for its more conversational tone and irregular rhyme scheme and line lengths. Warren chooses to highlight the notable characteristics of Lowell's stylistic changes that he and Jarrell were also aiming to achieve; he observes: "Two wonderful effects in there: the line 'mad scramble for their lives' and then the last line has sudden shifts of rhythm and general feeling in that poem. Great strokes, there, I think." Amid the muscular, pulsing rhythm of the poem, these two lines stand out as echoes of idiomatic speech, halting the forward-thrusting movement typical of Lowell's early work. Warren notes that the "idiom" of "mad scramble" is "very dramatic and 'quick' . . . That does something to the rhythm, doesn't it?" The same observation applies to the last line that Warren singles out. The four lines of dialogue at the end of the passage initially appear to be arranged as a conventional prayer; the antiquated language and the repetition of the line "If God himself had not been at our side" heighten the reader's expectation for a melodramatic flourish at the end. Instead, Lowell supplies, "Then it had swallowed us up quick." The informal phrase *swallowed us up* and the end result of being swallowed alive creates an anticlimactic, yet entirely human, ending to the desperate plea.

A final noteworthy comment, Lowell mentions to Warren that these lines, "the hard ones to get in," are "both slightly prosy and harsh." In a telling response, Warren replies, "Prosy and harsh, yet they come with a great shiver, both of them" ("Robert Lowell" 40). Here is evidence that Warren and Lowell mutually acknowledged the great potential power in mixing prose with poetry. Considering that Lowell would later praise Warren's *Brother to Dragons* as "prose genius in verse," that Warren would commend Lowell for *Life Studies,* and that Jarrell would extol both works, it is clear that part of moving forward stylistically meant redefining "poetry" to include highly conceptualized, metaphorical, musical "prose" (Lowell, "Warren's *Brother to Dragons*" 73).

Moving forward also included simultaneous shifts in content for all three writers. By no means were they one-minded on politics, especially early in their careers. Warren began as a conservative Southern Agrarian, Lowell an aristocratic northerner, and Jarrell a left-leaning Marxist. However, World War II succeeded in uniting these poets in shared doubt and cynicism for the future of America. In addition to stylistic similarities, there is also a philosophical overlap between Lowell's "Quaker Graveyard" and Warren's *Brother to Dragons.* Lowell's poem is filled with references to Herman Melville's *Moby-Dick,* including the lines: "Ahab's void and forehead," "The Pequod's sea wings, beating landward," and "The bones [that] cry for the blood of the white whale." Lowell later explains that the one image he would choose for America "would be one taken from Melville's *Moby Dick:* the fanatical idealist who brings the world down in ruin through some sort of simplicity of the mind." Lowell's belief is embodied in his poetic allusions to *Moby-Dick* in "Quaker Graveyard," while in *Brother to Dragons* Warren expresses a similar fear for America in his portrayal of the blindly idealistic Thomas Jefferson. The description Lowell provides for the "symbolic figure" of Captain Ahab functions doubly to describe Warren's Jefferson. Both are "doomed and ready, for their idealism, to face any amount of violence" (Lowell, "Endnotes" 1008). Though, as Warren reveals in *Brother to Dragons,* Jefferson isn't quite prepared to face such violence within his own family. Moving forward, we see Lowell, Warren, and Jarrell taking on violence, and the rest of America's most difficult challenges, in poetry that continues to sing with authenticity.

Robert Frost

A Unifying Figure to Guide Change

The latter part of the 1940s found Warren, Jarrell, and Lowell as close as ever. In April 1946, when Jarrell temporarily took the place of Margaret Marshall as literary editor of the *Nation,* his friends were very much in the forefront of his mind. Jarrell assured Marshall that he was up for the task, writing: "I'd become quite familiar with the way things were done at the *Southern Review*—Red Warren was one of my best friends while I was in college, and I visited him [at Baton Rouge] a lot" (M. Jarrell 152). It was also this "best friend" to whom Jarrell sent his first official letter as editor, begging for some reviews and poems to publish. Jarrell wrote to Warren: "I was awfully glad you like *Little Friend* so well. . . . Will you, if you have any time at all, do me a couple of reviews? If you're terribly rushed for time I could give you Briefer Notices. . . . But if you are too busy even for that please let me see your poems when you do get back to writing poetry" (160). This letter, typical of their correspondence during this time, reveals several things: the comfort with which they communicated, the respect Jarrell had for Warren's critical voice, the mutual esteem they held for one another's work, and Jarrell's unflagging confidence that Warren would return to writing poetry after his hiatus.

Just one year earlier, Jarrell had revealed to Lowell that he found Warren's preoccupation with anything other than poetry to be a waste. In a letter to Lowell in November 1945, Jarrell wrote, "Nothing is so foolish as doing what Red does; wasting your life on textbooks, criticism, and so-so novels when you are a good poet" (M. Jarrell 139). Of course, this was before the publication of *All the King's Men* (1946), but it is clear that Jarrell saw Warren—just as in their early days at Vanderbilt—foremost as a poet. In Jarrell's June 1946 letter to Warren, however, he recognizes the depth of Warren's talent for fiction and reveals a sincere appreciation for Warren's most recent novel: "I thought I ought to write you a fan letter about *All the King's Men*. It's an overwhelming book: I, and my wife, and four people I lent it to, and several people who've talked to me about it, were all like people in a movie advertisement—we'd had an 'experience,' and still felt stunned" (167). As further insight into the nature of Jarrell and Warren's literary connection during this time, when Tate requested a regional poem from Jarrell to fit the theme of the *Sewanee Review,* Jarrell responded: "The only Southern subjects I ever thought of writing about are you, Red, and Mr. Ransom—your poems, I mean" (qtd. in Beck, *Fugitive Legacy* 86). Indeed, all three "subjects" were present in Jarrell's work, but it is Warren's influence that is most identifiable in his post–World War II poetry.

In addition to Jarrell's continued association with Warren, the late 1940s brought him closer to Lowell than ever before. Not only was Jarrell instrumental in Lowell's success in *Lord Weary's Castle,* but he also served as a reliable friend through Lowell's bitter divorce from his first wife, Jean Stafford. Reportedly, when Stafford had trouble finding Lowell, she called the Jarrells, the only people in New York whom Lowell was seeing besides his mistress, Gertrude Buckman (Mariani 147). Lowell's letters confirm regular visits with the Jarrells during this time. In November 1947, Lowell wrote to Buckman, "Thanksgiving comes and with it the Jarrells"; and in December 1947, he regaled Elizabeth Bishop with a tale about how "Randall's something with people he doesn't like," going on to narrate a humorous interaction between Jarrell and a "pompous man of some political importance" from Harvard. To John Berryman in March 1948, Lowell related, "I've just gotten back from Greensboro where Jarrell's lost all his early enthusiasm for the faculty" (*Letters of Robert Lowell* 75, 77, 87), which, one supposes, was most likely inferior in Jarrell's mind compared to Lowell and the rest of their inner circle. Furthermore, as in Jarrell's letter to Warren, Jarrell also nudged Lowell to produce more poetry, questioning: "And the other new poems, where are they? You won't have any readers if you don't send out your new work" (M. Jarrell 168). Of course, Jarrell mutually benefited from Lowell's creative production since he published "as many Lowell poems as he could get his hands on" in the *Nation,* but he was also continuing the practice he had learned from the Fugitives in the 1930s by encouraging his friends to keep sacred the hierarchy of writing that held poetry at the pinnacle.

In a typical letter from this time period, Jarrell wrote to Lowell in April 1946: "When do you expect to come down? We're looking forward very much to having you here. . . . Be sure to bring all your new poems. Red was in town this week" (M. Jarrell 161). This note illustrates the genuine friendship between the two men, proves the deep interest Jarrell maintained for Lowell's poetry, and serves as proof that Warren's visit would have been a point of interest for Lowell. As further evidence of the Warren-Lowell literary connection, Lowell wrote to Buckman on Warren: "He's amusing, knows the people I do, and is instructive on intellectual things" (Berg Collection, Lowell Holdings in Backlog, box 97). Furthermore, in a letter to Louis Untermeyer in February 1947, Lowell wrote: "I'm sure your revised anthology [of American poets] will include Shapiro; but I hope it will also have selections from Randall Jarrell and Elizabeth Bishop and some of the later work of R. P. Warren" (Mariani 149). Of all the poets of this time period, Lowell was most eager to see the work of Jarrell, Bishop, and Warren alongside his own poems.[1]

Admittedly, the nature of this study necessitates a somewhat disproportionate emphasis on the relationships among Warren, Jarrell, and Lowell, but there are obviously additional elements that prompted these authors toward a poetic shift at midcentury. Looking past personal factors—including divorces and remarriages, physical and mental health issues, world travel, deaths of parents, and fatherhood[2]— that had an impact on their work, there are several literary influences worth noting. In studies of Jarrell and Lowell in particular, the role of William Carlos Williams is often highlighted because of his literary influence on and friendships with both poets. Jarrell published on Williams with warm praise such as, "*Paterson (Book I)* seems to me the best thing William Carlos Williams has ever written; I read it seven or eight times, and ended lost in delight" ("Poets" 226). Furthermore, Pritchard names Williams as "a stimulus [for Jarrell] toward composition by the musical phrase (in Pound's words) and toward the incorporation of more disparate kinds of materials and juxtapositions" in his poetry (180).

Lowell's biographer also emphasizes Williams's influence, describing Lowell at midcentury in "a war to decide the future of American poetry, . . . caught between his old aristocratic and classical allegiance for Tate and Eliot and his growing democratic allegiance for Williams" (Mariani 174). Williams's influence on Lowell is unquestionably important in terms of redefining the limitations of and possibilities for poetry, but it is not as immediately apparent in the structure of his verse as it is in Jarrell's. Lowell later recalls being "drawn" to Williams but also admits: "I differed so in temperament and technical training . . . that nothing I wrote could easily be confused with [his] poems" ("Endnotes" 992). Warren is not typically linked to Williams at midcentury, but one of his later works, *Chief Joseph of the Nez Perce* (1982), is notably reminiscent of *Paterson*. Like Williams, Warren inserts real history—from battlefield markers to interviews to *American Sculpture: A Catalogue of the Collection of the Metropolitan Museum of Art*—within his tale about Chief Joseph, a real-life Nez Perce chief.[3] Ultimately, while Williams may have influenced Jarrell, Lowell, and Warren in highly individualized ways throughout their careers, there is another more significant figure who played a direct role in these poets' similar, simultaneous midcentury shifts: Robert Frost.

Leading up to Frost's simultaneous resurgence in their work in 1947, the three poets spent a considerable amount of time together. Early 1947 brought Warren, Jarrell, and Lowell together at a writers' forum at the Woman's College in Greensboro, North Carolina. Warren was invited to give a lecture at the forum, for which, he explained, "one compensation would be seeing friends," including Jarrell and Lowell (Blotner 238). Lowell reported to Buckman on the event: "There's lots that will make good talk that would take forever to write. Red was wonderful and I impressed everyone that I shouldn't of" (*Letters of Robert Lowell* 61–62). Along with the formal lectures and forum events, the poets would have followed the social model they learned in their college years: poetry, alcohol, and more poetry.[4] A letter from Warren to Peter Taylor narrates: "I am looking forward with great pleasure to seeing you all. It's fine that Cal will be there, and John and Randall. Old home week, barbecue on the ground, beer in the keg, chicken-droppings on the grass where you sit" (Robert Penn Warren Special Collections Library, Blotner Papers). Jarrell's description of a visit from Lowell the same year further exemplifies what their time was like when they were together: "I have been talking and listening steadily for five days" (*Letters of Robert Lowell* 76). That year, in particular, they would have had a lot to discuss.

Following Jarrell's 1946 Guggenheim Fellowship, both Warren and Lowell each earned a Guggenheim and a Pulitzer Prize in 1947. Jarrell, who has never been as publicly acclaimed as his friends, was still enjoying success among literary circles from *Little Friend, Little Friend* and publishing additional poems that would be collected in *Losses*. In addition to their own poetic progress, evidence makes it safe to assume that they were also discussing Robert Frost. Pritchard can't quite explain Jarrell's newfound interest in Frost that year. He notes that in Jarrell's Kenyon days, he had been "contemptuous of Frost, but changed his mind after re-reading him in 1947 and giving a lecture on him at Indiana University. . . . In his own career, Jarrell had long aspired to get more 'speech' into his poems, but didn't think of Frost as a poet notable for such effects. It is likely that his conversations with Lowell, who was himself attempting to loosen up his forms so as to accommodate the sound of someone talking, spurred the interest in Frost" (160). It is understandable why Pritchard would posit that Jarrell's reevaluation had been inspired by Lowell. Lowell did, after all, take a bus trip with Theodore Roethke to Vermont that year to visit Frost at his farm, and both Lowell and Jarrell were aiming for a more conversational quality in their poetry (Mariani 152). However, what Pritchard fails to note is that Warren's renewed interest in Frost surfaced before that of Jarrell and Lowell. In fact, Warren presented a Hopwood Lecture earlier that year entitled "The Themes of Robert Frost,"[5] which is noticeably similar to Jarrell's later article "The Other Frost" (1947).

This overlap is significant for American literary history because the qualities of Frost that Warren, Jarrell, and Lowell emphasize, illustrate, and celebrate in lectures and in writing are precisely the characteristics that mark their midcentury poetic shift. Though they were already headed in this direction, Frost served as a steadfast signpost marking the path. An investigation into the lectures, articles, and letters from 1947 reveals how Warren, Jarrell, and Lowell looked to Frost as a model for the following: first, how to infuse ostensibly simple verse with multifaceted layers of meaning; second, how to utilize concrete details to create an authentic presentation of the world; third, how to capture the language of real men, both in diction and rhythm; and fourth, how to raise actual human experience to the universal level.

Warren begins "The Themes of Robert Frost" with his methodology for explicating Frost's poems: "We must be able to look forward as well as back as we move through the poem—be able to sense the complex of relationships and implications—before we can truly have that immediate grasp" (286). This statement directly echoes Jarrell's 1942 lecture on poetic structure, which calls for poems to be read for "extremely complicated systems of thoughts, perceptions, and emotions" ("Levels and Opposites" 392); this noticeable similarity points to the fact that both poets approached Frost from a similar mind-set, one that prompted a dynamic approach to explicating poetry.

Warren and Jarrell were equally impressed by the layers of complexity that underlie the deceptive simplicity of Frost's poetry and by the pointed inclusion of specific details that add to the desired overall effect. Warren observes that "Stopping by Woods on a Snowy Evening" may be said to "be simple. . . . But this does not mean that the implications of the event are not complex" ("Themes of Frost" 287), just as Jarrell later acknowledges, "It is easy to underestimate the effect" of Frost's poetry, in which "objects have the tremendous strength . . . of things merely put down and left to speak for themselves" ("Other Frost" 30). Furthermore, in the Jarrell Holdings of the Berg Collection, there are five pages, front and back, of handwritten notes by Jarrell on what he intended to ask Robert Frost in an interview for the Library of Congress. On page 4, by a scrawled title, "Stopping by Woods on a Snowy Evening," Jarrell penned, "What kind of a man, do you think, would write 'some people want you not to understand, reader, but I want you to understand me wrong?'" (Jarrell Collection, interview with Robert Frost, Library of Congress). Clearly, Jarrell was aware of the potential trappings of reading Frost's work merely on the surface level.

Frost's "Stopping by Woods on a Snowy Evening" is exemplary for displaying how complexity underlies his poetry. The simple nouns and corresponding modifiers—such as the "frozen lake," "harness bells," and "deep" woods—work together to create contrasts, thereby attaining meaning from the situation of the narrative and creating palpable tension within the poem. Readers sense that there is a sinister pull for the narrator, the tempting promise of solitude and silence in death. The beast cannot understand the human impulse to consider anything other than survival, his harness bells serving to alert the narrator—both literally and figuratively—of the danger of premature "sleep." Jarrell, Lowell, and Warren aim to imitate Frost's deceptive simplicity and skillful use of concrete details, as can be seen in Jarrell's "The Night before the Night before Christmas," in *Seven-League Crutches:*

> The girl trails toward the house
> And stares at her bitten nails, her bare red knees—
> And presses her chapped, cold hands together (20–22);

in Lowell's "Father's Bedroom," in *Life Studies:* "blue dots on the curtains / a blue kimono" (4–5); and in Warren's "The Hazel Leaf," in *Promises,* which has resonances of Frost's "Stopping by Woods" in style, content, and metaphysical underpinning:

Tonight the woods are darkened
>   You have forgotten what pain
Had once drawn you forth:
>   To remember it might yet be some pain.
>   But to forget may, too, be pain. (1–5)

In Warren's poem, there is the same lone traveler in the deep woods drawn deeper by the same unknown force, illustrated with the same simple language that speaks volumes. Warren's poem—and Jarrell's "Night" and Lowell's "Bedroom"—all contain the quality that Warren admires in Frost: they "drop a stone into the pool of our being, and the ripples spread." Warren claims that this powerful impact in Frost's work stems partly from the "simple contrasts" that transform into deeper layers of meaning ("Themes of Frost" 287, 288). Jarrell dutifully echoes Warren in his essay, claiming, "The contrasts [Frost] gets from his greyed or unsaturated shades are often more satisfying to a thoughtful rhetorician than some dazzling arrangements of prismatic colors" ("Other Frost" 32). The same may be said of those purposeful contrasts in the later poetry of Warren, Jarrell, and Lowell.

Another large part of what they collectively admired in Frost is how he presents these complex contrasts, effective points of tension, and surprising depth in his poetry, all while writing in the speech of ordinary men. Jarrell overflows with praise for how Frost "uses, sometimes with absolute mastery, the rhythms of actual speech" to achieve great ends ("Other Frost" 30). Lowell echoes this sentiment in an interview with Frederick Seidel as he admires Frost's "sense of rhythm and words and composition, and [how he gets] into his lines language that is very much like the language he speaks" ("Art of Poetry" 71). It is evident from poems as early as "The Ballad of Billie Potts" that Warren also aimed to bring his poems to life with vernacular speech, both in dialogue and breath-like rhythms.

Essentially, the authors traded the lofty, prophetic tone of Eliot and Tate for the living, breathing speech of Frost, as in Frost's "'Out, Out,'" a tragic narrative of a boy who chops off his hand while cutting wood and dies. The colloquial nature of the lines "stood beside them in her apron / To tell them 'Supper'" creates an understated tone, one that invokes everyday life on the farm, and makes the lines that follow all the more shocking, considering the saw's violent reaction to the simple word *Supper*. Furthermore, Frost mimics the natural pacing of speech, as aided by his punctuation choices. The dash after *leap* generates a long enough pause to lay subtle blame on the boy: "or seemed to leap— / He must have given the hand." Then, by juxtaposing the declarative statement "Neither refused the meeting" with an exclamation— "But the hand!—fault again shifts to the boy. The hand may have vehemently refused the meeting, but the boy did not refuse; therefore, "He must have given the hand." Like "Stopping by Woods on a Snowy Evening," the deceptively simple language and ordinary speechlike rhythms of men give way to larger philosophical depths, in this case the human impulse to be exculpated from guilt, as Frost ends his poem, "And they, since they / Were not the one dead, turned to their affairs"—a glimpse at one ugly and true side of humanity.

An additional element that all three poets admired in Frost is how he creates universal portrayals of rural life that are rooted in real human experience. Lowell praises the work of Elizabeth Bishop in 1947 by comparing her to Frost: "[Her work's] purpose is to heighten and dramatize the description and, at the same time, to unify and universalize it. In this, and in her marvelous command of shifting speech tones, Bishop resembles Robert Frost" ("Elizabeth Bishop's *North & South*" 77). Invoking a similar sentiment, in an analysis of "After Apple-Picking," Warren identifies Frost's aesthetic theory in one of the "implications" of the poem's meaning: "Art must stem from the literal world, from the common body of experience, and must be a magnified 'dream' of that experience as it has achieved meaning" ("Themes of Frost" 298). In other words, the key to effectively presenting human experience in poetry is to heighten the raw material through the perception and artistic lens of the creator. This important distinction sets the later poetry of Warren, Jarrell, and Lowell apart from the overly simplistic, truly *confessional* poems of poor poets. Warren explains how a poem can provide "a poignant chapter of biography. . . . But we may remember that the poem . . . is not an attempt merely to present the personal problem but an attempt to transcend the personal problem, to objectify and universalize, that we can distinguish the themes inherent in the poem as such from the personal theme or themes which remain irrevocably tied to the man" ("Poem of Pure Imagination" 349).

Though their post–World War II poetry increasingly contains personal, autobiographical elements, Warren, Jarrell, and Lowell succeed in raising such material to what they regarded as a universal level, just as Frost attempts in his pastoral scenes. For example, Lowell draws from his childhood memories of the "old South Boston Aquarium" to create a narrator who recalls:

Once my nose crawled like a snail on the glass;
my hand tingled
to burst the bubbles
drifting from the noses of the cowed, compliant fish. ("For the Union Dead"
    5–8)

Jarrell recollects his time in California:

My lifetime
Got rid of, I sit in a dark blue sedan
Beside my great-grandmother, in Hollywood. ("A Street off Sunset" 10–12)

And Warren portrays a sweet family moment:

You leap like a fish-flash in bright air,
And reach out. Yes, I'm well aware
That this is the spot, and hour,
For you to demand your flower. ("The Flower" 38–41)

In these poems, they are each employing concrete, sensory details to create a transcendent exploration of selfhood, not only for the narrator but also for those who share in his humanity.

Within these poets' midcentury quest for authenticity, there is also a noticeable shift from lyrical poems to narrative poems, replete with the realistic characters and dramatic scenes that were characteristic of Frost. Jarrell celebrates Frost's characters as "living beings he has known or created . . . with their real speech and real thoughts and real emotions," and further compliments Frost's "wonderful dramatic monologues . . . that come out of a knowledge of people that few poets had" ("Other Frost" 32, 34, 30). Of these memorable characters, one may recall the female narrator of Frost's "A Servant to Servants," who proclaims:

It's rest I want—there, I have said it out—
From cooking meals for hungry hired men
And washing dishes after them—from doing
Things over and over that just won't stay done. (49–52)

In these lines, readers can detect an authenticity that resembles the voices of Kate Chopin's *The Awakening* and Charlotte Perkins Gilman's "The Yellow Wallpaper." Readers might also recall the contemplative, relatable neighbor who narrates Frost's "Mending Wall":

> Before I build a wall I'd ask to know
> What I was walling in or walling out,
> And to whom I was like to give offense.
> Something there is that doesn't love a wall,
> That wants it down. (32–36)

Again, within these lines, one may hear the "real speech and real thoughts and real emotions" that Jarrell touted in Frost's work.

In addition to writing and speaking about Frost's admirable characteristics on their own, there is also tangible evidence that these writers were speaking to one another about Frost. For example, in the interview of Lowell conducted by Warren and Cleanth Brooks, Warren says to Lowell: "I remember now our talk with Frost some time back. He said: 'What makes a line stick in your head? . . . A good line's got to be catchy. A good poem's got to be catchy.' Now you want to say 'catchy' is based on a dramatic element in the poem." Lowell responds to Warren with an anecdote about meeting Frost: "[Frost] was the first poet I ever met who told me about this." Lowell describes how Frost read some Keats and pointed to a line, stating, "There it comes alive." From this discussion, both Warren and Lowell agree that "what we ultimately mean by 'dramatic' in poetry" is when the lines come alive ("Robert Lowell" 37–38). Looking at Jarrell's *Losses* (1948), Lowell's *The Mills of the Kavanaughs* (1951), and Warren's *Brother to Dragons* (1953), one could argue that all three poets had the "extremely wonderful dramatic and narrative element" of Frost in mind, though all three books show room for further growth in their subsequent poems ("Other Frost" 34).

If Jarrell's poems were divided into "early," "middle," and "late," *Losses* serves as the bridge or transition work between the fairly successful middle poems and the late poems that marked his greatest work in *The Seven-League Crutches* and beyond. William Doreski supports this progression in an observation that while Lowell's *Lord Weary's Castle* still conforms mostly to New Critical principles, the poems "in Jarrell's *Losses* were cut from a different cloth" (92); some of that cloth was cut based on Frost's designs, but there were also many elements of his own. In many ways, "Orestes at Tauris" embodies the incongruities of Jarrell's early and late poetic style. Despite his attempt at a Frost-like sustained narrative, Jarrell clings to the antiquity of his early years, portraying classical Greek figures in a story centered on the painful loss of a sibling. Though these characters are more intriguing than those in some earlier works, they remain static types, far from the flesh-and-blood characters with real thoughts and emotions that are depicted by Frost. Most notably, however, Jarrell's battle between the old high-minded classical tone and the newer conversational tone results in an accidental mock epic tone:

> Yet when she pressed it to your lips you gulped at it,
> And it was so thick and bitter with some drug
> Your teeth rang on the rim, you gave a long shudder,
> Snatched it, and poured the rest on the ground—
> Then you looked up at her and laughed.
> Her head began to swim away, you fell asleep. (135–40)

Amid the more classically oriented diction of "pressed it to your lips," "Your teeth rang on the rim," and "gave a long shudder," the moment Orestes "looked up at her and laughed" and then "fell asleep" seems woefully out of place, both in rhythm and diction. In comparison to Lowell, who successfully integrates "prosy and harsh" lines into "Quaker Graveyard" amid local details and time-appropriate references to World War II, Jarrell's shift in tone is entirely unexpected yet not in an effective way to pleasantly surprise readers with something new, as Lowell had achieved.

The same undesirable effect is replicated later in the poem, when Jarrell includes details that seem superfluous and inappropriate for the scene:

> Others . . . looked piteously
> From jewels sewn in their lids, into your eyes,
> As though to beckon you to their blind world.
> A man came walking through their midst, with clumsy steps.
> A long, white, and heavy coat, high shapeless boots,
> A broad-sleeved and knee-long coat, and great peaked hood:

Such garments, white as salt, hung covering him.
Come to the goddess, he swayed and stood. (157–64)

The imagery of jewels and creatures beckoning Orestes to the "blind world" builds suspense for the entrance of an impressive figure, yet Jarrell instead provides a description fit for the villain in a low-budget horror film. In addition to the questionable word choice of *walking, clumsy,* and *swayed,* the elaborate, somewhat feminine description of the garments seems incongruous in this scenario. Aside from the occasional bits of well-written vivid imagery, this poem serves most helpfully as an example of what Jarrell was leaving behind.

Other poems in *Losses,* such as "Moving" and "Lady Bates," represent the ways in which he was moving forward. "Moving," a poem with irregular line lengths and speechlike rhythm, contains powerful realistic imagery that is characteristic of Jarrell's later work, such as:

A smeared, banged, tow-headed
Girl in a flowered, flour-sack print
Sniffles and holds up her last bite
Of bread and butter and brown sugar to the wind. (5–8)

This passage functions similarly to Williams's "The Red Wheelbarrow," each line building on the last to create a complete realistic image. Far from the artificial, mannered verse in "Orestes at Tauris," the flexible form allows Jarrell to play with sounds and pacing in this poem. The four *-ed* adjectives in a row slow readers down, encouraging them to savor each additional description of the little girl. Jarrell's wordplay with near-homonyms *flowered* and *flour* similarly slow the pace, forcing a separate consideration for the "flowered" and "flour-sack" elements of her dress. The enjambment removes all sense of urgency, as the lines trickle onward until the last, significantly longer line, made longer still by the repetition of *and.* The next two lines make Jarrell's purpose clear: "Butter the cat's paws / And bread the wind. We are moving" (9–10). A noticeable contrast from the slow-paced first stanza, the second stanza begins with these short, clipped commands. As the rest of the work reveals, the poem captures the little girl's thoughts in a stream-of-consciousness style as she processes all that she will be forced to sacrifice for this move. The quick, imperative statements demonstrate a shift in tone. No longer is she holding on to her "last bite"; she is newly resolved to accept that she will "never again sing / Good morning, Dear Teacher, to my own dear teacher" (11–12), among other heartbreaking truths that bring to mind Ransom's "Janet Waking" and poor, dead Chucky the hen.

Similar in structure to "Moving," "Lady Bates" is also composed with irregular line lengths and irregular stanzas, allowing the narrative voice and content of the poem to determine the form. An example of the real-time revision technique described earlier, this poem also captures the spontaneous process of the mind:

> The lightning of a summer
> Storm wakes, in her clay cave
> At the end of the weeds, past the mock-orange tree—
> Where she would come barefooted, curled-up-footed
> Over the green, grained, rotting fruit
> To eat blackberries, a scratched handful—
> The little Lady Bates.
> You have played too long today.
> Open your eyes, Lady.
>   Is it a dream
> Like the ones your mother used to talk away
> When you were little and thought dreams were real?
> Here dreams are real. (1–13)

The first six lines tumble forward, like a story being told as the narrator recalls additional details on the spot. Like Lowell's sunflowers that become "pumpkins floating shoulder-high," this poem portrays a poet revising his details in order to capture a more realistic portrayal of the scene. The same improvisational technique marks some of Jarrell's more successful war poems, such as "A Camp in the Prussian Forest" and "Eighth Air Force." With the horrified voice of a subjective narrator, Jarrell captures the dramatic element that he appreciated so deeply in Frost's work.

Just as *Losses* serves as a bridge for Jarrell, *The Mills of the Kavanaughs* is Lowell's bridge from *Lord Weary's Castle* to his turning point work, *Life Studies*. The title poem of *Mills* is in fact reminiscent of Jarrell's "Orestes at Tauris," complete with the narrative form, classical references to Greek figures, formal language, and traditional structure marked by iambic pentameter and a regular rhyme scheme. Like Jarrell's, a descriptive prose paragraph of the historical situation also precedes Lowell's poem, the only difference being Lowell's contemporary plot line. Lowell depicts the reflections of Anne Kavanaugh, a young widow, as she recalls her husband's frightening decline into madness, partly a result of the announcement of World War II, and his ultimate death.

Indicative of impending style changes, Lowell struggled with this long poem from its inception. In the summer of 1947, Jarrell—high on his newfound appreciation of Frost's narrative skills—wrote to Lowell in response to an early version of "The Mills of the Kavanaughs": "I thought the writing was good but that it needed more story or argument" (M. Jarrell 177). Some years later, early in 1950, Warren and Lowell exchanged visits while performing readings at each other's universities. Mariani notes, without drawing a connection, that after these visits, Lowell "seemed to know that ['The Mills of the Kavanaughs'] was far too long on classical and biblical allusion and far too short on narrative" (191). It is safe to assume that the advice of both Jarrell and Warren on the poem's shortcomings had been in unison.

Though not entirely successful in his revision of "Mills," Lowell's failures aren't as detrimental as Jarrell's in "Orestes," since Lowell manages to maintain a consistent tone and is able to develop deeply haunting images and insightful psychological portrayals of his characters. Jarrell provides a summative statement in his review of The Mills of the Kavanaughs: "Mills" is "an interesting and powerful poem; but in spite of having wonderful lines and sections . . . it does not seem to me successful as a unified work of art, a narrative poem" ("Three Books" 258). Though aesthetics were still, and would always be, of great importance to all three poets, attention was increasingly focused on creating a successful narrative. In Louise Bogan's June 1951 review of Mills, she argues that despite the noticeable flaws, "Lowell's relation to his subjects . . . is absolutely and dramatically direct, and the smallest details of character and setting make an unforgettable impact upon the attentive reader because they are so clearly a living part of the poet's emotional and imaginative being" (qtd. in Axelrod, Robert Lowell 59). When reading Bogan's use of the words dramatic and living to praise Lowell's work, one cannot help but be reminded of Warren and Lowell's discussion of Robert Frost and their conclusion that "what we ultimately mean by 'dramatic' in poetry" is when the lines come alive.

The rest of Jarrell's review of *Mills* reaffirms the goal of authenticity that these poets shared at midcentury. Ultimately, Jarrell argues, in addition to improving his narrative voice, Lowell should increase the element of "spontaneity, the live half-accidental half-providential rightness" in his poems, and aim to create "real" characters, instead of those who "too often seem to be acting *in the manner of* Robert Lowell, rather than plausibly as real people act" ("Three Books" 258). Not surprisingly, after *Mills* was published, Lowell opted for a comparison to Frost in order to reflect on the failed elements of his own work: "I don't know how to describe this business of direct experience. . . . In Frost you feel that's just what the farmers and so on were like. It has the virtue of a photograph but all the finish of art" ("Art of Poetry" 71). Fittingly, the last sentence of this statement serves as a perfect description of what Lowell would later achieve in *Life Studies*.

A mirror of Jarrell's *Losses* in many ways, Lowell's *Mills of the Kavanaughs* also contains highly successful poems in addition to the less widely acclaimed long narrative poem. Jarrell includes an enthusiastic appraisal in his review: "'Mother Marie Therese' is the best poem Mr. Lowell has ever written, and 'Falling Asleep over the Aeneid' is—is better; *very* few living poets have written poems that surpass these" ("Three Books" 255). One may add "Her Dead Brother" to that group, though the incestuous subject matter may have prevented Jarrell, with his sensitive moral compass, from including it on his list. In many ways, "Her Dead Brother" foreshadows techniques that would become characteristic of Lowell's later work. Reportedly, Lowell lifted the theme of suppressed incest from a deeply private confession by his first wife about "some sort of sexual intimacy" between her and her brother during childhood (Mariani 149). In a practice that would become habit for Lowell, he drew from this personal experience to create a gripping piece of art.

As the speaker of this dramatic monologue mourns for her brother lost in battle, her tender, forbidden thoughts evoke a twisted empathy in a way that rivals Vladimir Nabokov's *Lolita*. Jarrell famously identified the "dark side" (or "other side") of Frost, a man who employed simple language to write poems that are far from "orthodox," often "extraordinarily subtle and strange" ("Other Frost" 30).[6] Though Frost's "darkness" did not include such blatant appeals to sexuality, in "Her Dead Brother," Lowell is similarly weighting deceptively simple lines with his own flavor of darkness: an artful display of double entendre.

The following stanza relates the initiation of incestuous feelings between brother and sister; theme appropriate, there are images and words pregnant with additional sexual references throughout these lines. For example, the siblings trek to the fort above the Sheepscot River armed with tools for exploration, "telescopes" and "leather handbooks," or instruction manuals. The surrounding syntax and imagery subtly hints where the real exploration may have occurred:

Summer was too short
When we went picnicking with telescopes
And crocking leather handbooks to that fort
Above the lank and heroned Sheepscot, where its slopes
Are clutched by hemlocks—spotting birds.

The ostensible reason for visits to the fort, "spotting birds," is purposely delayed for four full lines and further set apart by a noticeable dash. Furthermore, the sexually charged diction—*lank, slopes,* and *clutched*—and the fact that "hemlocks" are known for their poisonous properties adds to the illicit gestalt created by these lines.[7] Next there is the image of the phallic "four-foot milk-snake" that her brother discovers "in a juniper," a shrub with the feminine qualities of "fragrant wood and bluish-gray berrylike fruit" (*Webster's II*). In a highly metaphorical last line, "Father shellacked [the snake] to the ice-house door," thereby immortalizing the symbol of their immoral intimacy.

The next stanza continues with the double entendre but also demonstrates another technique that Lowell was to employ so handily in his late work:

No one could see us; no, nor catch your hissing word,
As false as Cressid! Let our deaths atone:
The fingers on your sword-knot are alive,
And Hope, that fouls my brightness with its grace,
Will anchor in the narrows of your face.
My husband's Packard crunches up the drive. (25–30)

Lowell juxtaposes classical allusions, such as "Cressid"—the Trojan woman who eternally betrayed Troilus—with banal images from daily life, such as when the narrator's "husband's Packard crunches up the drive." Never purely a confessional poet, as he had been mislabeled, Lowell combines the intellectual acuity of his former Fugitive training with the immediacy of his new poetic style in order to create poetry that breathes with life but also depth, rippling with the additional symbolic weight of historical and literary allusions.

Lowell also drew from his early style for the traditional ten-line stanzas of iambic pentameter and regular rhyme scheme in this poem. However, whereas his pulsing rhythm once seemed to buck against the noose of conventional forms, here he manipulates the constraints to his advantage. In a sense, Lowell employs these tighter forms as a technique to bridle, control, and temper the sensuality inherent in the poem; the formality keeps the difficult topic controlled, even if in structure only. This poem proves Jarrell's observation of *Mills* to be true: Lowell had "poured every variety of feeling and technique into it" (qtd. in Mariani 209). The experimental moves in structure, content, and style within this poem characterize Lowell's work for the rest of his poetic career and foreshadow the changes that occur in all three poets' turning point works.

4

The Turning Point
at Midcentury

AMERICA AT MID-TWENTIETH CENTURY

As the second half of the twentieth century began, the United States was deeply entrenched in problematic international relations. The country was still reeling from what Jarrell saw as the "anxious mortality that would haunt the postmodern world" after World War II, the arms race was heating up, and the Korean War had just begun (Travisano 180–81). William Faulkner, with his fingers on the pulse of the nation, encapsulated the mood of the times in his acceptance speech for the Nobel Prize in Literature, delivered on December 10, 1950: "Our tragedy today is a general and universal physical fear so long sustained by now that we can even bear it. There are no longer problems of the spirit. There is only the question: When will I be blown up? Because of this, the young man or woman writing today has forgotten the problems of the human heart in conflict with itself which alone can make good writing because only that is worth writing about." In the very same month, Warren echoed Faulkner's sentiment: "The world news gets me down. . . . The general picture is so grim that it makes all your ordinary pursuits, the business of literature and so forth, seem trivial in the face of the absolute bestial blankness of the objective world" (qtd. in Blotner 267). Indeed, these were depressing and anxious times, especially for the heightened awareness of many artists.

Despite, or perhaps because of, the unique challenges of the times, Warren, Lowell, and Jarrell responded to Faulkner's charge that it is "the poet's . . . duty . . . to write about these things" ("Nobel Prize"). Not only did they write about the pressing political and moral crisis of the United States, but they remained true to Faulkner's recipe for success by writing about the human heart in conflict with itself. In fact, one may easily recognize these three poets taking on the new role of poet-philosopher-historian and even public figure after World War II, a shift that would shape and influence the content and aesthetics of their pinnacle works and beyond. Jarrell experienced the last of his artistic growing pains with *Losses,* and Lowell with *The Mills of the Kavanaughs;* furthermore, the 1950s brought Warren out of his decade-long poetic hiatus, only for him to reemerge with a vast and brilliant creative energy that did not cease until his death in 1989.

All of Warren, Jarrell, and Lowell's aesthetic changes described thus far—the reduction in regular rhyme and meter; aim for authenticity in narrative, characters, and speech; newly conversational tone; increase in immediacy and spontaneity; and occasional polivocality—were fitting for the highly charged content of current political issues and recent events in American history. Therefore, the way Warren looks to poetry to "fulfill its function of bringing us face to face with our nature and our fate" reveals a trend among these poets who were all using art to voice their concerns for America in the postmodern era (Warren, "Use of the Past" 31). In responding to the nation's need, each poet wrote his best book of poetry to date within this decade.

JARRELL'S TURNING POINT

Jarrell, first to articulate his desire for the "next" thing in poetry, was also the first to reach his turning point with *The Seven-League Crutches* (1951). Considering the long road to the midcentury poetic shift that has already been described, the flaws in Adam Kirsch's following argument on Jarrell's poetic changes are obvious: "[Jarrell] would advance not by attacking the old values, but by almost naively discovering and practicing new ones" (154). Not only had Jarrell been finding shortfalls in the old values since "A Note on Poetry" was published eleven years earlier, he, along with his colleagues, engaged in a rigorous approach to shaping a new poetic style. As the letters and critical responses have demonstrated, Jarrell had a vision for what postmodern poetry should achieve, and this vision was shared by both Warren and Lowell.

Jarrell first signaled "The End of the Line" in 1942, but Warren's and Lowell's influence was crucial for rounding out his aesthetic principles. Warren and Jarrell were mutually interested in depicting an exploration of selfhood, loosening the poetic line, and experimenting with forms, but Warren further directed Jarrell's attention to the desirable authenticity in Frost and the dramatic value of a well-developed narrative poem. Lowell and Jarrell reciprocally encouraged one another to capture the element of *life* in verse, yet it was the politically active Lowell who fueled Jarrell's concern for the cultural crisis in America and pointed him to the merit in addressing current events. At the start of Lowell's review of *The Seven-League Crutches*,[1] after naming Jarrell "our most talented poet under 40," Lowell identifies how "Jarrell is able to see our whole scientific, political and spiritual situation directly and on its own terms" ("Randall Jarrell's Wild Dogmatism" 27). It is this fuller vision, especially in contrast to society's relative blindness, that would contribute to Jarrell's success as a writer.

When Jarrell's *Complete Poems* was published after his death (1969), Helen Vendler voiced a position that has too long clung to Jarrell's reputation: "[Jarrell] put his genius into his criticism and his talent into his poetry" ("Complete Poems" 37–38). It is unfortunate that Jarrell's legacy as a poet has been so far reduced beneath his role as literary critic because, while his criticism is insightful and sharp, his poetry, especially in *Seven-League Crutches* and beyond, truly deserves the praise Lowell lavished upon it in 1951. *Crutches* does not contain as many war poems as Jarrell's last two books, but its poems speak wisely of the postwar culture in ways that transcend that era to maintain value and relevance today. From soldiers to women and children, Jarrell's newfound poetic voice expresses the complexity and psychology of postwar times, all in skilled poetic verse.

Though Jarrell more vocally rebelled against the influence of Ransom and Tate, like Warren and Lowell he never abandoned his heightened attention to the effects of language instilled within him by his formalist training, nor did he abstain from the aesthetic experimentation of modernism. *Crutches* is therefore marked by flexible forms that maintain elements of structure. A mixture of equal parts dramatic monologue, polivocality, and direct address to an inferred listener, this book exemplifies the style of Jarrell's mature poetry. With the ever-present goal to achieve authenticity, Jarrell's stylistic changes enabled him to capture realistic moments, as in the life of a soldier in "Transient Barracks." In place of the strained, contrived lines of earlier poems such as "Orestes at Tauris," Jarrell employs the diction, rhythm, and colloquialisms of real speech, in both the body of the poem and the dialogue. Despite the absence of strict, consistent meter or rhyme scheme, there is a semblance of order, a hint of Ransom's balance and regularity. All lines contain either nine or ten syllables, except for two noteworthy lines that demand careful attention. First, line 12, which contains eleven syllables, captures the important moment when "the man sees his own face," a line unmistakably Warrenesque in its portrayal of a man coming—quite literally—face-to-face with himself. Second, line 20, with only five syllables, allows several beats to fill in the blanks of Jarrell's dialogue with the reader: "These are. Are what? Are." Though the poem begins with a bold trochaic line, the "marching" foot that embodies the spirit of the barracks, Jarrell quickly abandons this meter for iambic lines—a generous label, considering the many exceptions to the rule—until returning to that marching foot for the last three lines of military dialogue:

> The man sees his own face, black against lather,
> In the steamed, starred mirror: it is real.
> And the others—the boy in underwear
> Hunting for something in his barracks-bags
> With a money-belt around his middle—
> The voice from the doorway: "Where's the C.Q.?"
> "Who wants to know?" "He's gone to the movies."
> "Tell him Red wants to sign his clearance"—
> These are. Are what? Are. (12–20)

The way in which Jarrell invokes the implications of regular meter to create a desired effect, while simultaneously breaking the same rules to achieve a different desired effect, is further evidence that in his new poetic style, he does not leave the techniques of Ransom and Tate behind but, rather, employs their lessons in innovative ways. Lowell explains this phenomenon in his description of Jarrell's "Orient Express," a "brilliantly expert combination of regular and irregular lines, buried rhymes, and sestina-like repeated rhymes, in which shifts in tone and rhythm are played off against the deadening roll of the train" (Lowell, "Randall Jarrell's Wild Dogmatism" 28). Kirsch is accurate in asserting that Jarrell was "not attacking the old values," but there was nothing "naïve" about the way he mastered a blending of aesthetic forms, and Lowell was keenly aware of this fact.

In terms of content, deceptively simple like Frost's work, "Transient Barracks" contains several layers of meaning and several voices. In addition to the voice of the narrator, who describes the details of the scene from a detached point of view, readers are privy to the shaving man's immediate thought process when he looks in the mirror and identifies himself as "real," not a dream. Jarrell also gives voices to the actual soldiers, from the boy in underwear to someone slightly higher in rank.[2] A fifth and sixth voice depict an exchange between the poet and his imagined reader: "These are. Are what? Are." It is as if the poet is reassuring his audience that these images *are* real; this is a side of war unseen by most. The experimentation with poetic form and meter also allows Jarrell to present the dreamlike verses in "A Quilt-Pattern" and the stark yet stunning work of "The Face," with its referent-laden lines that require the reader's thought process to fill in the unspoken subcontext:

> Not good any more, not beautiful—
> Not even young.
> This isn't mine.
> Where is the old one, the old ones?
> Those were mine. (1–5)

Like "Transient Barracks," "The Face" is centered on a character in the midst of self-evaluation, once again in front of a mirror. By requiring the reader's participation to complete this character's personal reflection, Jarrell pushes the boundaries of the New Critical principle that a poem should be an independent and self-sufficient verbal object; Warren and Lowell would also increasingly follow this model.

In addition to the spontaneous element of Jarrell's work that invites reader participation, his goal of presenting real-life narratives and characters is also somewhat at odds with New Critical principles, which, in 1951, still held great influence in the literary world. At a time when many poems were "increasingly well wrought, autotelic, full of ironic tension, unified through paradoxical resolutions," Jarrell's poetry was already moving past this literary wave. Kirsch notes that "A Girl in a Library" is "historically significant, since such New Critical terms don't take us far in describing its style. But its more important significance has to do with the amount of 'life'—the illusion of a world going on—he managed to get into the experience of a poem" (178). As mentioned earlier, Kirsch mistakenly accuses Jarrell of blindly stumbling upon new techniques; however, it is precisely the element of "life" Kirsch praises that Jarrell had been encouraging Lowell to develop further in his work since 1945, when he recommended for Lowell to "start from a real point of departure in contemporary real life" and scolded him for "not putting enough about *people* in the poems" (M. Jarrell 139). It is also this element of life that Warren and Lowell had celebrated in Keats as the "dramatic" element one should aim to create in poetry. Finally, it is that very quality of life that all three poets came to admire so specifically in Frost's work in 1947.

After making significant headway in achieving authenticity and life with *Little Friend, Little Friend,* and even more so in *Losses,* Jarrell's colleagues recognized a new breadth and depth specific to *Crutches.* Lowell acknowledges Jarrell's innovation and progression in talent by noting, "In *Losses* and more rangingly in *Seven-League Crutches,* new subjects appear" (Lowell, "Randall Jarrell's Wild Dogmatism" 27). Jarrell had written to his second wife and constant companion, Mary von Schrader, that in *Crutches* he had started to consider himself as a "dramatic rather than a lyric poet" (qtd. in Pritchard 235). One may understand why from observing the dynamic storylines and rounded characters of "Nollekens," "Hohensalzburg: Fantastic Variations on a Theme of Romantic Character," "The Night before the Night before Christmas," and especially in "Seele im Raum" and "A Girl in a Library," both of which earn special recognition in Lowell's review. Returning, as ever, to Frost as a guidepost, Lowell comments, "In 'Seele im Raum,' [Jarrell] masters Frost's methods and manages to make a simple half-mad woman speak in character, and yet with his own humor and terror" ("Randall Jarrell's Wild Dogmatism" 28). To "maste[r] Frost's methods," according to Lowell, Jarrell, and Warren, would equate to achieving a writer's great victory; one may posit that Lowell saw Jarrell's "Seele im Raum" as a fantastical take on Frost's "A Servant to Servants," with the same admirable authenticity in the female narrator's voice.

Continuing the pointed praise, Lowell describes "A Girl in a Library," his "favorite" poem in *Crutches,* as "an immortal character piece" ("Randall Jarrell's Wild Dogmatism" 28). Jarrell's "girl" does seem to enter into existence from the page:

An object among dreams, you sit here with your shoes off
And curl your legs up under you; your eyes

Close for a moment, your face moves toward sleep . . .
You are very human. (1–4)

Here, in the character of the "girl," is, to quote Lowell, Frost's "farmers," with the "virtue of a photograph but all the finish of art" ("Art of Poetry" 71). One can almost see the girl's heavy lidded eyes, ready for sleep, and hear her feminine peel of laughter. The rest of *Crutches* contains similarly well-chosen details and concrete images that bring Jarrell's characters to life amid various backdrops of home life, history, fantasy, and dreamworlds. Travisano explains how both Jarrell's and Lowell's post–World War II work is written in "a style that would be able to explore lost worlds on many levels, in the realm of personal loss, in the realm of history, in the realm of myth." Ultimately, however, these ruminations are tied to the issue of selfhood, to Faulkner's "issues of the human heart," and the exploration of the personal, historical, and political backgrounds that inform "one's perceptions of the self" (Travisano 217).

After honing his poetic voice in *Crutches*, "a mode that was distinctly his," it was almost a decade before Jarrell's next book of poetry was published (Bryant 16).[3] During this time, he maintained close friendships with Warren and Lowell while continuing to write poems and work on other projects. A letter written by Jarrell on May 20, 1952, to Mary is representative of the anecdotes he shared about his time with "Red" Warren: "I'm on the train to New York. I certainly had a good time! Red was as gay as could be. . . . We read some Hardy poems after that [softball game], Red and Cleanth and I are all crazy about his poetry. . . . Red's almost finished a very long poem—a narrative several thousands of lines about Jefferson" (M. Jarrell 351). As in their earliest days together, visits entailed a combination of entertainment, poetry, and discussions about their own work. Mary recounted a similar gathering between Jarrell and Lowell in June 1953 in which the two authors reunited after being apart for some time: "[The reunion] was fond and playful. . . . Driving or walking on campus, they talked about Mallarmé, Williams, Eliot, and Whitman, and quietly seated at home, they continued. Lowell spoke in long, halting sentences that Jarrell darted in and out of but that Lowell, unperturbed, perfected as he went along, choosing just the right, most exact, precisely descriptive word" (381). These get-togethers were always marked by a meeting of the minds, a fruitful breeding ground for new advancements in American literature.

When Jarrell's *Poetry and the Age,* a study of modern poetry, was published in 1953, it served as yet another confirmation that his thoughts were in harmony with those of Warren and Lowell. In the introduction to a recent edition of Jarrell's book, William Logan states, "I once heard a poet say that poets in the fifties were afraid of three things: Randall Jarrell's reviews, Robert Lowell's poetry, and the atomic bomb" (xi). Though Jarrell's reputation as a fierce and accurate critic had already been established from the reviews he published in literary magazines, *Poetry and the Age* propelled him to a new level of critical acclaim among his contemporaries. John Berryman's review in the *New Republic* proclaims: "A salient truth about Jarrell, for the present reader, is that he is seldom wrong. . . . Everybody interested in modern poetry ought to be grateful to him" (12–13). This level of success inspired Logan's overall assessment of Jarrell's work: "When we read the poems, we hear a man trying to be a poet, trying with great skill and intelligence; when we read the criticism, we hear a man born to the trade" (xix).

There is much to be mined in Jarrell's insightful, frequently quoted collection, but for this study, it is most constructive to note points in which Jarrell's views mirror those of Warren and Lowell. Essays such as "The Obscurity of the Poet," "The Age of Criticism," and "Is American Poetry American?" demonstrate how Jarrell's increasing interest in cultural issues matched that of his colleagues, and the rest of the essays provide insight into Jarrell's stance on American poetry at midcentury. For example, his views on Frost that partly inspired the parallel stylistic changes of Jarrell, Warren, and Lowell are collected in *Poetry and the Age* within "The Other Frost" and "To the Laodiceans." In addition to Frost, however, Jarrell's comments on poets such as Wallace Stevens, Walt Whitman, and William Carlos Williams reveal his dedication to the stylistic changes he envisioned for himself after World War II—shifts that are also evident in the work of Warren and Lowell. In "Some Lines from Whitman," Jarrell comments: "If we compare Whitman with that very beautiful poet Alfred Tennyson, the most skillful of all Whitman's contemporaries, we are at once aware of how limiting Tennyson's forms have been, of how much Tennyson has had to leave out. . . . Whitman's poems *represent* his world and himself much more satisfactorily than Tennyson's do his. . . . Few poets have shown more of the tears of things, and the joy of things, and of the reality beneath either tears or joy" (128, 124). One might as well replace *Tennyson* with *Ransom* in this quotation in order to read Jarrell's opinion on the deficiencies of his former mentor's strict formalism and Jarrell's resulting appreciation of the opportunities inherent in utilizing more flexible forms. More than anything, Jarrell embraces looser forms in order to fit life—"the tears of things, and the joy of things, and the reality" in between—into his poetry.

In another essay that showcases Jarrell's aesthetic principles, he critiques Wallace Stevens's poetic practice: "[Stevens] often treats things or lives so that they seem no more than generalizations of an unprecedentedly low order. But surely a poet *has* to treat the concrete as primary, as something far more than an instance" ("Reflections on Wallace Stevens" 140). Jarrell, Warren, and Lowell increasingly aimed to capture concrete particulars in their poetry, leaving behind the generalizations and stereotypical characters that populate some of their early verse but with the goal of those particulars generating a universal meaning. Rounding out this argument on particularization versus generalization, Jarrell argues in "An Introduction to the Selected Poems of William Carlos Williams": "Williams' imagist-objectivist background and bias have helped his poems by their emphasis on truthfulness, exactness, concrete 'presentation'; but they have harmed the poems by their underemphasis on organization, logic, narrative, generalization" (244). Jarrell finds fault with both the overgeneralization of Stevens and the superficiality of Williams, whose objects simply stand as objects. In fact, Jarrell criticizes verse inspired by Williams's "no ideas but in things" for the absence of a greater context and points to the lacking coherence and depth necessary to create timeless poems that bear a wider resonance for mankind.

Jarrell, Warren, and Lowell worked toward a median point between particularization and generalization in which they could create concrete illustrations of the world that could also be magnified and appreciated on a universal level. After Jarrell's *Selected Poems* was published in 1955, James Dickey praised Jarrell for precisely this ability: "Through poems about what has happened to this man (or this child) in this time, we get, in an extremely detailed, moving, and 'true' way, the experience of our time defined. . . . This world is so real that the experienced world is transfigured and intensified, through the poem, into itself, a deeper *itself,* a more characteristic *itself*" ("Randall Jarrell" 37). This unique balance between the concrete and the ineffable, skillfully exemplified in the later work of Jarrell, Warren, and Lowell alike, is one that various contemporary southern poets—Dave Smith and David Bottoms, for example—still strive to emulate. Yes, *Poetry and the Age* serves as a snapshot of the literary and cultural issues of the mid-twentieth century, but thanks to Jarrell's foresight, it also foretells the future of American poetry. Namely, an effective way to write in the post–World War II era is to employ flexible forms, concrete details, and historical context in order to create "a world so real that the experienced world is transfigured and intensified" (Dickey, "Randall Jarrell" 37).

WARREN'S TURNING POINT

After Jarrell's turning point work and his accompanying views on poetry were published, it was Warren's turn to make his mark on American poetry. Following the publication of *I'll Take My Stand* (1930), the early established Fugitive practice of reexamining and reevaluating history—national, regional, and personal—continued to take precedence in Warren's work.[4] Through the thirties and forties, his national concerns were expressed mostly in poetry and fiction, but starting in the 1950s and continuing, increasingly, Warren was propelled into almost three decades of active involvement and commentary on national affairs—not only in his poetry and fiction but also in articles, lectures, and book-length works of nonfiction. Fittingly, the form and content of Warren's post–World War II poetry, like Jarrell's, is linked to the issue of selfhood for the modern man. Hugh Ruppersburg identifies that, by 1953, Warren increasingly explored "the individual's place in modern America and in the modern world," and Joseph Blotner similarly notes that Warren's "attempt to render the sweep of history, which had earlier prompted references to classic ages, focused powerfully now on the American past" (Ruppersburg 2; Blotner 289). Like Jarrell and Lowell, Warren amended his early aesthetic style in order to examine selfhood more fully amid the backdrop of real American life and history.

As discussed earlier, Warren, Jarrell, and Lowell conversed with one another about the plight of the nation and equally bemoaned society's obsession with the present that resulted in blindness to the past and the future. Warren observes, "A society with no sense of the past, with no sense of the human role as significant, not merely in experiencing history but in creating it, can have no sense of destiny" (*Democracy and Poetry* 56). For Warren, like his former mentor Tate, poetry could play a therapeutic role in reversing this pandemic blindness. Jarrell similarly identifies American society's collective tunnel vision and the writer's integral role in widening the lens; for the artist, Jarrell argues, "the present is no more than the last ring on the trunk, understandable and valuable only in terms of all the earlier rings. The rest of our society sees only that great last ring, the enveloping surface of the trunk; what's underneath is a disregarded, almost mythical foundation" ("Sad Heart" 74). Jarrell and Warren encourage readers to identify their place in history in order to foster the development of selfhood, of individual identity, through the way both authors integrate history into their later poetry. Beck observes, "Both [Jarrell and Warren] found in the re-creation of actual events a way of attacking the epistemological dilemma implicit in the recording of history" ("Fugitive Fugitives" 89); they were able to bring their version of truth to the historical facts.

An example of how these authors were presenting a "truthful" history in the post–World War II era can be seen in Warren's *Altitudes and Extensions* poem, "Wind and Gibbon," which depicts a man who, after being awakened by the sound of wind, begins reading a volume of Edward Gibbon's *The History of the Decline and Fall of the Roman Empire*. "This is History," the narrator proclaims, "solid as masonry," unlike the "morning paper" that will "gabble like paranoia, chitter in a strange tongue" (20, 17). The poem's title implies that readers are to take the wind and Gibbon in equal parts; it's not "Wind *with* Gibbon" or "Wind *like* Gibbon"; it is "Wind *and* Gibbon," which draws attention to their like characteristics. When the narrator picks up this book, he notes, "You do not hear the wind" (19). The wind's movement from the beginning of the poem, which "Suddenly, stops. Shifts. Again lifts" (8), is transferred to the movement of Gibbon's history, his "hot lava" that "Seethes over the conical brim of the world," flow[ing] "like incandescent irony," spilling "Over empires, imperial palaces" (29). After an eleven-lined vivid illustration of the motion of Gibbon's words, there is a hard break and one line that stands alone: "History is not truth. Truth is in the telling" (31). For Warren, Gibbon's writing is hot lava, capable of burning its path not only over "vineyard, sheepfold, stone hut, and villa" but also into the mind of his reader; this is one way not only to tell history but also to shape it. Lowell's letter to Alfred Kazin reiterates this idea: "While it was true that the historian didn't 'quite make history,' it was equally true that most lived history was 'hardly worth preserving, until the great historian' entered the mass of facts to shape them" (qtd. in *Lost Puritan* 373).

From the 1950s onward, Warren would both tell and shape history, beginning by shedding light on the true story of a brutal murder committed by President Thomas Jefferson's nephews in *Brother to Dragons: A Tale in Verse and Voices* (1953). After a decade of publishing only fiction and prose, Warren returned to poetry with an innovative style that paralleled the changes in Jarrell's verse. An echo of Jarrell's letter to Mary, Warren felt an increasing "dramatic impulse" that would "bring more flexibility to his poetic style" (Blotner 289). This impulse resulted in *Brother to Dragons*, a book-length dramatic narrative in which Warren builds on the interplay of styles from "Billie Potts" with a play-like format that includes eight characters who speak alternately in mostly blank verse. Though many critics name Warren's *Promises: Poems, 1954–1956* (1957) as the "turning point" in his career,[5] *Brother to Dragons*—with its elements of life, looser forms, experimental techniques, narrative retrospection, conversational tone, spontaneous voices, and realistic details—debuts many of the successful characteristics that earned *Promises* a Pulitzer Prize. John Burt summarizes, "*Brother to Dragons* ended [Warren's] poetic dry spell, and [he] was reborn as a poet with a different style, a different point of view, and different subject matter" ("Afterword" 480).

Warren labels *Dragons* "a kind of hybrid," with "a complicated narrative" and "many fictional problems," that is based on a real murder that occurred on the night of December 15, 1811, at Rocky Hill, near Smithland, Kentucky ("Self Interview" 2). This incident haunted Warren for the span of over four decades, as he worked intermittently for ten years on the poem's 1953 iteration and later heavily revised and published it anew in 1979 (J. Burt "Afterword" 465). *Brother to Dragons* tells the true story about how Lilburne Lewis, aided by his brother Isham, brutally butchered a young slave with an ax as punishment for breaking a pitcher that belonged to their mother. The intrigue of this story is heightened, of course, because Lilburne and Isham Lewis are nephews of President Thomas Jefferson, sons of Lucy Jefferson Lewis.

In this narrative poem, Warren controls a "séance" of "an array of historical and quasi-historical spirits" through a persona, a "cynical stand-in for himself," the R.P.W. character (Justus 61; and J. Burt, "Afterword" 465). Though always presented through the lens of art, the R.P.W. narrator reflects Warren's, Jarrell's, and Lowell's increasing tendency to insert their voices within the action of the poem. Like Jarrell, Warren's unique style allows for openness, spontaneity, colloquial speech, and even a "polyphony of voices" that succeeds in conveying authenticity (Blotner 290). Though there are many rich points of discussion for this work, it is most important for this study to highlight the elements that both Jarrell and Lowell emphasize in their reviews. Not surprisingly, they focus on the issues they had been discussing with each other for the past decade, those praised in Jarrell's *Poetry and the Age:* the dramatic narrative form, the believability of characters, and the level of life presented in the work.

Jarrell's review of *Brother to Dragons* is more favorable than Lowell's. Even before the work was published, Jarrell wrote to Mary: "When I woke up Sunday morning I had such a strong hunch that [Warren would] win the Pulitzer Prize that I told Red about it. I hope I turn out to be a prophet" (M. Jarrell 351). Arguably, as for Lowell's *Land of Unlikeness* and *Lord Weary's Castle* in the 1940s, Jarrell's review aimed to convince other readers to fulfill his prophecy. Jarrell begins "On the Underside of the Stone" claiming, "This is Robert Penn Warren's best book" (176). Even in a private letter to Warren in August 1953, Jarrell gushes: "It's one of the best long poems I've ever read, and everybody I've seen that's read it thinks so too" (M. Jarrell 385). According to Jarrell, Warren was hitting the mark for what he envisioned as the next thing in American poetry.

Lowell, though equally intrigued, was slightly more critical of Warren's work, most likely because of its connection to his own recent (and future) literary pursuits; *Brother to Dragons* resembles the length and range of Lowell's long narrative poem "The Mills of the Kavanaughs" published only two years earlier. Norma Procopiow proposes, "Lowell used the review [of Warren] to expose his dilemma about the proper limits of literary form, both thematic and linguistic" (304). Considering how Lowell seems to resolve some of these issues in the review and later in the format of his own book *Life Studies,* Procopiow's argument is quite convincing. As for Warren's unique form, Jarrell presents unabashed praise of Warren's achievement, and Lowell provides an admiring appraisal of the potential for Warren's new style. It is arguable that Lowell's *Life Studies* is, in fact, modeled after what he labeled as "the prose genius in verse" of Warren's *Brother to Dragons* ("Robert Penn Warren's *Brother to Dragons*" 68, 73).

In addition to aesthetic form, Jarrell's and Lowell's reviews linger over Warren's characters in *Brother to Dragons.* Considering their own efforts toward developing realistic characterization, it is not a surprise that both poets point to some places where Warren could improve in this category. Lowell comments, "These monstrous heroes are so extremely *literary* that their actual lives seem to have been imagined by anti-romantic Southern moderns" ("Robert Penn Warren's *Brother to Dragons*" 67), and Jarrell notes: "[The characters] say what people do not say, but would say if they could. When they are through we know them, and what they have done, very thoroughly, and we give a long marveling sigh." Even though these characters do not embody realistic qualities as effectively as those, say, in Frost's work, Jarrell acknowledges that Laetitia and "Ishey-boy" are "two of the most touching creations in American literature" ("On the Underside" 176). Lowell likewise admires how *Brother to Dragons* ultimately "triumphs through its characters, most of all through . . . Lucy and Laetitia Lewis" ("Robert Penn Warren's *Brother to Dragons*" 70).

It is easy to see why Lowell admires Warren's portrayal of Lucy, especially in passages that demonstrate her true-to-life motherly guilt over her sons' actions:

> I did the best I could. No, that's a lie.
> I did not do my best. I died. I know
> That if you love enough, and well, no death
> Can come to kill you while there's need of you.
> And there was need of me. Yes, if I had lived,
> My love, somehow, might have sustained my son.
> It might have been to him like a hand stretched out.
> And for my other son, my love, somehow,
> Might have been at least some light against the ignorant torpor
> That breathed from the dark land. Yes, if I had loved,
> Loved well enough to live, the tiptoe horror
> Had not come sly and thus insinuated
> Itself in my name to my dearest son.
> This was my crime. (p. 22)

The first line, "I did the best I could. No that's a lie," is reminiscent of the improvisational technique that marks some of Jarrell's best verse, including "Eighth Air Force" and "Transient Barracks," both narrated by soldiers caught in honest acts of self-evaluation, questioning themselves as the lines unfold down the page. It is also understandable as to why both Jarrell and Lowell praise Warren's portrayal of Laetitia's earthy, honest voice. Here, for example, Laetitia describes the murder from her point of view:

Yes, yes, that's right, it just filled up the room,
And the dark outside the room, and the whole world,
Or seemed to. Yet it wasn't loud, far off,
Being so far off, down there in the meat-house.
But soon as I heard it, it was like the world
Just started screaming by itself, and like I
Had just been waiting for years for it to start,
And all my life had been waiting for it, and every
Dead leaf in the woods just screamed just like a tongue,
A little tongue, not loud, and maybe you couldn't
Hear one alone, it was so weak, but together
All screaming they made a big scream filling
Up all the world, and filled my head, and my poor head
Was one big hollow echo full of dark,
Big as the world, and the whole world, all the mountains,
The rivers, creeks, and fields and hills and woods and every
Leaf screaming in the dark, and all the stars,
Was in my head and lost, and my poor head
Kept whirling bigger. And I tried to scream. (pp. 50–51)

To quote Lowell, Laetitia's description may be too *literary* to pass as authentic dialogue, but there is no denying the power in Warren's image of the surrounding natural objects collectively "screaming in the dark," horrified by the murder that just took place, a murder that is unnatural in itself. The clear distinctions between Lucy's and Laetitia's voices in syntax, diction, and tone, and the seamless changes from one to the other, rightfully encourage critics to honor the "texture gained by the variation of speech styles," most notably the freest, most realistic voice of R.P.W. (Bradbury, "Warren as Poet" 74).

R.P.W.'s conversational tone combined with realistic facts often cuts through the rest of the voices in order to present the "correct version" of history. John Burt posits, "The poem is intended as a critique of the American sense of national innocence, which Warren fears may lead America into an aggressive self-righteousness" ("Afterword" 479). An embodiment of Warren's criticism for such naïveté, Jefferson speaks in dreamy, idealistic language about the existence of the old house: "It is not gone, for I who never saw it, / See it, see it now," only for R.P.W. to interrupt and set the facts straight:

> I assure you it is gone. I know the place.
> Up Highway 109 from Hopkinsville,
> To Dawson Springs, then west on 62,
> Across Kentucky at the narrow neck,
> Two hours now, not more, for the road's fair. (pp. 14–15)

The concrete details and trustworthy ethos of R.P.W.'s character allow his voice to surface as the pragmatic truth teller. This effect is often repeated throughout the poem, such as when R.P.W. sheds realistic light on Laetitia's soulful prayer: "You don't ask much. Yet you ask everything, / And maybe just the one thing God can't give" (68). Or when he interrupts Isham in an effort to keep his story on track:

> To be more systematic, first things first,
> And let whatever the deuce this last thing is
> Go till the last. Suppose I summarize.
> Correct me when you wish. (117)

The presence of this lifelike voice that captures both immediacy and spontaneity continues to appear more frequently in Warren's later work as well as in that of Jarrell's and Lowell's.

In addition to commenting on Warren's form and characters, both Jarrell and Lowell praise *Brother to Dragons* for the essential element most highly coveted by these authors in their post–World War II poems: the ability to bring life into poetry. Lowell, continuing with his subtle criticism, notes: "Though tactless and voluminous, [*Brother to Dragons*] is also alive." As a result, Lowell concedes that despite the flaws he identifies in the review, "Warren has written his best book" ("Robert Penn Warren's *Brother to Dragons*" 68). Jarrell echoes Lowell's praise: "There is a wonderful amount of life in it," and elaborates by noting, "The poem is a net, wide enough, high enough, deep enough, to have caught most of the world inside it" ("On the Underside" 177). This "wider net" is a fitting metaphor for all three poets' work at midcentury and beyond.

Also experimenting with genre, in 1954 Jarrell tried his hand at achieving authenticity in his first and last "novel," *Pictures from an Institution.* The book was so clearly based on autobiographical truth that even Jarrell was hesitant to refer to the book as a novel. He instead described it to Lowell as "well, not really a novel, but a prose comedy" (M. Jarrell, *Randall Jarrell's Letters* 285). Most critics agree with Jarrell's self-assessment. Far from Warren's masterpiece *All the King's Men* and his other great works of fiction, *Pictures* is, more than anything, a collection of Jarrell's humorous musings on academia. J. A. Bryant Jr. confirms, "The voice and mind of the narrator—as in the poetry and the essays—are unmistakably those of Randall Jarrell" (118). The narrator's wit and insight are delivered distinctly in Jarrell's voice, from the snarky critiques of life at Benton to the highly authentic character sketches of Gertrude Johnson and President Robbins, whom, the narrator observes with disdain, "'did not have his Ph.D.'—but had that bothered one administrator upon this earth?" (*Pictures* 23). Like the mixed reviews Warren received from Lowell and Jarrell for *Brother to Dragons,* Jarrell earned some praise and some constructive criticism from his friends for *Pictures.*

In light of Warren's most recent attempt at blending genres in *Dragons,* it is telling to read Lowell's and Warren's reactions to Jarrell's work. Jarrell's biographer acknowledges: "Jarrell's mixed feelings about what he had done in *Pictures* came out in letters he wrote to Lowell as the book was nearing publication in the spring of 1954, and to Warren after its publication a year later" (Pritchard 243–44). Despite Jarrell's hesitations, his colleagues mostly supported *Pictures.* In response to Lowell's flattering letter, Jarrell gushed with gratitude: "Your comparisons and nice sayings for *Pictures from an Institution* were as winning as comparisons well could be—I love being compared to Pope and Arnold and now Cocteau, by you" (M. Jarrell 377). Most significant for this study, in Lowell's letter to Bishop he observes: "Fiction or not, it's rather terrific writing" (qtd. in Mariani 228).[6] Following Lowell's praise for Warren's hybrid of prose and verse and now his appreciation of Jarrell's hybrid between fiction and autobiography, it is clear that seeds were being planted in Lowell's mind. Lowell once stated, "If a poem is autobiographical—and this is true of any kind of autobiographical writing and of historical writing—you want the reader to say, this is true" (Seidel, "Interview" 272). This very element of being "true" is precisely what Lowell appreciated in Jarrell's novel and what readers would soon see in Lowell's *Life Studies.*

Not surprisingly, Warren's reaction to Jarrell's novel was similar to Lowell's. Jarrell related to Warren the difficulty he had in creating a work "in which the main structure isn't a plot or story," thereby admitting that these were truly "pictures," or snapshots from his real-life experience (qtd. in Pritchard 243–44). Warren responded: "I'm very keen about it. You really make the characters come over, with fullness, and make their world credible. . . . The only criticism I have has to do with the way some of the first part of the book is done. . . . It is, at times, a little too essayistic in the beginning. And sometimes the wit is 'set-up'—doesn't spring right out of things. . . . It's a very impressive book, a really fascinating book, and nobody but you could have written it" (Clark, Hendricks, and Perkins, *Selected Letters*, 4:51). Warren's note demonstrates how he continued to encourage Jarrell toward the common goals they had identified in the late forties. He praises Jarrell's rounded characters and the realistic portrayal of "their world," yet he critiques the artificial moments in which the scene seems manufactured rather than natural. It is as if Warren echoed the advice Jarrell himself gave to Lowell in 1945, in which Jarrell condemned the "too-mannered, mechanical, wonderfully contrived" elements of Lowell's poetry (M. Jarrell, *Randall Jarrell's Letters* 139). Jarrell's response to Warren's criticism is typical. He first characteristically jumps to defend his work but then yields to Warren's sage advice with a conciliatory tone: "Your letter about *Pictures* was such a joy to me. . . . About the first part: I see what you mean and you may be right, . . . maybe it's too superficial and essayistic" (399). Though Jarrell spent most of the fifties exploring other genres, his projects—and Warren's and Lowell's reactions to them—confirm that all three writers maintained a unified vision for American literature.

It is safe to say that Warren's Pulitzer Prize–winning *Promises* could be considered a quintessential work for this exact unified vision shared among the trio. Composed of narrative sequences, as opposed to the play-like format of *Dragons, Promises* achieves many of the same successes, though to an even greater degree. Most notably, Warren skillfully integrates history—national, regional, and personal—into narratives that burst with real life and the dramatic quality that these three poets equally sought after. The theory that Warren derives from Frost's "After Apple-Picking" doubles as a description for his pursuit in this significant book: "Art must stem from the literal world, from the common body of experience, and must be a magnified 'dream' of that experience as it has achieved meaning" ("Themes of Frost"

298). Throughout *Promises,* Warren presents a living microcosm, a slice of life, with the complex thought processes and dialectics encouraged by Jarrell, underlying ostensibly simplistic depictions of the world. In order to achieve authenticity in this living microcosm, similar to the turning point works of Jarrell and Lowell,[7] Warren expands his use of autobiographical narrative in *Promises.* James H. Justus observes, "Despite the foreign setting of *Promises,* the volume contains more poems about the poet's Kentucky childhood and about America generally than are found in previous volumes" (72). The experimental narrative style and reliance on local content that were first exhibited in "The Ballad of Billie Potts" are revamped in *Promises* and increasingly become the norm for Warren's later poetry.

One poem that demonstrates all of these characteristics working together is "Dragon Country: To Jacob Boehme," which brings together elements of Warren's boyhood memories with ancient folklore and current politics in a narrative poem that recounts the legendary tale of a Kentucky county notorious for unexplained deaths and disappearances. Like Frost, and the contemporary work of Jarrell and Lowell, Warren invokes colloquial speech to depict images from real-life experience in order to frame the poem:

> I was only a boy when Jack Simms reported the first depredation,
> What something had done to his hog pen. They called him a God-damn liar.
> Then said it must be a bear, after some had viewed the location,
> With fence rails, like matchwood, splintered, and earth a bloody mire. (5–8)

Also like Frost, Warren's deceptively simple lines are loaded with multiple layers of meaning. Hilton Kramer describes Warren's language in *Promises* as "at once grave and earthly, an instrument of metaphysical discourse that lives on easy, intimate terms with the folklore of the past. This is a poetry . . . filled with dramatic incident, vivid landscapes, and philosophical reflection" (13). Kramer's observation serves as a particularly fitting description for "Dragon Country," a poem that contains the dramatic incident of unsolved deaths—"the wagon turned on its side" and "Jebb Johnson's boot, with the leg, what was left, inside" (14, 35)—and the vivid landscape of political issues: "We were promised troops, the Guard, but the Governor's skin got thin / When up in New York the papers called him Saint George of Kentucky" (25–26), along with the realistic backdrop of the struggling southern region:

Yes, other sections have problems somewhat different from ours.
Their crops may fail, bank rates rise, on rumor of war loans be called,
But we feel removed from maneuvers of Russia, or other great powers,
And from much ordinary hope are now disenthralled. (41–44)

These lines could have easily been drawn from Warren's own Kentucky upbringing.

Finally, the poem, which serves as an imaginative explanation for the depopulation of the rural South, is heightened by philosophical reflection. The poem ends:

But if the Beast were withdrawn now, life might dwindle again
To the ennui, the pleasure, and night sweat, known in the time before
Necessity of truth had trodden the land, and heart, to pain,
And left, in darkness, the fearful glimmer of joy, like a spoor. (49–52)

This narrative reflection sheds light on the human need for both mystery and consequence. The poem concludes that "the Beast," which has been identified as the source of the county's "evil" and suffering, actually enlivens and animates the otherwise sleepy town. The human heart requires the threat of evil to create the "fearful glimmer of joy," which, far from the joy of the lifeless "pleasure" described in the absence of the Beast, is a joy that ignites the human heart's desperate search for "truth"—an apt image for Warren himself.

Another one of Warren's poems that exemplifies these poets' vision for American poetry is the sequence "Promises," which makes up the latter two-thirds of the book. Within this sequence, Warren is once again integrating national, regional, and personal history while creating lines that resonate on a universal level. This group of poems is dedicated to Warren's son, Gabriel, but his "you" takes on universal significance. "XI. Infant Boy at Midcentury, 1. When the Century Dragged," contains these prophetic lines:

You enter an age when the neurotic clock-tick
Of midnight competes with the heart's pulsed assurance of power.
You have entered our world at scarcely its finest hour,
And smile now life's gold Apollonian smile at a sick dialectic.
. . . .

To pause, in high pride of undisillusioned manhood,
At the gap that gives on the new century, and land,
And with calm heart and level eye command
That dawning perspective and possibility of human good. (5–8, 21–24)

Though these quatrains address real post–World War II fears for the timing of Warren's son's birth, the message also speaks to a generation of parents and, through the description of the son's smile as "Apollonian"—a reference to the ancient god of prophecy, intellectual pursuits, and the protection of the young—the passage becomes an amplified commentary on the history of the world. Victor Strandberg notes, "Warren devotes [*Promises*] to a scrutiny of experience, his own and his generation's, in order to derive a vision of the total meaning of experience, encompassing its past, present, and future, its heritage and its promises" (*Colder Fire* 174). Essentially, Warren achieves in *Promises* what he, along with Jarrell and Lowell, admired so deeply in Robert Frost: he creates what they considered universal portrayals of life that are rooted in real human experience.

A final poem that exemplifies one more pattern found throughout *Promises*, "Court-martial," collapses the past with the present to explore "life's long irony" in a narrative about a grandson who tries "somehow, to untie / The knot of History" of his grandfather's war stories (41–42). As Joseph Blotner points out, in *Promises* Warren "had given additional evidence of his technical mastery of form at the same time that he was broadening his subject matter. He was using the direct conversational mode where it helped him to ask the fundamental ontological questions that obsessed him" (315). Like *Brother to Dragons* and even Jarrell's *Pictures, Promises* increasingly draws from personal material and American history to simulate an act of self-reflection that includes readers in those ontological questions, as in "Court-martial":

In the dusk by his chair
I undertook to repair
The mistakes of his old war.
Hunched on that toy terrain,
Campaign by campaign,
I sought, somehow, to untie
The knot of History,

For in our shade I knew
That only the Truth is true,
That life is only the act
To transfigure all fact,
And life is only a story
And death is only the glory
Of the telling of the story. (36–49)

Like *Brother to Dragons*, the narrator contemplates the "real version" of historical facts as he tries to parse Truth from his grandfather's tales of battle; for Warren, to know the past is to know the self, and this great quest served as rich fodder for his post–World War II poetry.

The end of Warren's "Court-martial" notably echoes Jarrell's "Transient Barracks"; Jarrell's line reads, "The thing about you is, you're *real*," and Warren's: "The world is real. It is there" (133). Warren thereby captures the narrators' mutual search for discovering and presenting what is real in this world. Whether recalling boyhood in "Gold Glade"; relating more recent personal experiences in the sequence "To a Little Girl, One Year Old, in a Ruined Fortress"; addressing the reader with a conversational *you* in "Country Burying" and "Summer Storm"; remaining observantly detached in "School Lesson Based on Word of Tragic Death of Entire Gillum Family," "Founding Fathers, Nineteenth-Century Style, Southeast U.S.A.," and "Dragon Country: To Jacob Boehme"; or speaking to his son directly in poems like "Lullaby: Smile in Sleep," Warren's poetic and prophetic voice in *Promises* records the narrator's attempt to comprehend the world—events, places, and people—in its entirety, a description also perfectly apropos for Lowell's *Life Studies*.

Randall Jarrell, Army Air Force, enlisted in October 1942. Photo taken May 30, 1945. *Courtesy of UNC Greensboro University Archives, Randall Jarrell Papers, Mss 009.*

Robert Lowell, undated.
Courtesy of Greenslade Special Collections & Kenyon Archives, Kenyon College.

Friends and collaborators: Randall Jarrell and Robert Penn Warren, 1963–64.
Courtesy of UNC Greensboro University Archives, Randall Jarrell Papers, Mss 009.

Roommates: Randall Jarrell, Robert Lowell, and Peter Taylor.
Photo taken at the 1948 Arts Forum.
Courtesy of UNC Greensboro University Archives, Randall Jarrell Papers, Mss 009.

Robert Penn Warren and mentor John Crowe Ransom.
Courtesy of Greenslade Special Collections & Kenyon Archives, Kenyon College.

UNC Greensboro chancellor Otis Singletary, Robert Penn Warren, and Randall Jarrell, 1963.

Courtesy of UNC Greensboro University Archives, Randall Jarrell Papers, Mss 009.

5

Reconsidering *Life Studies* & Lowell's Career

For *Life Studies* (1959), Lowell had a similar aim to that of Jarrell in *The Seven-League Crutches* (1951) and Warren in *Promises: Poems, 1954–1956* (1957): to comprehend and, in turn, authentically reflect the world around him with concrete details that transcend ordinary life to connect to a more universal level for readers. Because of the increased autobiographical content, the looser forms, and the mixture of poetry and prose in this book, critics often argue that *Life Studies* marks an entirely new phase for Lowell. The truth is, however, it is a continuation of the direction he had been following with Jarrell and Warren since the early 1940s. For this reason, before examining the text, it is necessary to call into question some widely accepted theories on *Life Studies*, from the way it defines Lowell's career to the way it defines the literary canon. Stated plainly, Lowell's success as a poet—and his place in literary history as one who helped to shape American poetry at midcentury—can be attributed more accurately to the influence of the southern Fugitives and their circle than to a mislabeled breakthrough into "confessional" poetry.

According to most sources of the canon, Lowell serves as an exemplary figure for the breakthrough narrative of literary history that was created and upheld by critics who were working to classify poetic trends of the second half of the twentieth century. That often-repeated narrative, which has recently come under fire for its reductive nature, would have readers believe that Lowell fills the mold of one who wrote "several books of highly praised New Critical well-wrought urns (objective and impersonal)," then suddenly "understood that poetry could be fragmentary, subjective, and personal," thereby resulting in *Life Studies*, a watershed in twentieth-century poetry (Longenbach 5). James E. B. Breslin, in *From Modern to Contemporary: American Poetry, 1945–1965* (1985), and David Perkins, in *A History of Modern Poetry: Modernism and After* (1987), develop similar arguments from this flawed point of view in their respective texts, as does Sandra M. Gilbert, in "Mephistophilis in Maine: Rereading 'Skunk Hour'" (1986): "*Life Studies* is famous for two things: First, it marked a decisive break with the formal verse patterns and dense, metaphorical rhetoric of the early poetry that had established Robert Lowell as a leading poet in the high Modernist mode. Second, it repudiated the key Modernist ideal of authorial impersonality on behalf of what seemed at the time to be barefaced self-revelation, thus ushering in the 'confessional' mode that dominated American poetry in the 1960s" (80). Stripped of nuance, Gilbert's argument works primarily to fit Lowell, and other poets like him, into a neat category. Essentially, critics understood Lowell's career as being cut in two distinct halves: first, the pre–*Life Studies* works, replete with identifiable influences of formalism, modernism, and New Criticism; and second, works including *Life Studies* and those that came after, which eschew all previous influences in favor of a raw, confessional mode. As time passes and the gift of hindsight presents itself, critics are questioning these originally hard-drawn lines and—in the words of Lawrence Kramer—aiming "to fray the edges" of the "orthodox understanding" of Lowell and *Life Studies* ("Freud and the Skunks" 81).

In addition to the more complex counterarguments to this commonly adopted narrative, there is the simple fact that the overemphasis on *Life Studies* and relative neglect of Lowell's subsequent works leads the less conscientious reader to believe that *Life Studies* is essentially the end of the line for Lowell. Such a viewpoint prevents readers from understanding Lowell's career, more accurately, as "an attractively circuitous muddle" (Longenbach 9). Like Jarrell after *The Seven-League Crutches* and Warren in the works that follow *Promises*, Lowell continued to experiment with style after *Life Studies*. In an interview with Frederick Seidel late in Lowell's life, he admits that "there's another point about this mysterious business of prose and poetry, form and content, and the reasons for breaking forms. I don't think there's any very satisfactory answer. I seesaw back and forth between something highly metrical and something highly free; there isn't any one way to write" ("Interview" 269). Just as critics almost always overlook the role of

Warren and Jarrell's influence on Lowell's work, they also tend to ignore that *Life Studies* is the furthest point in the swing of the pendulum on Lowell's line of "closed" to "open." In the works after *Life Studies*, Lowell "seesaws" between the freer forms that marked his influential book and more conventional forms, such as the fourteen-line sonnet structure to which he adheres throughout *Notebook, 1967–68* (1970); *History; For Lizzie and Harriet;* and *The Dolphin* (all 1973). Even a quick glance at these later poems reveals that Lowell never returned wholly to his pre–*Life Studies* style but instead—like Jarrell and Warren after their seminal works—continued a search for authenticity in whatever form seemed appropriate for the content.

Aside from the misrepresentation of Lowell's pendulum swing, the basic premises of these canonical arguments are to some extent accurate. The characteristics of Lowell's early work do indeed include tight forms with classical characteristics, and in the 1940s and beyond, Lowell, Warren, and Jarrell were working toward creating more conversational verse with a less rigid aesthetic. However, it is problematic to espouse the arc of Lowell's work as merely a chronological shift between mutually exclusive binaries: closed to open, formal to free, rigorous to loose, impersonal to raw, and objective to subjective. Not only does this stance preclude an understanding of the overlap in Lowell's work—for example, in the ways that *The Mills of the Kavanaughs* (1951) serves as a bridge to *Life Studies*—but it also presents a mistaken depiction of Lowell's development as a poet.

As an example of Lowell's misidentified artistic route, Breslin tells the story of Lowell's career by equating modernism "with formalism, mere craft, and stultifying hierarchy—to account for the 'breakthrough' of American poetry at large," and furthermore, focuses on William Carlos Williams's influence on Lowell because "it's easier to contrast [Williams's] values with the New Criticism, telling the story of Lowell's career as a linear trajectory" (Breslin 9). Within these myopic depictions, Breslin and other critics frequently ignore the early and late points of Lowell's career in order for him to fit more precisely into the category of previously "stilted" poets—John Berryman, W. S. Merwin, Adrienne Rich, and Theodore Roethke among them—who were able to break free from the chains of the "anxiety of influence" that once bound them.[1] The breakthrough narrative, however, is particularly inadequate for Lowell.

In an interview with Frederick Seidel, Lowell reveals that before he arrived on Allen Tate's doorstep in 1937, he was already writing in the style of

Williams: "I wasn't a very good writer then. . . . I was trying to write like William Carlos Williams, very simple, free verse, imagistic poems" ("Interview" 280). Lowell's comment is reminiscent of Jarrell's critique of Williams's imagist-objectivist background, which, though it "helped his poems by their emphasis on truthfulness, exactness, concrete 'presentation,'" also "harmed the poems by their underemphasis on organization, logic, narrative, generalization" (Jarrell, "Introduction to Williams" 244). Though Jarrell did not reach this conclusion until later in his career, Lowell recognized at twenty years old that his earliest Williams-inspired poetry required additional complexity and depth, such as what he admired in poems by John Crowe Ransom and Allen Tate.

Therefore, when critics, such as Adam Kirsch, argue that 1952 was "around the time Lowell was turning into a Williams disciple," they are ignoring Lowell's original preoccupation with Williams's style. Ian Hamilton astutely asserts that in the 1950s, "although Lowell was in regular admiring contact with the older poet at this time and had been particularly dazzled by a reading Williams had given at Wellesley in 1956 . . . , he knew that the lessons he could learn from him would always be of the most general kind: loosen meter, abandon rhyme, use ordinary speech, introduce more characters, and so on. Even the very personal poems that Williams was writing in the mid-fifties were of a radiant simplicity that Lowell could marvel at but never think to copy" (232). A more accurate version of Kirsch's earlier assertion is that Lowell was a true "Williams disciple" in the late thirties. By the fifties, however, he was a wisely discerning author who—though reinvigorated by Williams's freer structures and use of the American idiom after his immersion in Ransom's formalism and Tate's high modernism—was also well aware of the limitations of imitating Williams's verse. The last line of Hamilton's quotation further complicates Kirsch's claim and calls into question Perkins's point that Lowell is "conceal[ing]" his "rigorous artistry" in later work (Perkins 348). Never entirely in line with the "radiant simplicity" of Williams in later years, even Lowell's seemingly simple, so-called confessional poems are multidimensional and attentive to the implications of language and aesthetics. To reiterate, Lowell never abandoned Ransom's principle that form and content are inextricably linked. His artistry was not "concealed" in *Life Studies;* it was merely taking on a new shape.

Though Kirsch neglects to mention Lowell's initial encounter with Williams, part of his argument is valuable for dismantling the conventional stance on Lowell's "breakthrough" at midcentury. Kirsch perceptively acknowledges the significant connections among Lowell, Jarrell, and Williams in the fifties; in particular, he highlights how Lowell's (reawakened) appreciation of Williams coincides with Jarrell's influential essay on the author. Furthermore, Kirsch points to the fact that Jarrell praises Williams "for being 'spontaneous, open, impulsive, emotional, observant,'" which, Kirsch notes, are "just the qualities that would distinguish *Life Studies* from *Lord Weary's Castle*" (18). Supporting a main tenet of this study, Kirsch recognizes that Jarrell's appreciation of Williams had an indirect impact on Lowell's style that was as influential as the direct impact Williams had on Lowell's work. In the same way that Warren's renewed interest in Robert Frost in 1947 inspired Jarrell to see Frost's work in an inspiring new light, Jarrell's essay on Williams encouraged Lowell to return to that poet's work with newly eager eyes. As has been described at length, Warren, Jarrell, and Lowell gradually came to develop a mode that was distinctly their own: a mode that was not born from a violent "breakthrough" but, instead, from innovative collaboration paired with a painstakingly deliberate mining of the giants in American poetry—Ransom, Tate, Eliot, Frost, and Williams among them.

Another example of a critic who purports the breakthrough narrative in an effort to explain Lowell's career, Richard Fein articulates a common viewpoint on Lowell's work: "*Life Studies* . . . not only takes its place along the route of American poetry, it helps establish the terrain. . . . Lowell's career measures the development of modern poetry from the hard surface, the intellectually brilliant writing . . . to a poetry that does not exactly deny this tendency but that is low-keyed, approaching the informalities and laxities of prose" (68–69). Fein is not exaggerating the lasting impact of Lowell's *Life Studies* on contemporary American poetry, nor is he mistaken in his description of the prose-like elements in Lowell's book. However, the subtext of Fein's purposely vague language regarding the "brilliance" of Lowell's book—"a poetry that *does not exactly deny* this tendency"—implies a lesser degree of intellectual rigor in *Life Studies*. Taking this argument a step further, M. L. Rosenthal does not bother hedging in his critique of *Life Studies*, describing this work as "impure art . . . unpleasantly egocentric. . . . Since its self-therapeutic motive is so obvious and persistent, something of this impression sticks all the way" ("Poetry as Confession" 51).

Fein's implication that *Life Studies* is somehow inferior in intellect and Rosenthal's interpretation of the book as self-therapy are two claims against which Lowell's reputation still struggles. In fact, recent critics have pointed to the ways in which these two misconceptions have contributed to the perpetration of the woefully inadequate term *confessional* to describe Lowell's work. Frank Bidart reports that when Rosenthal coined the label "confessional," Lowell "winced at the term," aware of its damaging implications.[2] Considering that Bidart—a famous poet who learned a lot from Lowell—similarly had to throw off a reputation as a confessional writer, he does a particularly fine job of reconceptualizing this term, arguing against its connotation of a "helpless outpouring, secrets whispered with an artlessness that is their badge of authenticity" and instead favoring an interpretation of "Lowell's candor" as "an illusion created by art" ("On 'Confessional' Poetry" 997). Steven Gould Axelrod, James Longenbach, Thomas Travisano, and Christian Sisack similarly identify the integral role of artistry in even Lowell's most personal, intimate poetry.[3] Now that critics are starting to realize "Lowell's [late] poetry is too highly crafted, sophisticatedly ironic, and explicitly heterogeneous to be considered 'raw,'" it is time to interpret Lowell's *Life Studies*, and the works that follow, as evidence of Lowell's continuation on the path alongside Warren and Jarrell, rather than as a radical break from everything that had come before (Sisack 270).

By examining the years between *The Mills of the Kavanaughs* and *Life Studies*, one may identify contributing factors to Lowell's style change aside from the overemphasized influence of Williams, the frequently discussed connection to Elizabeth Bishop, or the often referenced 1957 West Coast reading tour during which Lowell gained exposure to the Beat poets and proclaimed: "I became sorely aware of how few poems I had written, and that these few had been finished at the latest three or four years earlier. Their style seemed distant, symbol-ridden, and willfully difficult. I began to paraphrase my Latin quotations, and to add extra syllables to a line to make it clearer and more colloquial. I felt my old poems hid what they were really about, and many times offered a stiff, humorless, and even impenetrable surface" ("On 'Skunk Hour'" 227). As mentioned earlier, part of what inspired Lowell—along with Warren and Jarrell—toward more colloquial, conversational verse in the fifties was a desire to enter an accessible colloquy with readers (in this case listeners). Rosenthal condemns the poems in *Life Studies* for being merely self-therapeutic, and Tate wrote to Lowell in 1957, warning him: "*All* the poems about your family . . . are definitely *bad*. . . . Quite bluntly, these details . . . are of interest only to you. . . . They have no public or literary interest" (I. Hamilton 237). Whereas Rosenthal and Tate saw these "self-centered" poems as the negative result of a poet turning too far inward, Lowell deemed his more flexible forms and increased autobiographical content as the result of shedding his "prehistoric monsters" in order to bring his poems more in line with an authentic portrayal of real life, a mission also shared by Warren and Jarrell ("On 'Skunk Hour'" 227).

Lowell remarked that while his reading tour pushed him even farther from dense classical references and difficult diction—a track he had already begun treading in *Lord Weary's Castle* and *The Mills of the Kavanaughs* as a result of Jarrell's suggestions—he was "no convert to the 'beats.'" In Lowell's 1960 acceptance speech for the National Book Award, he made a thinly veiled swipe at Allen Ginsberg, claiming that contemporary verse was "often like an unscored libretto by some bearded but vegetarian Castro." In fact, Lowell instead attributes his style changes to another factor that draws him in line with Warren and Jarrell at this time: "What influenced me more than San Francisco and reading aloud was that for some time I had been writing prose" ("On 'Skunk Hour'" 227). Not a coincidence, Lowell began writing prose shortly after both the publication of Warren's *Brother to Dragons* in 1953, which Lowell reviewed as "prose genius in verse," and Jarrell's *Pictures from an Institution* the next year, which Lowell praised: "Fiction or not, it's rather terrific writing" (Lowell, "Robert Penn Warren's *Brother to Dragons*" 73; S. Hamilton 201). It is difficult to gauge how much Jarrell actually pushed Lowell toward prose writing, but Jarrell did write to Lowell after *Pictures* encouraging him to also "write a prose book of some length," adding, "I still don't want to say *novel*" (M. Jarrell 285); and Lowell did, soon after, begin writing autobiographical prose similar to the personal mode of Jarrell's book.[4]

Furthermore, around the time that Lowell was crafting new poems for *Life Studies*, he was once again in the regular routine of sending drafts of his poems to Jarrell for his valued commentary; on October 11, 1957, for example, he enclosed a rough copy—unsigned and undated, complete with typos—of what would become his brilliant "Skunk Hour" (Berg Collection, Lowell Collection, Outgoing Correspondence to Jarrell). He wrote to Jarrell: "I've been writing poems lately again. . . . [and] loosening up the meter . . . I am heavily in your debt. I've been going through your [1955] selected poems quite a lot, and marvel again how supple . . . and personal they are" (S. Hamilton 295–96). A passage from Lowell's "91 Revere Street" perfectly encapsulates what Warren, Jarrell, and Lowell worked to achieve in their simultaneous move toward looser, more autobiographical poetry: "There, the vast number of remembered *things* remains rocklike. Each is in its place, each has its function, its history, its drama. . . . The things and their owners come back urgent with life and meaning—because finished, they are endurable and perfect" (p. 122). Once rendered into poetic form, the "things" of their individual and collective pasts are crystallized into art forms, capable of being magnified and raised to the universal level. Purely retold memories are merely "confessions," but once arranged with a skillful, artistic eye, they become finished works of art with the urgency of life that all three authors admired in Robert Frost in the late 1940s and forevermore strived to re-create in their own work.

While it is likely that Jarrell's *Pictures* and *Selected Poems* had an effect on the production of Lowell's "91 Revere Street,"[5] it is almost undeniable that Warren's *Brother to Dragons* had an impact on Lowell's style shift in *Life Studies*. Lowell's contentious relationship with *Brother to Dragons* is described earlier in this study. Essentially, since *Dragons* was similar in length and tone to Lowell's recently published poem "The Mills of the Kavanaughs," Lowell was particularly critical of Warren's work, perhaps fueled by a sense of competition or even self-doubt. There is no denying that Lowell was also wildly impressed by *Dragons,* naming it "a model and an opportunity" and daring to hope "its matter and method will become common property," which is just what Lowell appears to have done ("Robert Penn Warren's *Brother to Dragons*" 68). Norma Procopiow argues that Lowell's review of *Brother to Dragons* was "the prolegomena for the poetic of *Life Studies*," forcing Lowell to contemplate the difficulties he had with his own writing: "how to mix dialogue with narrative voice; how to sustain a long poem without growing 'puffy, paralyzed, and pretentious'; how to achieve the historical sense with documentary detail" (304). The flaws (and the successes) that Lowell identified in Warren's work served as teaching points as he shaped and altered his poetic style for the second half of the century. In fact, John Burt, editor of the forthcoming new edition of *Brother to Dragons*, argues that *Dragons* "certainly posted the direction Lowell himself was shortly to follow in *Life Studies* and *For the Union Dead*" ("Afterword" 486).

There is evidence to suggest that Warren's influence on Lowell's creation of *Life Studies* is greater than Norma Procopiow, John Burt, and other critics have previously acknowledged. In the early fifties, the relationship between

Warren and Lowell was strongly grounded in a mutual respect for one another's literary opinions and work. In a telling letter from March 10, 1950, Lowell wrote to Warren after reading poems at the University of Minnesota, where Warren was teaching at the time: "Your hospitality leaves one rather breathless and gasping, and I almost forgot to thank you, and tell you I enjoyed it all tremendously—particularly talking with you. . . . Your section on the sources of poems covers more than I would have imagined possible in the space.[6] One thing that might be added would be translations—prose originals of Shakespeare and Jonson; Pound's 'Seafarer' with a literal translation—some of Wyatt; . . . then Valery's idea of revision as both improvement and change. . . . Wish we could move the restaurant where I had the double martini and you, no longer on the wagon, here next week for Dylan Thomas's reading" (S. Hamilton 154–55). The tone and content of this letter reveals the genuine friendship between the poets, which is strengthened by long talks, mutual interests, and shared martinis. It also depicts both men on an equal playing field, with Lowell providing thoughtful advice for Warren's current literary project.

Some years later, Warren wrote to Lowell: "I wish you had been with Peter [Taylor] and me when we had our trip to Naples. . . . I'm glad you like some of the poems. . . . I enclose one begun last summer and just now finished" (Clark, Hendricks, and Perkins, *Selected Letters* 4:249). Lowell remained a sounding board for Warren, for both his works in criticism and poetry. Warren even trusted Lowell's judgment in matters of administration in academia. On August 26, 1959, Warren wrote to Bruce Dearing: "You ask about a writer who might be brought to your university [University of Delaware]. Certainly Snodgrass is a poet of high quality. I know nothing about him as a teacher, but I hear from my friend Cal Lowell that he is a fine person. I am sure that would be a good appointment" (4:261). Based on their connection, it was surely with an invested, carefully attentive eye that Lowell read and reviewed Warren's long, experimental poem, *Brother to Dragons*.

Lowell's review of *Dragons* reveals sincere admiration for Warren's unique ability to blend poetry and prose in order to create a dramatic narrative poem that is desirably "alive." Lowell extols Warren's new approach: "I feel not only that Warren has written a successful poem but that in this work he most truly seems to approach the power of those writers one has always felt hovering about him, those poetic geniuses of prose, Melville and Faulkner. In Warren's case, it is the prose genius in verse which is so startling" ("Robert Penn Warren's *Brother to Dragons*" 73). Warren's distinctive hybrid form would have seemed all the more "startling" to Lowell, who was still reeling from his struggles with "Mills" and, in his words, was "finding that your old style won't say any of the things that you want to" (S. Hamilton 196). He further complained to Jarrell, "It's been tough getting down to writing. . . . [because of] a wavering between a desire not to repeat, and the void and formlessness of what I haven't tried" (Berg Collection, Lowell Collection, Outgoing Correspondence to Jarrell). In light of these comments, he would have been all the more receptive to imitating Warren's style. One may recall the moment in Warren's interview of Lowell in which after Lowell identifies some of his own lines as "both slightly prosy and harsh," Warren replies, "Prosy and harsh, yet they come with a great shiver, both of them." It is significant that shortly after this conversation, Warren published *Brother to Dragons* and Lowell, *Life Studies*. Lowell recognized in Warren a stylistic method to bring new life to the forms of their shared mentors: "It is the prose genius in verse which is so startling"[7]—the "prose genius in verse" that would define Lowell's success in *Life Studies*.

Without acknowledging the connection to Warren, Lowell's biographer Paul Mariani reflects on this period for Lowell: "The essential element missing . . . , he'd come to see, was a sense of lived experience . . . a poetry that went beyond poetry to incorporate the living river of voices, rich and diverse in its sources, that made up this construct called America" (*Lost Puritan* 243). Mariani might as well be referring directly to the particular elements Lowell admired in Warren's *Brother to Dragons*: the "sense of lived experience" that Lowell celebrated in his review; the "poetry that went beyond poetry" into the less exclusive, more inclusive realm of prose; and the "living river of voices, rich and diverse," which is a pinpoint perfect description of the literal voices—in dialogue—of the characters in Warren's long poem. From the unpretentious, honest vernacular of Laetitia to the intellectual, idealistic Jefferson and especially the prophetic, autobiographical R.P.W., one may easily recognize what inspired Lowell in Warren's work.

Indeed, in addition to style, Warren's work also inspired Lowell to refresh his content. Back to a reconsideration of the confessional paradigm, the influence of Warren's *Brother to Dragons* quite simply deserves more recognition for Lowell's autobiographical turn in *Life Studies*. James H. Justus points to this very element in Warren's work: "The use of himself, both as a persona and as a fully developed character, is one aspect of *Brother to Drag-*

ons that justifies the frequent observation that it marks a watershed in Warren's career, that it is the enabling work that allowed the later poetry to develop in a more open and confessional manner" (61). In other words, though *Life Studies* earned Lowell the position as poster boy for the confessionals, Warren had already made notable strides in this genre six years earlier. By further exploring this turn to "confession," careful readers quickly realize that it is not confession at all but, instead, a meticulously crafted, multilayered style of narrative poetry that allows Warren and Lowell to find their own artistic voices by pushing on the boundaries of their mentors' conventions.

In terms of the aesthetics tied to Warren and Lowell's artistic voices, recall Fein's quotation in which he points to the "low-keyed" nature of Lowell's *Life Studies* as it "approach[es] the informalities and laxities of prose" (68–69). It is difficult to ignore the similarities between Lowell's "laxities of prose" and those—as Lowell enthusiastically describes them—in the "unfaltering, unstitled blank verse" of Warren's *Brother to Dragons* ("Robert Penn Warren's *Brother to Dragons*" 67). For example, Warren draws on memories of his family for many passages of R.P.W.'s dialogue, such as:

> It was remembering my father that flushed these thoughts.
> But now speculation settles like the dust
> When wind stops, and there is only the great quiet of the
> > sunlit space,
> For I recall one Sunday afternoon,
> How, after the chicken dinner and ice cream,
> Amid the comics and word of the world's disaster,
> I saw him sit and with grave patience teach
> Some small last Latin to a little child. (p. 30)

and:

> The grave of my father's father is lost in the woods.
> The oak-root has heaved down the headstone.
> I should not know how to come there. Who knows now?
> My father himself has, no doubt, lost that orientation.
> He says: "About this time, about December,
> I recollect my father, how he'd take
> Some yellow percoon, just the root, and mash it,

And bark of prickly ash, and do the same,
And cram it in a gallon jug, with whisky."
"What for," I said, "—to make a kind of drink?"
"Why, no," he said, "it's medicine to take."
He'd set the jug near three months on a shelf.
To wait and make the medicine come true.
And spring came on, and then he'd call us boys—
All boys, we were a house of boys he had—
And line us up and give it, morn and night.
"What for?" I said. And he: "Why, Son, I reckon
It's old-folks talk, but then they held it true,
How in the spring you had to thin the blood." (pp. 204–5)

Though Lowell's portrayal of his prominent New England family differs in content and tone from the tales of Warren's South, with its "percoon" and "gallon jug," both speakers draw on autobiography and insert bits of dialogue to create authentic, yet artistic, images of real life. The similarities are most obvious in Lowell's "91 Revere Street," which—as part 2 of *Life Studies*—is most notable for its prosaic characteristics:

I used to sit through the Sunday dinners absorbing cold and anxiety from the table. I imagined myself hemmed in by our new, inherited Victorian Myers furniture. (147)

My father had been born two months after his own father's death. At each stage of his life, he was to be forlornly fatherless. He was a deep boy brought up entirely by a mild widowed mother and an intense widowed grand-mother. (126)

"A penny for your thoughts, Schopenhauer," my mother would say.
"I am thinking about pennies," I'd answer.
"When *I* was a child I used to love telling Mama everything I had done," Mother would say.
"But you're not a child," I would answer. (128)

Reminiscent of Warren's lines, Lowell's memories of Sunday dinners, faded recollections of grandparents, and snippets of remembered conversation with his parents characterize the supposedly revolutionary and confessional style of this major work in *Life Studies*.

In addition to the more obvious link between *Dragons* and "91 Revere Street," each poem in part 4 of *Life Studies* maintains the same Warren-esque blend of autobiography, poetry, and prose-like characteristics. From the more eminent "My Last Afternoon with Uncle Devereux Winslow," "Sailing Home from Rapallo," "Waking in the Blue," "Memories of West Street and Lepke," and "Skunk Hour" to the lesser-known "Dunbarton," "Grandparents," and "Terminal Days at Beverly Farms," these dramatic narrative poems—with their "laxities of prose"—are remarkably similar to Warren's style. Though Lowell's diction reveals his narrative voice, the content, tone, and style of "Dunbarton" exemplify some parallels of Lowell's narrator to R.P.W.'s voice in *Brother to Dragons*. Lowell's lines read:

> He was my Father. I was his son.
> On our yearly autumn get-aways from Boston
> to the family graveyard in Dunbarton,
> he took the wheel himself—
> like an admiral at the helm.
> . . . .
> Grandfather and I
> raked leaves from our dead forebears,
> defied the dank weather
> with "dragon" bonfires.
> . . . .
> In the mornings I cuddled like a paramour
> in my Grandfather's bed,
> while he scouted about the chattering greenwood stove. (10–14, 35–38,
> 58–60)

Both poets present narrators who discuss and visit family grave sites with their fathers while engaging in explorations of the self amid both familial and regional history—a metaphysical journey that becomes ever more important in the later poetry of both authors.

In the same way that Warren's *Brother to Dragons* deserves more credit for influencing Lowell's autobiographical turn in *Life Studies*, his 1957 work *Promises: Poems, 1954–1956* should also be referenced in context of the praise Lowell received for organizing his poems into intricately plotted sequences. Upon the publication of *Life Studies,* Rosenthal remarked: "The completed *Life Studies* is a sequence in which interrelationships create a larger context that deepens the impact of the individual poems. Lowell's achievement, critics have generally agreed, is complex in that he broke new ground, not only in the individual poems, but in the group as a whole by further extending the modern concept of the poetic sequence" (qtd. in Doreski 120). While other contemporary poets were also experimenting with the powerful effect of creating these interrelationships, scholars have established Warren among the most successful in the art of the poetic sequence. Randolph Runyon's *The Braided Dream* is a book almost entirely dedicated to Warren's mastery of the sequence technique, which reportedly surfaces in *Promises* (Runyon 2). James A. Grimshaw similarly marks the sequence as one of the defining characteristics of Warren's mature poetry, claiming: "The years 1953 to 1966 show Warren moving more into his own voice in his poems. His poetry of this period exhibits an increased use of poetic sequences" (123); and Hilton Kramer notes that the books of Warren's later phase "must, indeed, be taken whole, for they trace a particular course of feeling and thought. . . . The long-breathed utterance that shapes this style does not invite or reward interruption" (15).

In addition to the numerous scholars who confirm Warren's implementation of the poetic sequence before the publication of Lowell's *Life Studies,* there is also proof that this topic was directly addressed between Warren and Lowell. Warren expressed his approval for Lowell's use of the sequence technique in a letter: "One more thing I want to say, out of the many that could be said: it is remarkable how each book of yours gives the impression of a unity, and this one [*Near the Ocean*] most of all, the quality of a long poem rather than a collection" (Clark, Hendricks, and Perkins, *Selected Letters* 4:501). There is a hint of teacher's pride for a "pupil" who successfully followed instruction; at the very least, there is evidence that both poets maintained a similar vision for the purposeful effect of this significant element in American poetry.

As is to be expected, Jarrell also had a hand in directing Lowell's poetic shift at this point. On October 11, 1957, Lowell wrote to Jarrell: "I've been writing poems lately again, my first in a good four years. And I want to try them out on you! . . . I've been loosening up the meter, as you'll see, and horsing out all the old theology and symbolism" (S. Hamilton 295).

Jarrell must have eagerly critiqued and responded to Lowell's poem because less than two weeks later, Lowell wrote that it was "terribly refreshing to know that you and Mary liked my *Skunks* ['Skunk Hour']. I've been working like a skunk, doggedly and happily since mid-August and have seven or eight poems finished (?) some quite long and all very direct and personal. They are mostly written in a sort of free verse. . . . I'll get them typed for you next week and mail them off. I'll be very sad if you don't like them. I don't see how I could ever have finished *Lord Weary* without your quips and praise" (297–98). Similar to their correspondence from a decade earlier, this letter reveals Lowell's unyielding respect for Jarrell's critical opinion and also proves that they continued to discuss their poetic changes in matters from style to content.

Lowell proudly reported to Elizabeth Bishop that in addition to the approval of "Skunk Hour," Jarrell provided a general note of praise on his recent work: "The motion has changed and is much clearer and easier" (S. Hamilton 299). The "motion" to which Jarrell refers is created by Lowell's irregular meter and line lengths; his newer poetry moves along the rhythms of speech, as is exemplified within the sestets of "Skunk Hour." In place of the heavily metered stresses and unrelenting sustained rhythms, here Lowell loosens the firm grip on his lines in order to capture the immediacy of experience.

Yet one more element of this *Life Studies* argument is introduced in a letter from Lowell to A. Alvarez in 1959: "Jarrell's is the only criticism I've had that bit in very deep. Of course, it's too favorable probably, but I have other reasons for liking what he says. I take rather his line on American poetry" (S. Hamilton 337). Indeed, as Lowell made waves in literary history with the publication of *Life Studies*, he was remarkably in line with Jarrell's and Warren's views on American verse. Ironically, perhaps due to the greater critical attention Lowell has attracted over the years, scholars often read the situation conversely. After the publication of Jarrell's *The Woman at the Washington Zoo* in 1960, Jarrell was understood as having taken Lowell's line on American poetry. Helen Vendler remarks that for Jarrell, there was a "growing drift from the personal that was not reversed until *The Woman at the Washington Zoo.* . . . This reversal . . . brings Jarrell into the Confessional School" (98–99). Another judgment based on the breakthrough narrative, Vendler's statement clearly misses the mark.

One critic who did not miss the mark was John Crowe Ransom; as Stephen Burt acknowledges, "Some of Jarrell's best interpreters were his contemporaries" and those who knew him well (xvi). Ransom's contribution to *Randall Jarrell, 1914–1965* credits Jarrell for the poetic technique of infusing prose-like characteristics into poetry, not Lowell or even Warren. As would be expected from Ransom, he critiques the stylistic technique that strays far from his own: "I don't know if the combination of prose properties and poetic properties in the same piece is as good as either prose or poetry by itself; the prose and the poetry seem to adulterate one another" ("Rugged Way" 170). Though he may not have approved of the innovative strategy, he was able to see that though Warren and Lowell did have a large part in developing this style—Warren in *Brother to Dragons* and *Promises* and Lowell in *Life Studies*—Jarrell's poetry in the 1940s already contained conversational, prose-like elements that most likely inspired the other two authors. Another flaw in the reductive breakthrough narrative, Warren was also mistakenly deemed as a subscriber to "Lowell's" revolutionary poetic form. Joseph Blotner explains: "Warren was caught . . . in 'a massive shift in national cultural sensibility, away from the . . . high Modern period . . . and toward the loosely structured, transparently readable, Whitmanesque style of the "New American Poetry," whose rising prophets in the 1950s were Beat and Confessional poets'" (337). By illuminating the relationships and correspondences between Warren, Jarrell, and Lowell at this time, readers should have a clearer picture: Warren and Jarrell played just as much a part as Lowell (if not more) in founding the "New American Poetry" of the 1950s.

A close examination of an archetypal poem of this New American Poetry, Lowell's "For the Union Dead" finally sets the record straight about America's so-called confessional poet. This poem, written just months after *Life Studies* was published, is one that, while often identified as confessional, has multiple layers of meaning and depth as well as structural complexity. As Lowell admitted later in his life: "I think anyone could tell that my free verse was written by someone who'd done a lot of formal verse. . . . [*Understanding Poetry*] is in my blood very much . . . . You felt you had to get away from that at all costs. Yet it's still in one's blood. We're trained that way and I admire Tate and Ransom as much as ever" (Alvarez, "Robert Lowell in Conversation" 82). As much as the breakthrough narrative proponents lead readers to believe that Lowell's split from his mentors was final and decisive, this poem proves otherwise; it also establishes a pattern that identifies Lowell's mature poetry for the rest of his life, the unique formula of Lowell's late work. On January 30, 1960, Lowell wrote to Jarrell: "I'm deep in translations and have only finished one poem of my own since last winter. . . . One wants a whole new deck of cards to play with, or at least new rules for the old ones" (S. Hamilton 359). By capturing a blend of private autobiography and public shared history within a carefully organized, complex poem that transcends a strict adherence to conventional forms, Lowell's "For the Union Dead" establishes those "new rules."

Aside from being "one of [Lowell's] most characteristic poems," "Union Dead" is also generally accepted as his "most accomplished and critically acclaimed political poem" (Doreski and Lowell 30; E. J. Smith 293). Even Lowell, who was hesitant to name "Union Dead" as his best poem, ultimately chose it for Whit Burnett's anthology entitled *This Is My Best* (Doreski 47). He also admitted to Tate, "The 'Union Dead' poem took all winter and I suppose it is the most composed poem I have ever written" (S. Hamilton 373). His selection of the phrase *most composed* is telling. "Union Dead" is free from the stringent and rigorous forms that marked Lowell's early work, yet it is still crafted in regular quatrains, and the ideas are carefully connected through logical associations. After Warren names Lowell's "Union Dead" as one of Lowell's "best" during an interview, Lowell explains his aesthetic choices to Warren: "The parts hold together yet there's no meter. And the quatrain is, in a certain sense, an artificial one. It's sometimes kept and sometimes run on and the lines vary greatly in length; they may be three or four syllables or fifteen, yet I feel the quatrain is important" (Warren, "Robert Lowell" 47). Remarkably significant for the works that follow *Life Studies*, Lowell points to how he loosens the conventional form while still relying somewhat on the old tradition to add a semblance of structure to his work. Like Lowell's "Union Dead" and other poems throughout the rest of his career, Warren's later work is also often marked by some regular poetic conventions, and Jarrell's "The Lost World" even boasts a terza rima format; however, as in Lowell's poem, the autobiographical threads and conversational diction imbues a notably "free" quality in these poems despite the regularities in form.

In addition to its formal elements, the content of "Union Dead" is also characteristic of Lowell's later work. In a letter to Richard Tillinghast, Lowell explains: "'Union Dead' . . . [is] a public 'ode' tho autobiographically truth. . . . I was trying to give the 'free verse' of *Life Studies* greater resonance and rhetoric (sound effects, history)" (S. Hamilton 519). Essentially, Lowell infuses the autobiographical elements of the poem with multiple allusions that resonate deeply with his audience. Lowell once suggested to Hamilton in an interview: "You say I have become more overtly concerned with public events, but true public poetry must come as an inevitable accident" ("Conversation with Hamilton" 269). Lowell's "Union Dead" manifests autobiographical, historical, and cultural layers that are intricately linked to the exploration of man's place in the modern world; this arguably qualifies as true public poetry rendered inevitable by Lowell's personal interests and public persona. Some background on each of these layers will provide a richer context for an explication of this complex poem.

First, and most easily recognizable, is the autobiographical plotline of Lowell's contemplation of the "old South Boston Aquarium," the "Boston Common," and the "Civil War relief" of Colonel Shaw, which serve as landmarks of his childhood ("For the Union Dead" 1, 13, 23). Mark Rudman reports that the Boston Common is a ten-minute walk from 91 Revere Street, where Lowell lived as a boy, and further asserts: "[Lowell] probably passed it every day. No matter how public a statement the poem makes, its focus is personal and specific" (133). In addition to relying on childhood memories for parts of the poem, the autobiographical element stretches to the present. "For the Union Dead" is the fifth and final version of the poem that Lowell crafted specifically for the 1960 Boston Arts Festival, for which he was commissioned. The year he read his poem aloud, the Boston Common had actually been partially dug up for construction of a massive underground parking garage (Thurston 97). These details help to create a vision of the prophetic poet delivering his poem to a flesh-and-blood audience with the backdrop of ugly, mechanized "progress" looming ominously in the background. Lowell was a longtime citizen of Boston, and he was drawing upon personal memories to shape this reflective poem, but in addition to these factors, he was also a renowned poet lamenting the current state of modern society.

Second, the historical layer takes into consideration the symbolic values of these civic locations, monuments, and images. For an American reader or listener, it is nearly impossible to split Boston from its greater historical significance as one of the oldest cities in the United States, as the intended "city on a hill" for the first Puritan settlers. Essentially, the Boston Common, which is both the heart of Boston and the focusing point of this poem, is a metonym for the center of America. The St. Gaudens monument of Colonel Shaw also serves to evoke the history of Robert Gould Shaw, a soldier who led the first black regiment of the Civil War into a battle at Fort Wagner that ended in bloody defeat in 1863. The Shaw monument, both in real life and in Lowell's poem, speaks volumes without words. Lowell draws on this historical figure in order to address contemporary themes of race and misappropriated honor. Finally, Lowell's references to "Hiroshima boiling" and the "drained faces of Negro school-children" recall the atomic bomb dropped on Japan and the plight of African Americans before obtaining equal rights ("For the Union Dead" 56, 60). Like much of Warren's later work, such as *Chief Joseph of the Nez Perce* (1982) and "New Dawn" (1985), Lowell's "Union Dead" forces readers to face the difficult truth of America's history.

Third, Lowell invokes Christian imagery to issue a prophetic warning that is designed to resonate with his audience. The Bible was a large part of Lowell's early learning. In an interview with Alvarez, Lowell speaks about his upbringing "as an Episcopalian Protestant with a good deal of Bible reading at school" and further relates that, as students, "we were rather saturated" with the Bible ("Robert Lowell in Conversation" 40). It was somewhat shocking when—the progeny of Puritan, Unitarian, and Episcopalian clergy, the descendant of Jonathan Edwards, the man who had once told a friend that Catholicism was the religion of Irish servant girls—Lowell eventually converted to Catholicism.[8] After his baptism in 1941 on Louisiana State University's campus, his first wife, Jean Stafford, recalled how Lowell went to Mass at six thirty every morning, said grace before and after meals, attended benediction in the evening, and prayed two rosaries a day. Even more, he "read only religious books and talked about nothing but the existence of God" in the years after his conversion (Mariani 93–94). Though he left the Catholic Church only five years later, while simultaneously obtaining a divorce from Stafford, he received an inundation of religious knowledge during that time period.

In the 1944 introduction to *Land of Unlikeness*, Tate describes Lowell as a "Catholic poet" whose "Christian symbolism is intellectualized . . . it points to the disappearance of the Christian experience from the modern world, and stands, perhaps, for the poet's own effort to recover it" (1). By the time Lowell wrote "Union Dead," his religious faith was far less fervent, yet the Christian themes of his younger years remained a potent force in his poetry. Lowell revealed to Frederick Seidel: "In many ways [my late poems] seem to me more religious than the early ones. . . . It seems to me it's clearer to me now than it was then, but it's very much the same sort of thing that went into the religious poems—the same sort of struggle, light and darkness, the flux of experience. The morality seems much the same" ("Interview" 250). While

Lowell does not include paraphrases from Genesis, Exodus, and Matthew, as in his earlier "Quaker Graveyard in Nantucket," or adhere to the exact conventions of apocalyptic literature, as in "Where the Rainbow Ends," his later poetry still invokes universally accepted Christian symbols. With the Christian symbol of the fish, the Christlike figure of Colonel Shaw, the imagery of hell, and the Calvinist theology of Boston as "damned," the religious undertones of "Union Dead" provide a deeper, prophetic layer to this poem (Perkins 409). Returning to Tate's quotation, Lowell still points "to the disappearance of the Christian experience," but his aim changes from recovering faith to exposing how his modern audience has replaced religious devotion with a zeal for wealth and commercialism—a message that is unmistakably reminiscent of Jarrell's *A Sad Heart at the Supermarket.*[9]

Lowell's artistic hand combines these three layers of autobiography, history, and religion into a powerful, lasting poem that embodies the best qualities of his late poetry. The epigraph of "For the Union Dead," "Relinquunt Omnia Servare Rem Publicam," serves to encapsulate the underlying theme of Lowell's poem. The statue of Colonel Shaw made by Augustus St. Gaudens bears Charles W. Eliot's Latin inscription that is translated: "He leaves all to serve the state." Lowell, however, slightly modifies the wording for his epigraph: "They leave all to serve the state," thereby including the African American soldiers who also sacrificed their lives in the Civil War (Rudman 141):

> Parking spaces luxuriate like civic
> sandpiles in the heart of Boston.
> A girdle of orange, Puritan-pumpkin colored girders
> braces the tingling Statehouse,
>
> shaking over the excavations, as it faces Colonel Shaw
> and his bell-cheeked Negro infantry
> on St. Gaudens' shaking Civil War relief,
> propped by a plank splint against the garage's earthquake. (17–24)

By pointing to the statehouse, which "faces Colonel Shaw" as if in combat, Lowell implies that the legislators are opponents to the "They"; this move forces a comparison between the honorable Shaw and his soldiers versus the state lawmakers who, in the South, were preventing the "Negro schoolchildren" from attending the same schools as white children (21, 60). From the context of the rest of the poem, the modification from *He* to *They* also implicates Boston society—which runs on a "savage servility" that "slides by on grease"—as another opponent (67–68). Essentially, Lowell's modification of the Latin statement reflects "contempt for a society which is violent, cringing and servile in front of money values," a society that no longer honors Colonel Shaw nor the values of one who leaves all to serve the state (Nelles 640).

Moving into the body of "For the Union Dead," Lowell's autobiographical underpinning is prominent in the first several stanzas, in which the narrator observes the "old South Boston Aquarium" with its windows "broken" and "boarded" (1–2). The second stanza of the poem recalls the childhood excitement and innocence of the young boy as his nose "crawled like a snail on the glass" (5). This line is followed by two short lines that, when read aloud, indicate a quicker pace induced by the excitement of the child as his "hand tingled / to burst the bubbles" (6–7). With a hard break and the start of a new quatrain, the narrator jumps back to the reality of present day. He reports, "My hand draws back," as if, while recalling himself as a child, he instinctively outstretched his adult hand to burst the bubbles in his recollection (9). In stanza 5, the word *tingled* is deliberately repeated, though instead of describing the innocent child hand "tingling" with anticipation, it refers to the "tingling Statehouse, / shaking over the excavations," braced for construction of a nearby parking garage. The childlike joy and appreciation for the natural "vegetating kingdom" shifts noticeably to the narrator's focus on the statehouse (10).

This building serves as a synecdoche that represents the governing body responsible for choosing to press forward into the progress of "barbed and galvanized" fences, "steamshovels," and endless "parking spaces" that indicate the dehumanizing elements of industrialization (12, 14, 17). The words *grunting, cropped up, gouge,* and *underworld* produce a sense that digging this parking lot is a physical violation of the city of Boston. Lowell gives this industrial scene symbolic weight by choosing the phrase *Puritan-pumpkin colored girders* to "[brace] the tingling Statehouse" (19–20). He harks back to Boston's founders, emphasizing the word *Puritan* with alliterative *p*'s. Clearly, "Puritan-pumpkin colored" support beams are a poor substitute for Puritan ideals to support the statehouse. In *Life Studies,* Lowell expresses contempt for other historical figures who also maintained "Statehouses."[10] Through employing the tropes of metonymy and synecdoche, Lowell not only magnifies his personal disdain for disreputable leaders; he also depicts the city of Boston as a symbolic figure for other American cities similarly enduring the negative effects of statehouses that tingle with the double-edged promises of industrialized growth and prosperity.

These first five quatrains are the most autobiographical in nature, but when the figure of "Colonel Shaw" enters in the sixth stanza, the poem turns more heavily toward historical and religious allusions. Though Lowell's personal faith was not as strong as it once was, he knew that Christian images would resonate profoundly within his American listeners and readers. Almost four hundred years earlier, Puritan leaders intended for Boston to be "the founding of the exemplary Kingdom of God . . . in the desolation of the Americas" (Sarwar 117). There is clearly an ironic connotation to this history in "Union Dead" and—as other critics have noticed—to the distinct Calvinist theology of the modern man as "powerless and foredoomed" (Mazzaro 85).[11] It is therefore not a coincidence that "Union Dead" is laden with fish imagery, invoking the Christian symbol of the fish that has represented Christ since the first century CE. The images of the dilapidated aquarium, which was once full of fish, along with the "bronze weathervane cod" that "has lost half its scales," serve as metaphors for a city that has lost its faith, or at least put its faith in something other than Christ (1, 3). "The airy tanks are dry" without "cowed," "compliant" followers to fill them, and the boy's experience with the "vegetating kingdom / of the fish and reptile"—a reference to the Garden of Eden—is traded for "press[ing] against the new barbed and galvanized / fence" (4, 8, 10–13). The galvanized steel of enterprise replaces the vegetation of paradise, and the "grunting" "steamshovels," a synecdoche for the machinery of industrialization, are responsible for creating hell on earth, "their underworld garage" (13, 16).

The emphasis on St. Gaudens' monument of "Colonel Shaw / and his bell-cheeked Negro infantry" adds to the Christian themes (21–23). In this poem, the monument of Shaw and his "bronze Negroes" "sticks like a *fishbone* / in the city's throat" (28–30; emphasis added). On the secular level, a memorial that honors African Americans would have caused some discomfort for the white Boston community during the beginning of the civil rights movement (a cause that both Warren and Lowell actively supported). On a religious level, the fishbone refers to the statue of Colonel Shaw, thereby establishing him as a Christ figure in Lowell's poem. The descriptions of Shaw's leadership—"wrenlike vigilance"—the way "he seems to wince at pleasure," and his ultimate martyrdom all link him to Jesus Christ.

The next section, stanzas 10–13, also has a dual secular and religious meaning. The Colonel "rejoices in man's lovely, / peculiar power to choose life and die" (37–38). In an interview with Alvarez, Lowell explains: "We've always had the ideal of 'saving the world.' And that comes close to perhaps destroying the world" ("Robert Lowell in Conversation" 41–42). After atomic warfare was introduced, "saving the world" militarily, like Colonel Shaw and his men aimed to do, runs the risk of nuclear annihilation. This horrifying image contributes to the apocalyptic message of the poem but also holds further religious significance. When Christ sacrificed his life, souls could enter Heaven; when the Christ figure Colonel Shaw "rejoices in man's lovely, / peculiar power to choose life and die," he affirms mankind's free will to live and to die for a cause.

Colonel Shaw is drawn twice more in parallel to Christ: "when he leads his black soldiers to death, / he cannot bend his back" just as Christ is nailed to a cross when he leads humankind to redemption (39–40). Finally, as Colonel Shaw's "body was thrown / and lost with his 'niggers,'" Christ's body was also thrown in an unmarked tomb after dying nearby society's outcasts (51–52). Boston's people can no longer appreciate the sacrifice of Colonel Shaw and his men, nor do they maintain the Puritan faith their city was founded upon. In Fein's words, "We can measure our plight by our society's inability to appreciate and comprehend Shaw and the significance of his statue which barely survives" (114). Along with the "stone statues" that "grow slimmer . . . each year" from deterioration, the "flags" that "quilt the graveyards of the Grand Army of the Republic" become "frayed," and what Americans once valued is replaced by the "Mosler Safe," which is strong enough to "[survive]" an atomic "blast" (45–46, 43–44, 57–58).

Another character who serves a historical and symbolic function in this poem is that of William James.[12] The poem relates, "Two months after marching through Boston, / half the regiment was dead" (25–26). Historically, James performed the dedication of the monument in 1897, and so it rings true that he "could almost hear the bronze Negroes breathe," since their memory was still so fresh and alive for the Boston community (28). Those statues now "grow slimmer . . . each year" as they waste away physically from prolonged exposure to the elements and are banished emotionally from the city's collective consciousness as time passes. In place of "statues for the last war," on "Boylston Street" there is "a commercial photograph" that "shows Hiroshima boiling," a metaphor that America has become a country that would sacrifice everything for the sake of commercialism (56–58). Indeed, the future looks grim for a society that would use the horror of the atomic bomb for the benefit of advertisement.

By shedding light on America's dangerous path forward, Lowell develops his apocalyptic prophecy. The poem's narrative shift from innocent childhood to the painful awareness of adulthood in a city consumed by greed and commercialism clearly has a more universal significance than a mere personal reflection. Parallel to Warren's mature poetic techniques, Lowell's poetic strategies layer the regional significance of Boston and its surrounding landmarks with metonymic value for the rest of the nation. Furthermore, Boston not only signifies the rest of America but also becomes the biblical Babylon on the brink of apocalypse. In particular, Lowell invokes Christian symbols and imagery to draw an analogy between Boston and the doomed cities in the Book of Revelation. "For the Union Dead" does not depict complete destruction or a new world purged of evil, and so it does not fulfill all conventions of the apocalyptic literary tradition; however, there are enough elements of the Last Judgment and hope for the Second Coming to support a reading of a visionary narrator issuing a prophetic warning to his audience.

The message of this poem, however, is not that citizens should return to zealous religious beliefs. Instead, Lowell draws the conclusion that the people of Boston, and the people of America, have traded their God for wealth and progress much like the biblical cities awaiting an apocalypse. The closing portion of "Union Dead" echoes the judgment of Babylon found in the Book of Revelation: "Fallen, fallen is Babylon the great! . . . Alas, alas, the great city, clothed in fine linen, in purple and scarlet, adorned with gold, with jewels, and with pearls! For in one hour all this wealth has been laid waste!" (18:2, 16–17). Just as Babylon hoarded its fineries only to be destroyed by the apocalypse, so, too, does Boston protect its wealth above all things. Mazzaro asserts, "Lowell associates the materialistic exploitation of one's fellowman with the decay of Christianity and the evils of capitalism" (21). In an apocalyptic tone, Lowell's poem warns, "The ditch is nearer" as "There are no statues for the last war here" (53–54). The "ditch" of oblivion is close for those who no longer honor the soldiers but instead have found a material substitute for their praise.

"Colonel Shaw / is riding on his bubble" in the second-to-last stanza of the poem; "he waits / for the blessèd break" (61–64). At this point in his life, Lowell most likely did not believe in an impending Second Coming, but he did fear that humans would bring the end of the world upon themselves. This fact makes the Christ figure of Colonel Shaw even sadder and more ironic as his statue slowly wastes away, waiting for the "blessèd break"—a phrase widely accepted as an allusion to a biblical apocalypse and subsequent new world order. The last stanza returns aptly to fish imagery. "The Aquarium is gone," and just as the "vegetating kingdom," or Garden of Eden, is replaced by industrialization in the beginning of the poem, the Christ image of the fish is replaced by "giant finned cars" that "nose forward *like* fish" (65, 66; emphasis added). Machinery, "progress," now reigns "everywhere" (65). Stripped of an appreciation for heroes such as Colonel Shaw and Christ, humans are doomed to live according to a barbaric, "savage servility" that "slides by on grease" (67–68). Boston, the community that once stood as a religious beacon, the city on the hill, is reduced to a place of worship for industrialization, commercialism, and prosperity.

Though less apocalyptic in tone, Jarrell similarly bemoans the current state of modern America in *A Sad Heart at the Supermarket,* a book Lowell praised as [its] author's *Culture and Anarchy,*" with "essays that speak with prophetic distress about our culture" (Mariani 305). Creating a similar image to Lowell's Mosler safe, Jarrell argues: "The act of buying something is at the root of our world; if anyone wishes to paint the genesis of things in our society, he will paint a picture of God holding out to Adam a check-book or credit card or Charge-A-Plate" (*Sad Heart* 66). Once again in tune with Lowell and Jarrell, Warren also points to the failure of society for prioritizing commercialism over a sense of identity: "Americans, by and large, have had little use for the past except for purposes of interior decorating, personal vanity, or pietistic and self-congratulatory celebrations" ("Use of the Past" 31). This shared concern for America, as well as the changes in both content and style depicted here at midcentury, would continue to characterize the work of Warren, Jarrell, and Lowell through the rest of their careers, starting with the 1960s.

6

The 1960s

"The Times They Are A-Changin'"

THE SWINGING SIXTIES

An escalation from the nation's turmoil of the 1950s, the 1960s marked a period of great change and shifting consciousness for America and for the world. The Cold War raged on, heightened by the failed Bay of Pigs invasion, the Cuban missile crisis, and the highly controversial war in Vietnam. As millions of children from the post–World War II baby boom entered young adulthood, the decade became characterized by revolutionary thought and opposition to conservatism. The civil rights movement, supported by President John F. Kennedy, Martin Luther King Jr., and President Lyndon B. Johnson, made great strides for African Americans and women via the Civil Rights Act of 1964, and contentious debate and protest, particularly on college campuses, became commonplace for a generation that craved change. A far cry from what Lowell described in "Memories of West Street and Lepke" as the "tranquilized Fifties," many Americans identified this decade as the "Swinging Sixties," a time that continued to inspire artists—Warren, Jarrell, and Lowell among them—in all genres to respond to the incendiary world events. Thrust into the limelight due to notable success in American letters, Warren, Jarrell, and Lowell served as public spokesmen in the 1960s, and national concerns took shape in their poetry, fiction, and nonfiction alike.

By this point, as Warren, Jarrell, and Lowell were well-established authors writing the "New American Poetry" that defined the second half of the century, the 1960s brought prolific literary achievements for each author. Warren published several excellent books of poetry, including *You, Emperors, and Others: Poems, 1957–1960* (1960); *Selected Poems: New and Old, 1923–1966* (1966); *Incarnations: Poems, 1966–1968* (1968); and one of his masterpieces, *Audubon: A Vision* (1969), in addition to two influential nonfiction works, *The Legacy of the Civil War* (1961) and *Who Speaks for the Negro?* (1965), and several other fiction and nonfiction works. After nine years without publishing any new books of poetry, Jarrell penned his best, *The Woman at the Washington Zoo* (1960) and *The Lost World* (1965), and also published his noteworthy book of essays *A Sad Heart at the Supermarket* (1962), along with some translations, before his untimely death in 1965. After Lowell's watershed *Life Studies* in 1959, he followed with several books of translated poems (1961 and 1969) as well as his first and only play, *The Old Glory* (1965), and two books of poetry, *For the Union Dead* (1964) and *Near the Ocean* (1967). Though each of these works is deserving of a comprehensive analysis, for the purposes of this narrative, this chapter will focus on the ways in which these authors' work and lives continued to intersect in this decade.

One thing that brought Warren, Jarrell, and Lowell together since their days at Vanderbilt was a shared devotion to the impact of history, past and present, on American society. In light of their increasing political activity in the 1960s and beyond, it is enriching to consider the political endeavors of these writers, especially seeing how these roles shaped the content and aesthetics of their poetry. Though it seems commonplace today for politics to serve as the main point of discourse in a work of literature, it was far from the norm in American poetry until this decade. Lowell, the former jailed conscientious objector to World War II, was ever more outspoken on his political beliefs, whether he was speaking at the Cultural and Scientific Conference for World Peace (1949), the Boston Arts Festival (1960)—at which he read his highly political poem "For the Union Dead"—or at the Library of Congress, where he delivered a short speech on the Gettysburg Address (1964). Lowell even sounded off in a 1962 issue of the *Partisan Review* on the "Cold War and the West" by stating: "No nation should possess, use or retaliate with its bombs. I believe we should rather die than drop our own bombs" (S. Hamilton 295). He is also remembered for the provocative statements in his final prose piece, which serve as a final barb to the American government: "Politics? We live in the sunset of Capitalism. We have thundered nobly against its bad record all our years, yet we still cling to its vestiges" ("After Enjoying" 991). One act of resistance, however, that drew Warren to Lowell's side was when Lowell declined President Johnson's invitation to the White House Festival of Arts as an act of protest against the president's policy on Vietnam. In a public letter to President Johnson, Lowell stated, "Every serious artist knows that he cannot enjoy public celebration without making subtle public commitments" ("To President" 371). In his letter, Lowell further explained that while he supported Johnson's domestic choices, he "can only follow our present foreign policy with the greatest dismay and distrust" (S. Hamilton 459). An act that solidified their shared political views, Warren joined eighteen other influential writers and artists in signing Lowell's published letter. Warren later explained to Lon Cheney: "Yes, I did associate myself with Cal Lowell's statement. . . . I was for anything that would get the issue in the open. . . . I also recognize a distinction between the arts and politics, but it is not an air-tight distinction: I don't think that Cal's position is the only one but I did—and do—think that it is a tenable one" (Clark, Hendricks, and Perkins, *Selected Letters* 4:450–51). By stating that the distinction between arts and politics is not "air-tight," Warren speaks also for Lowell and Jarrell, the three of them routinely allowing politics to paint the background, and oftentimes the foreground, of their literary works.

Scholars as they were, all three authors approached politics with an academic attention to detail. William Bedford Clark acknowledges that during this time, Warren "not only followed the headlines assiduously but also was keenly attuned to the drama and dynamics of history itself"; therefore, Clark advises scholars to "situate [Warren's] correspondence from this period against the backdrop of his age, a time of intense collective anxiety born of mounting global conflict" (*Selected Letters* 4:3). This statement could be expanded to include all of Warren's written works, and the same consideration should be made for Lowell and Jarrell. Though not as much in the public eye as Warren and Lowell, Jarrell did not avoid addressing cultural issues. From the Marxism inherent in his poetry of the 1930s and 1940s to the social criticism of "mass culture" he expressed in poetry and prose during the 1950s until his death in 1965, Jarrell was highly opinionated on matters of the times (S. Burt 26, 76–84).[1]

As in the 1950s, the three men communicated regularly about cultural issues and often proved to be like-minded in their responses. For example, Jarrell wrote to Lowell in November 1960: "Did you see a piece of mine . . . named 'A Sad Heart at the Supermarket'? It rather goes with your . . . poem ['For the Union Dead']" (M. Jarrell 446). Jarrell is referring to the similar way both his prose piece and Lowell's poem bewail society's destructive tendency to praise and prioritize commercialism over human life, religion, and all else. Furthermore, Warren wrote to Jarrell: "I have lately finished your *Sad Heart,* with the greatest pleasure. I wrote a note to Pat Knopf about it, trying to define my admiration. . . . It's a delightful, not to say, pointed, book" (Clark, Hendricks, and Perkins, *Selected Letters* 4:331). Completing the literary circle, in an interview of Lowell by Warren and Cleanth Brooks, Lowell reads "For the Union Dead" aloud, and Warren responds: "Very fine. That's one of your best, I expect. One of your very best" ("Robert Lowell" 47). Warren's comments of praise do not offer direct evidence that Warren approved of Lowell's use of poetry as a vehicle for political thought, but considering Warren's statement that the distinction between arts and politics is not air-tight and taking into account his own integration of politics in his poetry, one may gather that Warren's approval of the poem had more far-reaching implications.

All three poets, more than ever, lamented in unison, publicly and privately to one another, about America's reverence for money and material things. Jarrell states: "The act of buying something is at the root of our world"—and the resulting disregard for history and intellectualism ("Sad Heart" 75). The following instance reveals a similar attitude among Jarrell, Warren, and Lowell toward society, history, and the need to address both in writing. In March 1961, Jarrell wrote to Warren commending his "live" and authentic portrayal of the Civil War: "I have wanted to write you about your Civil War piece in *Life.* . . . The amount of knowledge in it, the amount of attention you paid to the noblest and basest things in the war, and the thoroughly live and thoroughly dignified style were all just extraordinary." Furthermore, in November 1961, Jarrell wrote to Lowell addressing the current state of the world: "I feel about the world, now, just as you do: it's heartbreaking. Who would believe even people could get things to this point?" Finally, in October 1961, Warren addressed an audience of two thousand in a tribute to Jarrell and praised him: "His severe passion for high standards of intelligence and reason have turned inward into a self-demanding scrupulosity in his own writing that is seasoned by humor with an undertone of piety for human failing and human feeling" (M. Jarrell, *Randall Jarrell's Letters* 448, 451, 449). Clearly, all three artists were inspired to capture the issues of the world, and man's struggle within it, in their writing. This shared concern for America determined much of the content of all three poets' later works and influenced their stylistic choices. The aesthetic changes made at midcentury—the loosening of forms; preference for the concrete over the abstract; the attempt to infuse life into poetry by creating authentic characters, rhythms of speech, and conversational diction; and partiality for narrative over lyric poems—were maintained and heightened by a greater attempt to communicate directly with the reader. For Warren, Jarrell, and Lowell, the distressing events of the second half of the twentieth century called for a colloquy with their audience that would attempt to direct their attention away from superficial nonsense and toward the important work of self-reflection.

JARRELL ADDRESSING AN AUDIENCE WITH WARREN & LOWELL

By the time *The Woman at the Washington Zoo* was published in 1960, Jarrell's two-year term as the poetry consultant to the Library of Congress (1956–58) had further heightened his awareness of America's cultural crisis. William Pritchard reports, "The more he saw of [America] the more appalled he was at what he saw" (*Randall Jarrell* 267). Along with Lowell's public political statements and Warren's growing involvement in national issues, Jarrell felt an increasing responsibility to publicly address these matters in both poetry and prose. On March 15, 1959, Lowell reported to John Berryman: "I am just back from Greensboro, where Randall and [I] enjoyed (?) ourselves lamenting the times. It seems there's been something curious twisted and against the grain about the world poets of our generation have had to live in" (S. Hamilton 338). There was a palpable sense that poets were in this struggle together: a grand effort to discover, interpret, and expose the *something curious* that plagued Lowell, Jarrell, and their contemporaries.

Through the mid- to late fifties, Jarrell produced essays for his second book of literary criticism and social commentary, *A Sad Heart at the Supermarket* (1962), while learning from Warren and Lowell how to address these issues in verse without destroying the integrity of the art form. From published reviews and personal correspondences, many of which have already been recounted, there is no question that Jarrell praised and supported both Warren's and Lowell's literary works from the late fifties. When Warren was awarded the National Book Award in 1958 for *Promises: Poems, 1954–1956*, it was Jarrell who presented the address on behalf of the committee. In his speech, Jarrell referred to Warren's works as examples of particularly worthy literature. After claiming that it is Warren's "superego, or muse, or demon, that makes him write poems like *Brother to Dragons* and *Promises*," Jarrell concludes, "We are safe as long as Warren's superego survives" (M. Jarrell, *Randall Jarrell's Letters* 429). Just two years later, in 1961, at the Woman's College of the University of North Carolina, Warren gave a talk on Jarrell, chiding him gently with memories of that "tall, skinny young man—just getting acquainted with the art of the razor" who was "even at the time of the Sophomore Survey, a poet" (University of North Carolina at Greensboro, Digital Collections, "Warren on Jarrell"). They had now been expressing deep appreciation of and admiration for one another publicly and privately for almost four decades.

Around the same time, Jarrell wrote to Lowell: "It certainly was fun talking to you for so long. . . . I was delighted that you're writing some new poems, just as I've been delighted (for about six weeks) to be writing one myself" (M. Jarrell 429, 428). As Jarrell turned his full energy back to poetry, his attention lingered predictably on the most recent works of Warren and Lowell. In particular, Jarrell praised "the pathos of the local color of the past" in *Life Studies* and pointed to the "largeness and grandeur" in Lowell's poems, which "exist on a scale that is unique today" (qtd. in Pritchard, *Randall Jarrell* 287). Essentially, Jarrell admires Lowell's ability to write poems on topical, local subjects that can also be raised to a scale of "largeness and grandeur"—a characteristic common to the mature poetry of Jarrell, Lowell, and Warren alike. These writers, by tapping into the shared human experience through integrating autobiographical material, created personal poetry that simultaneously resonates on a universal level.

In response to the reviews of Lowell's *Life Studies*, Jarrell approvingly professed to Lowell: "They were good—they hardly *could* have been better. I hope you get all the prizes this spring to wind it up properly" (M. Jarrell, *Randall Jarrell's Letters* 443). Lowell did, in fact, win the National Book Award for *Life Studies* in 1960, and Jarrell followed him in 1961 with the same award for *The Woman at the Washington Zoo*. Much like when Warren, Jarrell, and Lowell were all awarded Guggenheim Fellowships between 1946 and 1947, the back-to-back National Book Awards again established these authors as forerunners in American literature and publicly linked them to one another during times of great literary success.

Of course, Warren and Lowell weren't the only influences on Jarrell during this time. William Wordsworth, for example, is often cited as one of Jarrell's biggest influences (S. Burt 23). There is no question that Jarrell looked early to Wordsworth while developing his practice of emulating idiomatic speech, nor is it difficult to identify Jarrell's replication of the technique in which Wordsworth's narrators interact with an imagined listener. However, the influence of Jarrell's closest contemporaries on the development of Jarrell's "interpersonal style" should not be underestimated. Not to minimize the struggles that faced Wordsworth and his fellow Englishmen in the early nineteenth century, but for Jarrell, the urge to reconnect to the outside world stemmed from the particular sense of isolation that plagued modern Americans. It is therefore important to consider Jarrell's interpersonal style within the context of his connection to Warren and Lowell, writers who similarly faced the unique anxiety and modern loneliness characteristically felt by Americans at mid-twentieth century.

In line with this willingness to address current issues, the last five years of Jarrell's life and poetic production are marked by his head-on confrontation with history. Stephen Burt, Jarrell's highly insightful biographer, explains how Jarrell "insisted that some sense of our presence in our own history, and of our inward difference from the rest of the world, remained prerequisite for our life with other people, for aesthetic experience, and even ethical action" (xii). In other words, Jarrell saw an awareness of history as crucial for human beings to function in society. Warren articulates an almost identical ideology in later works, such as *Democracy and Poetry* and "The Use of the Past," but this theory also underlies parts of Warren's work from the 1960s—in poetry, fiction, and prose. In *Legacy of the Civil War,* Warren credits "history" for giving man "a program for the future" and "a fuller understanding of ourselves" (100). *Who Speaks for the Negro?* further links an awareness of history to ethical action, as Jarrell did. Long after Jarrell's death, Warren continues in this vein, passionately insisting that "the past is . . . the great pantheon where we can all find the bearers of the values by which we could live. It gives us the image of a community and of a role, an identity, within that community, the image of a self to be achieved" ("Use of the Past" 50). The concept of shaping an identity through confronting the past became a notable theme in Jarrell's final works.

Along with the historical emphasis of Jarrell's last works, in assessing the stylistic changes involved in the transformation from Jarrell's early to late work, J. A. Bryant Jr. observes that "the best" of Jarrell's poetry is "deeply personal . . . whether he was employing the device of monologue or that of the you-address favored by his friend and early mentor Robert Penn Warren"

(9). Essentially, Bryant attributes Jarrell's poetic achievement partly to the techniques he honed alongside Warren and Lowell. Though Warren successfully integrates autobiographical material in *Promises* and beyond, Lowell is also closely associated with the phrase *deeply personal poetry,* and while Lowell is equally concerned with communicating directly with his audience in *Life Studies* and after, Bryant specifically names Warren and his particular "you-address" technique as responsible for advancing Jarrell's style. As much as Jarrell was an innovator in this literary circle, he was also an insightful scholar who drew from his colleagues for guidance when prudent.

By understanding the essential role Warren saw the past playing for society, one may also understand that by employing Warren's you-address in his later poetry, Jarrell is not merely imitating a rhetorical flourish; he is adopting Warren's technique and underlying principles in order to urgently encourage readers toward locating their place in history. Even early intimations of Warren's you-address encourage readers to engage in self-reflection. In "Terror," for example, published in *Eleven Poems on the Same Theme* (1942), Warren employs the you-address while his narrator contemplates that named human emotion, terror, in situations such as this illustration of German Nazis:

> Blood splashed on the terrorless intellect creates
> Corrosive fizzle like the spattered lime,
> And its enseamed stew but satiates
> Itself, in that lewd and faceless pantomime.
> You know, by radio, how hotly the world repeats,
> When the brute crowd roars or the blunt boot-heels resound
> In the Piazza or the Wilhelmplatz,
> The crime of Onan, spilled upon the ground;
> You know, whose dear hope Alexis Carrel kept
> Alive in a test tube, where it monstrously grew, and slept. (51–60)

With the pointed words *you know* and the accurate presentation of history, Warren inserts his reader, willingly or unwillingly, into the action of the poem. Even if the reader does not in fact "know" firsthand of the violence and bloodshed tied to Nazi Germany, Warren implores him or her to bear witness to these significant moments in the history of humanity. In adopting

Warren's technique, Jarrell also creates poetry that demands the participation of his reader.

Jarrell's later poems "seek to establish a nexus of recognition between reader and speaker, speaker and listener, actor and observer" (29); this technique is reminiscent of Warren's implementation of the you-address in *Eleven Poems*, "The Ballad of Billie Potts," and especially *Promises*, in which Warren begins to employ the you-address more frequently, whether to address his daughter, Rosanna, his son, Gabriel, or that other "you" who can be interpreted as Warren's own psyche or that of an intelligent reader. In Jarrell's turning point work, *Crutches*, he also begins experimenting more with the you-address, as can be seen in the poem "A Soul":[2]

> In the castle someone is singing.
> "Thou art warm and dry as the sun."
> You whisper, and laugh with joy. (9–11)

At this point his career, Jarrell most often addresses a specific character within the poem, such as soul-lover in this poem, the great-grandmother in "A Rhapsody on Irish Themes," the devil in "A Conversation with the Devil," or the female narrator's reflection in "The Face":

> I know, there's no saying no,
> But just the same you say it. No.
> I'll point to myself and say: I'm not like this. (16–18)

As demonstrated in these lines, in addition to the engaging you-address, Jarrell also frequently leaves lines half-finished, a stylistic choice that forces the reader to actively fill in the unspoken words of the conversation. Though these techniques demand reader participation, the you-address in Jarrell's *Crutches* does not implicate a wider audience as strongly as the *you* in poems such as Warren's "Terror" or "Infant Boy at Midcentury":

> When the century dragged, like a great wheel stuck at dead center;
> When the wind that had hurled us our half-century sagged now,
> And only velleity of air somewhat snidely nagged now,
> With no certain commitment to compass, or quarter: you chose to enter.
> (Warren, "When the Century Dragged" 1–4)

To return to a previously discussed debate between particularization and generalization, Jarrell's *you* is originally much more particularized, whereas Warren strives to weight his direct address, his *you*, with an additional layer of "generalized" meaning, one more universal and applicable to his readers.

By the time *The Woman at the Washington Zoo* was published, however, Jarrell's you-address was decidedly more Warrenesque. Russell Fowler's argument adds support to this assessment: "The poems of [Jarrell's] late period, the products of endless technical experimentation and revision, are intended as psychic 'catalysts'" ("Jarrell's 'Eland'" 189). Similar to Warren's later work, *Washington Zoo* contains poems that intentionally provoke readers to engage in self-reflection, not merely to produce answers for the anticipated response of Jarrell's characters but to produce their own answers after contemplating the metaphysical dilemma at hand. Stephen Burt asserts, "Jarrell and his personae turn at climactic moments to projected or imagined listeners, to a 'you,' to receive or confirm the experience in the poem" (28); both Warren and Jarrell replicate this real act of communication in poetry in order to create opportunities for art to be a potent force in society.

Jarrell's "Jamestown," for example, is particularly reminiscent of Warren's content and style. A first-person narrator contemplates "The True Historie" of Jamestown, Virginia, the first permanent English settlement in America. A mirror of Warren's technique, Jarrell's narrator invokes prominent historical figures—John Smith and Pocahontas—in order to contemplate the validity of American history and man's place within it:

—Is nothing here American?
John Smith is squashed
Beneath the breasts of Pocahontas: some true Christian,
Engraving all, has made the captain Man,
The maiden the most voluptuous of newts.
Met in a wood and lain with, this red demon,
The mother of us all, lies lovingly
Upon the breastplate of our father: the First Family
Of Jamestown trembles beneath the stone
Axe—then Powhatan, smiling, gives the pair his blessing
And nymphs and satyrs foot it at their wedding.
. . . .
The two lived happily

> Forever after. . . . And I only am escaped alone
> To tell the story. But how shall I tell the story?
> The settlers died? All settlers die. The colony
> Was a Lost Colony? All colonies are lost. (4–14, 19–23)

Though the elements of fantasy—nymphs, satyrs, and witches—are distinctly Jarrellian, his narrator's consideration of and desire for righting the "True Historie" is conspicuously Warrenesque. The questions "how should I tell the story?" and later

> No world, there is only you. But what are you?
> The world has become you. But what are you?
> Ask;
> Ask, while the time to ask remains to you. (45–48)

conduct the same metaphysical investigation that is often at the heart of Warren's poems. The narrator implores you, the reader, to also consider his own essence in the context of the world surrounding him. Jarrell's "what are you?" directly echoes Warren's line from "The Ballad of Billie Potts": "Think of yourself at dawn: Which are you? What?" (144). Readers can interpret this echo as a reflection of Jarrell's lasting connection to and admiration for Warren.

Similarly, one may acknowledge the more personal poetry Jarrell generated in his last years to the influence of his dear friends Lowell and Warren. Helen Vendler observes how, in "The End of the Line," Jarrell associated "idiosyncratic individualism" with modernism, and she therefore posits: "This sense led early to a growing drift from the personal that was not reversed until *The Woman at the Washington Zoo* and *The Lost World*" ("Complete Poems" 98). In light of literary history, Vendler's comment highlights the fact that the late fifties and early sixties, in general, marked a departure from the disdain and contempt poets once felt for personal, intimate poetry. The success of the Beat poets and other writers who included private subject matter—such as W. D. Snodgrass, John Berryman, and, of course, Warren and Lowell—reintroduced an opportunity for writers to explore autobiographical material in artful ways.

Though some reviewers criticize the autobiographical nature of Jarrell's title poems, several critics, including Lowell, have deemed *Lost World* as Jarrell's finest (Bryant 153). Stephen Burt, for example, observes, "Jarrell seems to have been developing quietly a new direction for his poetic talent that would not bear its fruit until the year of his death, when he published *The Lost World*" (131). Part of Jarrell's "new direction" entails the occasional break from his guarded dramatic monologues in favor of the first-person Jarrellian narrator. The poems in *Lost World* most clearly demonstrate the direct influence Warren and Lowell had on Jarrell's personal poetry, but *Washington Zoo* also contains evidence of this impact. "In Those Days," for example, includes lines of an adult narrator reflecting on childhood memories:

> How poor and miserable we were,
> How seldom together!
> And yet after so long one thinks:
> In those days everything was better. (13–16)

"The Elementary Scene," "Windows," "Aging," and, a fitting title for Jarrell, "The Lonely Man" similarly present a point of view that—like Warren's voice in *Brother to Dragons* and *Promises* and Lowell's voice in *Life Studies*—is unmistakably inspired by Jarrell's real experiences.

Another element of Jarrell's work that can be partly attributed to Lowell's influence is his inclusion of twelve translations in *Washington Zoo*.[3] Jarrell's letters reveal that, more than anyone else, Lowell was his main point of contact regarding the subject of translating poetry. It is further evident that Jarrell drew encouragement and inspiration for this pursuit from Lowell, whose *Phaedra* translation was published the same year as *Washington Zoo*, with *Imitations* just one year later. In a characteristic chain of correspondences, Jarrell reported to Lowell in early 1960: "I'm translating too, just like you" (M. Jarrell 442). Lowell, in turn, wrote to Jarrell: "I have read your bunch of translations with increased wonder. It's amazing how close you are, and yet the solemnity and vibrance remain. I think I even prefer you at times to the original" (S. Hamilton 359). Perhaps one reason Lowell took such a liking to Jarrell's translations is because their personal tone and style of highly accessible verse happens to closely resemble Lowell's own style in *Life Studies*.

One last notable issue in *Washington Zoo* that ties Jarrell, Warren, and Lowell together is a factor that also shaped Jarrell's nonfiction work *A Sad Heart at the Supermarket*—that of the influential role of the American cultural crisis. Chapter 4 notes specifically how all three poets shared an almost crippling fear of "the big bomb" throughout the post–World War II era. Nelson Hathcock reports that for Jarrell specifically, "the existential terror of the arms race was indeed a reality for Jarrell, 'the bomb' its overarching trope" ("Standardizing Catastrophe" 125). Around the time Jarrell was writing poems for *The Washington Zoo*, Mary Jarrell reported: "Cal Lowell's letters at this time were full of the grim realities of the bomb and mass death, and they stuck in Randall's mind and made him sad. 'But Cal is right,' he said and wouldn't be comforted. 'What an age to be part of!'" ("Group of Two" 289). A poetic manifestation of this shared fear, in addition to Jarrell's "Jerome," is the poem "The End of the Rainbow," which directly echoes, responds to, and borrows from Lowell's "Where the Rainbow Ends," the closing poem of *Lord Weary's Castle*.

Further acknowledging the relationship between these two poems, Jeffrey Meyers draws a connection between them, though he attributes a vicious competition between the artists as the reason Jarrell chooses to implicate Lowell's work. Contrary to this contentious reading, this study has demonstrated that the relationship between the two was congenial and supportive. Without an understanding of their mutually beneficial professional and personal relationship, however, one may understand why Meyers would argue that "as [Jarrell and Lowell] measured each other's faults as well as strengths, Jarrell began to reveal his poetic debts to Lowell. The influence was obvious to both poets, who began to mock each other publically, if not in print. The Title of Lowell's 'Where the Rainbow Ends' (1946) reappeared in Jarrell's 'The End of the Rainbow' (1954)" (44). Far from "mocking" one another, it is evident that Jarrell was offering a literary nod to Lowell. Still keeping Warren abreast of his literary successes, Jarrell wrote to Warren about his poem in July 1954, excitedly reporting: "I've just finished a long poem ["The End of the Rainbow"] I wrote for my first six weeks out here—I think it's one of the best I've ever written so, as you can imagine, I really feel good" (M. Jarrell 399). Contrary to Meyers's account, these do not sound like the words of a poet who crafted a poem with the specific intention to "mock" Lowell. Instead, Lowell appears to have inspired Jarrell to create a poem that greatly pleased him.

At first glance, Lowell's and Jarrell's poems are quite different from each other in both style and content. Lowell's poem, as was typical of his earlier style, is constructed into three ten-line stanzas of iambic pentameter with a repeating *abcbcadeed* rhyme scheme. Jarrell's poem, on the other hand, defies traditional formulas. A mixture of narrative, dialogue, dream sequence, and spontaneous interjections, Jarrell's chaotic form resembles the underlying apocalyptic theme that unites his work with Lowell's. Jarrell's first lines reference Lowell's poem while simultaneously establishing distance (literal and figurative) from it. Lowell begins: "I saw the sky descending, black and white, / Not blue, on Boston where the winters wore," thereby setting the scene in his hometown of Boston. Jarrell starts: "Far from the clams and fogs and bogs /—The cranberry bogs—of Ipswich," purposely pointing to the fact that his "rainbow ends" far from Lowell's Massachusetts (where Jarrell's female character is from) and instead in a place connected to Jarrell's childhood, "The sun of Southern California" (9).

Just as Lowell's poem follows a traditional format, it also satisfies the typical conventions of apocalyptic literature, as defined by M. H. Abrams: "Revelation . . . is the concluding book of the biblical canon which presents, in the mode of symbolic visions, a series of events, even now beginning, which will culminate in the abrupt end of the present, evil world-order and its replacement by a regenerate mankind in a new and perfected condition of life" (343). A quick list of the apocalyptic imagery in Lowell's poem reveals a faithful representation of this traditional literary representation of apocalypse: "Hunger," "worms will eat the deadwood," "scythers, Time and Death," "locusts," "scorched-earth," "judgment rising and descending," "dead leaves char the air," "Revelations," "serpent-Time," "serpents," "victim," "lion, lamb, and beast," "furnace-face," "marriage feast," "exile," and "dove has brought an olive branch." Lowell's poem moves from desperate end-times to an abrupt abolishment of evil, in line with the apocalyptic mode, as the narrator describes:

> I saw my city in the Scales, the pans
> Of judgment rising and descending. Piles
> Of dead leaves char the air—
> And I am a red arrow on this graph
> Of Revelations. (14–18)

Finally, "the dove of Jesus," or the Second Coming, brings "an olive branch," a symbol for peace and a "new and perfected condition of life," completing the regeneration of a new world.

Jarrell's poem also follows the formula for apocalyptic literature, but—

like his aesthetic form—his poem is far less conventional in fulfilling the checklist of necessary characteristics. As with Lowell's poem, a scan of Jarrell's apocalyptic imagery reveals the pattern of end-times, followed by an abrupt end to "evil," and finally, the creation of a new peaceful world. As the poem unfolds, a series of key images reveal this apocalyptic arc: "tadpoles feathering," "burnt hands," "face is masked," "seals are barking," "Death," "darkness," "Proverbs," "evil communications," "a detour of the path / Of righteousness," "God," "soul," "praise Heaven!" "Scriptures," "the earth / Lies light upon the old, and they are wakeful," "wakeful," "wakeful," "wakes," "Father," "colors," "warm," and "safe." Far from the traditional biblical tone of Lowell's poem, however, Jarrell's poem centers on a woman, named "Content," who has much in common with the despairing female in the title poem who longs to "change," who craves a "new and perfected condition of life." Content is unmarried and without children (other than her beloved pet dog, Su-Su IV), and through a series of memories of a past lover, surreal dream sequences, and an imagined conversation with Death, she comes, in the end, to accept her life as "a success." Ultimately, Jarrell transforms Lowell's biblical apocalypse into a psychological apocalypse that results in newfound peace for Content's soul at the end of the rainbow.

LOWELL AS PUBLIC FIGURE

In the same way that Warren, Jarrell, and many of their contemporaries were moved to respond to the provocative national events of the sixties, Lowell naturally gravitated toward his role as poet-prophet-philosopher during this time. His noteworthy political acts were, more significantly, paired with a level of increased cultural awareness in his poetry from this decade. Like "For the Union Dead," most works from this period—particularly *For the Union Dead* (1964), *The Old Glory* (1965), and *Near the Ocean* (1967)—address historical issues in a style that pointedly engages the reader or listener. To quote Herbert Leibowitz: "[Lowell's] poetic voice emerged from a talking contest with his ancestral voices: literary, familial, historical; the qualities of his rhetoric . . . are frequently the qualities of American rhetoric, just as the private experiences he transcribes are the salient features of American experience" (199). A quotation that would also suit Warren and Jarrell, Leibowitz's argument highlights the integral role of the past in Lowell's later work as well as his ability to create personal poetry that doubles as a microcosm of the larger American gestalt.

Lowell's translations from the early sixties demonstrate continuity from *Life Studies* and corroborate the vision Lowell had for American poetry. Highly reminiscent of the explanation Lowell provided Warren on his stylistic choices for "Union Dead," Lowell explains that in *Phaedra—A Verse Translation of Racine's Phèdre* (1961), "my couplet is run on, avoids inversions and alliteration, and loosens its rhythm with shifted accents and occasional extra syllables. I gain in naturalness and lose in compactness and extra syllables" ("On 'Skunk Hour'" 230). In other words, just as in "Union Dead," the format of Lowell's *Phaedra* pushes the boundaries of convention in order to increase authenticity, or "naturalness," of speech without abandoning structure altogether. Confirming the additional political impetus that was characteristic of his work from this time, Ian Hamilton notes: "In many reviews [*Phaedra*] was coupled with *Imitations* as further evidence of Lowell's cultural imperialism" (290). Part of defining American poetry for Lowell meant transforming international masterpieces into his own uniquely determined style. Lowell reports that in *Phaedra*: "I have translated as a poet, and tried to give my lines a certain dignity, speed, and flare" ("On 'Skunk Hour'" 231).

With the same promise of originality, Lowell's *Imitations* was also published in 1961. Unfortunately for Lowell, though this book earned the Bollingen Prize for Translation in 1962, it stirred intensified versions of the same critiques drawn by *Life Studies*. Steven Gould Axelrod's words encapsulate this criticism: "The volume became at last nearly as personal a document as *Life Studies*. . . . The voice, inevitably, was his own. Disguised as a collection of translations, the volume in actuality exposes Lowell's crisis of consciousness resulting from his contemplation of suicide" (*Robert Lowell* 135). As the visceral connection of these works to Lowell's personal life fades over time, critics might begin to acknowledge the high level of skill in at least a handful of these poems that earn merit as fine works of original art.[4] For the purposes of this study, however, it is worth noting that even this book marks a connection to Warren and Jarrell.

Lowell's introduction to *Imitations* announces his desire for this book to "be first read as a sequence, one voice running through many personalities, contrasts and repetitions. I have hoped somehow for a whole" (195). As mentioned earlier, this technique of creating sustained poetic sequences is one that was notably successful in Warren's *Promises* and one that Warren directly encouraged Lowell to continue. Coming full circle, a letter from Jarrell to Lowell in response to a negative review of *Imitations* reveals his support for Lowell's work: "I saw that stupid review [of *Imitations*] in *Time*—*Time's* the cheapest magazine in the world and Dudley Fitts the cheapest poetry reviewer. . . . I certainly did enjoy *Imitations*. It's all live English, a real book to read from beginning to end" (M. Jarrell 451). In addition to displaying steadfast loyalty to his friend, Jarrell's specific praise of Lowell's "live English"—a goal toward which they had been working since the 1940s—and of his sequence technique points to the fact that Warren, Jarrell, and Lowell continued to share the same goals in the early sixties.

More so than in his translations, Lowell's next work, *For the Union Dead*, demonstrates the lingering influence of Warren and Jarrell. In the first half of the 1960s, all three authors were still in close contact with one another. Lowell recalls a dinner at the White House in honor of the French minister of culture at which he and "Red Warren . . . had a frantic search for the men's room" (Mariani 306). Aside from this humorous anecdote, Lowell and Warren maintained their relatively frequent correspondence regarding poetry, personal lives, and political issues. Jarrell, always a more constant presence in Lowell's life, also continued to coach Lowell in his work, both privately and publicly. At the National Poetry Festival in Washington, D.C., on October 22, 1962, Jarrell presented a lecture entitled "Fifty Years of American Poetry," in which he spent a disproportionately long time discussing the achievement of Lowell's poetry; in particular, he lauded Lowell's later work, in which the author "has allowed facts to lead their own lives, and his poetry accordingly has gone on developing in grandeur and in power" (qtd. in Bryant 95).[5]

Other contemporary critics did not necessarily agree with Jarrell's fervor for Lowell's late work, especially for that created after *Life Studies*. Significant to this study, Lowell's later work is now rightfully being credited as more universally applicable and farther reaching than its original reputation as scribblings of a "megalomaniac" in search of mental therapy (Doreski and Lowell 45). More recent scholarship has rescued *For the Union Dead* from the "severe attacks" it initially received for what was critiqued as an excessive outpouring of personal emotion; or, as Robert Bly believed, "something rare, a book of poems that is a melodrama" (Rudman 106; Bly 74).[6] Critics arguing from this position often point to Lowell's final line in "Eye and Tooth" as a case in point; Lowell's narrator laments: "I am tired. Everyone's tired of my turmoil." Now that scholars are rethinking the confessional paradigm, one may return to Lowell's *Union Dead* and his other late books with renewed appreciation. To quote Alicia Ostriker, "Lowell [has] been misread as merely personal, merely self-indulgent, merely sick" (2). Contrary to what critics have argued, Lowell's late style is not merely the result of manic or melancholic episodes; it is, instead, further evidence that Lowell continued to pursue the goals for finding form that suits its content as initially set alongside Warren and Jarrell.

Similar to the mode of "For the Union Dead," the poem that serves as the title poem for Lowell's 1964 book, Lowell frequently returns to the formula of layering autobiographical, historical, and cultural elements within various gradations of open to closed aesthetic forms in order to address national issues and challenge his modern audience. Axelrod confirms: "In *For the Union Dead* [Lowell] reveals to us a consciousness shaped not just by individual experience and cultural inheritance but by its continuing exposure to our collective social and political ills" (*Robert Lowell* 144). The way "Union Dead" embodies this method was carefully addressed in the last chapter, but a close examination of other poems in *For the Union Dead* yields comparable results. "Middle Age," "Florence," "Going to and fro," "Myopia: a Night," "Beyond the Alps," and especially "The Public Garden" are similarly based in private, autobiographical experience that can be metonymically and symbolically expanded into a wider public relevance and further mined for their prophetic messages based on Christian imagery and historical allusions.

"The Public Garden" serves as a particularly important poem for this study, considering the direct role Jarrell had in shaping it. When Lowell's original version of this poem, "David and Bathsheba in the Public Garden," was published in *The Mills of the Kavanaughs* (1951), Jarrell's review attacked its weaknesses: "The organization and whole conception of 'David and Bathsheba in the Public Garden' are so mannered and idiosyncratic, so peculiar to Mr. Lowell, that the poem is spoiled, in spite of parts as beautiful as that about the harvest moon. . . . Someone is sure to say about this poem that you can't tell David from Bathsheba without a program: they both (like the majority of Mr. Lowell's characters) talk just like Mr. Lowell" ("Three Books" 254). It is significant to note that the rewritten version of this poem follows Jarrell's advice precisely. Most noticeably, it achieves an authenticity that was severely lacking in the "mannered and idiosyncratic" original.

As with many of Lowell's rewrites, these two poems are founded on the same basic plotline: a once passionate union between a man and woman fades into impotence and infertility. Whereas Lowell invokes the Hebrew Bible's intricate plotline of King David and his seduced lover Bathsheba in the original poem, the rewrite merely alludes to "Eden" and "Jehovah" while skillfully maintaining the rich tone of desperate longing, loneliness, and nostalgia for what once was. While the underlying plot remains the same, the form is completely changed. Jarrell complains that one cannot tell the difference between Lowell's David and Bathsheba without a program, so Lowell eliminates the program altogether. The original poem is composed of two distinctly labeled sections—"I. David to Bathsheba" and "II. Bathsheba's Lament in the Garden"—each containing three twelve-lined stanzas. The newer version is transformed into a shorter, thirty-lined, free verse poem; the structuring stanzas and "mannered" dialogue between the characters are noticeably absent.

A side-by-side comparison of some lines reveals Lowell's choice to trade the original stilted language and diction for a freer, more conversational and contemporary tone:

David and Bathsheba in the Public Garden

I. David to Bathsheba

Worn out of virtue, as the time of year,
The burning City and its bells surround
The Public Garden. What is sound
Past agony is fall: . . .

II. Bathsheba's Lament in the Garden

The lion frothed into the basin . . . all,
Water to water—water that begets
A child from water. And the jets
That washed our bodies drowned
The curses of Uriah when he died
For David; . . .

The harvest moon, earth's friend, that cared so much
For us and cared so little, comes again;
Always a stranger! Farther from my touch,
The mountains of the moon . . . whatever claws
The harp-strings chalks the harper's fingers. Cold
The eyelid drooping on the lion's eye
Of David, child of fortune. I am old;
God is ungirded; open! I must surely die. (1–4, 49–54, 65–72)

The Public Garden

Burnished, burned-out, still burning as the year
you lead me to our stamping ground.
The city and its cruising cars surround
the Public Garden. All's alive—
the children crowding home from school at five,
punting a football in the bricky air,

. . . .
The park is drying.
Dead leaves thicken to a ball
inside the basin of a fountain, where
the heads of four stone lions stare
and suck on empty faucets. Night
deepens . . .

. . . .
And now the moon, earth's friend, that cared so much
for us, and cared so little, comes again—
always a stranger! As we walk,
it lies like chalk
over the waters. Everything's aground.
Remember summer? Bubbles filled
the fountain, and we splashed. We drowned
in Eden, while Jehovah's grass-green lyre
was rustling all about us in the leaves
that gurgled by us, turning upside down . . .

The fountain's failing waters flash around
the garden. Nothing catches fire. (1–6, 10–15, 19–30)

In addition to the diction change, the mode of address is significantly altered. Instead of indicating dialogue with a traditional employment of quotation marks, Lowell opts for creating an implied listener in his newer poem—just as Warren and Jarrell do in their later works. Warren's you-address and Jarrell's "interpersonal you," as have already been discussed, are replicated here in Lowell's mature poetic voice in lines such as "you lead me to our stamping ground" and "Remember summer?" Lowell also opts to save the "parts as beautiful as that about the harvest moon" that Jarrell favored and chooses to add more "beautiful" imagery, such as the evocative depictions of summer, the bubbling fountain, and a "grass-green lyre" that introduces musicality into the scene.

In addition to reflecting Lowell's continued respect for and adherence to Jarrell's suggestions for his work, this poem also serves to bolster the argument that Lowell's title poem is the rule and not the exception in *For the Union Dead*. Though, like "Union Dead," this poem centers on physical landmarks and personal experiences from Lowell's life, it cannot be interpreted merely as a self-involved purge of emotion. Axelrod argues that "it is here [in *Union Dead*] . . . that Lowell tests for the first time his fully matured poetic voice. . . . He here speaks in a voice that will last him a lifetime, a voice capable of transmitting the full range and intensity of his unique sensibility and experience, a voice indebted to Tate and to Williams but ultimately liberated from both" (152). The voice that is "indebted to Tate and Williams yet liberated from both" is the same mature poetic voice of Warren and Jarrell in the fifties and sixties: all three poets drew from personal experience in order to create poetry that is alive and authentic. They discovered a balance between the overburdened complexity of Tate and the superficial simplicity of Williams in order to present the world through the eyes of a narrator whose experience, though personal, is raised to a level that can be considered universal.

Lowell once stated, "If a poem is autobiographical—and this is true of any kind of autobiographical writing and of historical writing—you want the reader to say, this is true" (Seidel, "Interview" 272). One way that Lowell, Warren, and Jarrell achieved this goal is by infusing their personal poetry with realistic, concrete details of the world around them. In Warren's

"A Vision: Circa 1880" (1960), for example, he recalls a visit to his father's hometown:

> That scene is Trigg county, and I see it.
> Trigg County is in Kentucky, and I have been there,
> But never remember the spring there. I remember
> A land of cedar-shade, blue, and the purl of limewater,
> But the pasture parched, and the voice of the lost joree
> Unrelenting as conscience, and sick, and the afternoon throbs,
> And the sun's hot eye on the dry leaf shrivels the aphid,
> And the sun's heel does violence in the corn-balk. (19–26)

Jarrell similarly depicts a realistic scene from his memories of Hollywood in "Children's Arms" (1965):

> On my way home I pass a cameraman
> On a platform on the bumper of a car
> Inside which, rolling and plunging, a comedian
> Is working; on one white lot I see a star
> Stumble to her igloo through the howling gale
> Of the wind machines. On Melrose a dinosaur. (1–6)

Lowell utilizes this technique in "The Public Garden" by including imagery based on what one would actually notice while standing in Boston's Public Garden, such as "the jaded flock / of swanboats [that] paddles to its dock" (8–9) and

> From the arched bridge, we see
> the shedding park-bound mallards, how they keep
> circling and diving in the lanternlight. (16–18)

Perhaps lines like these are what inspired critics, such as Bly, to describe Lowell's work as "banal and journalistic," but taken as a whole, these observations add to the overall sense of authenticity for all three poets (Bly 74). Like some of America's best fiction writers—Melville, Wharton, Willa Cather, Faulkner, Hemingway, and Toni Morrison included—Warren, Jarrell, and Lowell succeed in immortalizing their era through a carefully selected, artistically illustrated inclusion of tangible details.

Jarrell, unsurprisingly, expressed support for Lowell's *Union Dead*, as he and Lowell were in unison on much of its subject matter. Further evidence of Jarrell's likely influence on this work, while Jarrell was in Washington, D.C., for his stint as consultant in poetry to the Library of Congress, he wrote to Hiram Haydn in 1957 that all that summer he had been feeling "depressed about the United States now, and kept thinking of an imaginary piece called *A Sad Heart at the Supermarket.*" Once that "imaginary" piece came to fruition, Jarrell included these lines: "To [the artist] the present is no more than the last ring on that trunk, understandable and valuable only in terms of all the earlier rings. The rest of our society sees only that last great ring, the enveloping surface of the trunk; what's underneath is a disregarded, almost mythical foundation" (*Sad Heart* 74). Perhaps this image was on Lowell's mind when he later wrote his 1964 poem "July in Washington":

> The elect, the elected . . . they come here bright as dimes,
> and die disheveled and soft.
>
> We cannot name their names, or number their dates—
> *circle on circle, like rings on a tree*—   (11–14; emphasis added)

It is clear that, like Jarrell, Lowell was feeling "depressed" on the topic of Washington, D.C.

Warren, similarly like-minded on this topic, also wrote to Lowell to express his appreciation for *Union Dead:* "It is a splendid book, truly. 'For the Union Dead' is, for me, the big show piece. It is quite wonderful. Close behind—maybe not behind at all but less obviously 'big,' less 'public'—I find 'Soft Wood,' with its extraordinarily powerful ending created from such simplicity. And 'The Severed Head,' . . . 'The Drinker,' 'The Scream,' and 'The Old Flame.' What a book they make!" (Clark, Hendricks, and Perkins, *Selected Letters* 4:428). Warren's letter is noticeably less specific and less lengthy than the praising notes written to Lowell about his previous works, but Warren's favored poems are worth noting. It is not surprising that Warren enjoyed the big, public "Union Dead" and the more subtle, simple "Soft Wood," especially since he was also honing his political and personal poetry at the time. Less obvious, however, is the fact that he includes "The Scream" in his list of favorites. This poem, Richard Fein notes, "which brings to mind some of Randall Jarrell's moving poems about the plight of childhood, is a touching statement about the child as orphan" (95). Here are some of Lowell's heartbreaking lines:

> A scream! But they are all gone,
> those aunts and aunts, a grandfather,
> a grandmother, my mother—
> even her scream—too frail
> for us to hear their voices long. (36–40)

Fein's comparison of Lowell's work to Jarrell's poems is on point, though as Sister Bernetta Quinn argues, "Every critic of Randall Jarrell has noted his predilection for children, as foci of narration and dramatic characters." One must add that, as Quinn articulates in "Warren and Jarrell: The Remembered Child," Lowell's "The Scream," centered on the "[child] who had the experience and who did not miss the meaning," is equally reminiscent of the "remembering" children narrators of Warren's poems (32, 24).

WARREN & HISTORY IN THE 1960S

In poetry as well as prose, the 1960s brought Warren increasingly face to face with America's history. The primary message of Warren's poetry, like his prose, was for Americans to understand the historical weight of contemporary issues and to respond accordingly with a moral awareness and a sense of responsibility to improve the situation at hand. Though Jarrell's assessment of society was slightly more cynical and Lowell's more pessimistic, all three authors increasingly relied on such historical backdrops for depicting narrators in the midst of metaphysical ruminations on their place in the world.

Thanks to the influence of the Fugitives, history was ever present even in Warren's earliest works, but by the 1953 edition of *Brother to Dragons,* that history had shifted from classical allusions to a focus specifically on "the American past" (Blotner 289). Warren's post–World War II emphasis on the American past pairs with his larger philosophy: that Americans must know and understand the past in order to develop their sense of self. In "Poetry and Selfhood," Warren argues that poetry is "nourishment of the soul, and indeed of society, in that it keeps alive the sense of self and the correlated sense of a community" (92). Warren's awareness of this power—and the need for it—increases within his later poetry, as his unique poetic techniques help to foster a sense of community by demanding the participation of his readers.

As Warren navigates the new territory of addressing America's history alongside its modern cultural crisis, he looks to both Jarrell and Lowell as guides. Particularly, he followed Jarrell's lead in writing about war, one of Jarrell's areas of expertise. In the case of Jarrell's "Losses" (1944) and Warren's "Harvard '61: Battle Fatigue," from *You, Emperors, and Others* (1960), Warren responds directly to Jarrell's poem, including echoes of his original words. Both poets minimize the gravity of death in the first line: Jarrell begins, "It was not dying: everybody died," which Warren paraphrases, "I didn't mind dying—it wasn't that at all." Jarrell's poem is told from the point of view of "we" young World War II soldiers who die (and kill) innocently as mechanized instruments of war. Warren's poem is part of a two-part sequence entitled "Two Studies in Idealism: Short Survey of American, and Human, History," which depicts Civil War soldiers—the first narrator southern, the second narrator northern.

In Jarrell's poem and Warren's two poems alike, each narrator finds a way to justify death. In Jarrell's "Losses," the innocent soldiers follow orders unquestioningly: "They said, 'Here are the maps'; we burned the cities" (28). Warren's soldiers rationalize their acts through the respective moral codes instilled within them by their upbringing. For the southerner, there are simply "two things a man's built for, killing and you-know-what," and for the northerner, "It behooves a man to prove manhood by dying for Right." By playing off these stereotypes—Jarrell's innocent soldier and Warren's ignorant southerner and exhaustingly didactic northerner—both poets force readers to consider the often inflated, sometimes fabricated causes for war and death. Emphasizing this point, the narrators experience moments of doubt that momentarily cloud their idealistic logic.

Jarrell pointedly repeats a version of the first line of "Losses" in the last stanza, only to call its legitimacy into question with a *but* clause:

> It was not dying—no, not ever dying;
> But the night I died I dreamed that I was dead,
> And the cities said to me: "Why are you dying?
> We are satisfied, if you are; but why did I die?" (29–32)

Warren also implements a *but* clause to introduce a moment of uncertainty for the southerner in "Bear Track Plantation: Shortly after Shiloh," though the narrator simply reverts to an unenlightened validation of his beliefs:

> But now I lie worrying what look my own eyes got
> When that Blue-Belly caught me off balance. Did that look mean then
> That I'd honed for something not killing or you-know-what?
> Hell, no. I'd lie easy if Jeff had just give me that ten. (17–20)

The northerner, true to stereotypical form, never admits a flaw in his reasoning but instead condemns the world's logic with a renewed sense of haughty disgust; perhaps the *right*eous proclamation is more of a reminder for himself than anything else: "And I was dead, / too":

> Dead, and had died for the Right, as I had a right to,
> And glad to be dead, and hold my residence
> Beyond life's awful illogic, and the world's stew,
> Where people who haven't the right just die, with ghastly impertinence.
> (24–29)

Both Jarrell and Warren reveal that when the significance of death is undervalued during wartime, blindness—whether caused by innocence or idealism (both inextricably linked)—is often to blame for the destructive consequences. Warren's title, "Two Studies in Idealism: Short Survey of American, and Human, History," confirms the larger implications of this message. The apparently gratuitous commas that hug the phrase *and Human* require the reader to consider *American* and *Human* separately—a reminder that the falsely justified idealism that caused blindness for both sides of the American Civil War is often repeated in Human History.[7]

This ideology and the resulting desire to expose the truth about history came to define the underlying principles of Warren's prose works in the 1960s. Arguably a catalyst, though not the sole cause, Warren's public commentary on national matters was reignited by his friend and colleague at Yale, historian C. Vann Woodward (Blotner 343). Woodward challenged fellow historians, in his book *The Burden of Southern History*, to mark the bicentennial by remaining true to the facts, having a "special obligation of sobriety and fidelity to the record," so as not to "flatter the self-righteousness of neither side" (87). Most likely encouraged by the fact that Woodward dedicated this book to him, Warren accepted Woodward's challenge and responded with *Legacy of the Civil War: Meditations on the Centennial,* published in 1961. This book, in which Warren names the Civil War as "the greatest event of our history" for "the American imagination,"[8] contains the seeds of what would later grow into Warren's *Democracy and Poetry* and "The Use of the Past" (*Legacy* 3). In *Legacy,* Warren claims, "History cannot give us a program for the future, but it can give us a fuller understanding of ourselves . . . so that we can better face the future" (100). For Warren, a realistic grasp of the past facilitates the development of selfhood and identity.

After Woodward's challenge was met, Warren continued to be vocal on issues of American events, past and present. *Legacy of the Civil War* was followed, in 1965, by *Who Speaks for the Negro?* in which Warren "calls on Americans to respond appropriately to the moral demands of a historical situation" and encourages them to come to terms with the past for the good of the nation's future (Ruppersburg 22). The quotation Warren selects to introduce his book hints at the guilt he felt for the old views expressed in "The Briar Patch":[9] "I believe that the future will be merciful to us all. Revolutionist and reactionary, victim and executioner, betrayer and betrayed, they shall all be pitied together when the light breaks."[10] Warren's urge to shed light on the wrongs of the past, his own as well as society's, inspired him to write a book that literally gives voice to "the people . . . who are making the Negro Revolution what it is—one of the dramatic events of the American story" ("Foreword" 1).

Warren's journalistic style includes context and commentary on extensive interviews with African Americans ranging from Joe Carter, a reverend of West Feliciana Parish in Louisiana, to Martin Luther King Jr. and Malcolm X. In his foreword, Warren explains that the purpose for writing this book was "to find out something, first hand, about the people." It is therefore no surprise that the concept of identity is a common link throughout *Who Speaks.* When Warren asks Dr. Felton Grandison Clark of Southern University about the "Negro Revolution," Clark responds: "It's part of a world movement for freedom, for a sense of identity." At this point, Warren pauses the transcript of the interview to interject: "I seize the word *identity.* It is a key word. You hear it over and over again. On this word will focus, around this word will coagulate, a dozen issues, shifting, shading into each other. . . . how can the Negro define himself?" (*Who Speaks* 17). A familiar concept for

Warren scholars, *Who Speaks* is centered on the topic of defining the self and discovering identity.

The first question Warren poses to Malcolm X is about "the Negro's sense of a lack of identity." When Malcolm X suggests that "it is necessary to teach him that [the Afro-American] had some type of identity, culture, civilization before he was brought here," he is foreshadowing Warren's "The Use of the Past." Within Warren's reaction to Malcolm X, one may recognize those arguments formulating: "The purpose of the self-improvement [for Black Muslims] is . . . to become worthy of the newly discovered self, as well as of a glorious past and a more glorious future" (*Who Speaks* 252–54). Essentially, what Warren gains from his exploration of the African American experience is a common thread that unites humanity: the need to understand the past in order to discover selfhood and pave the way for a "more glorious future." This is a sentiment echoed by Jarrell, who observes, "The climate of our culture is changing. . . . The American present is very different from the American past: so different that our awareness of the extent of the changes has been repressed" ("Sad Heart" 86). For both Warren and Jarrell—and Lowell, whose later poetry reflects a similar theory—society suffers deeply from selective blindness to the past.

INFLUENCER & INFLUENCED: THE TABLES KEEP TURNING

Jarrell mirroring Warren and Lowell, Lowell imitating Warren and Jarrell, Warren echoing Jarrell and Lowell—and the pattern continues. Through the rest of the decade, there are dozens more examples of notable exchanges of influence; even after Jarrell died, in 1965, Warren and Lowell continued to shape one another's work. Exemplary of the typical pattern, there is one exchange worth noting in which Lowell affects Warren and another in which Warren influences Lowell. For the first exchange, readers may return to Lowell's *Life Studies*. As already established, Warren deserves more recognition for Lowell's style changes and autobiographical turn in *Life Studies*. However, Lowell—in turn—inspired Warren anew with his execution of those changes. After the publication of *Life Studies*, Warren wrote Lowell a letter expressing sincere appreciation for and deep understanding of what he deemed as Lowell's intentions for the book: "For some time I have been meaning to write and say how much I rejoice in the reception your book is having. It is a strong, original, and memorable book. . . . I see what you are up to—or think I do— . . . many [of the poems] bring wonderful dramatic flashes, and sudden glints of language. It is in no way a disparagement—quite the contrary—to say that I feel this is a transitional book. To say so is to say that you are vitally in motion, and that the achievements are, as the best achievements should be, marks along the way. Needless to say, we are happy to have the book come to us from your hand" (Clark, Hendricks, and Perkins, *Selected Letters* 4:256–57).

As Warren congratulated Lowell on achieving their shared goal of transcending formalism and high modernism to create something new, it is arguable that Lowell was still lingering in Warren's mind the year *You, Emperors, and Others* was published. On May 24, 1960, Warren wrote to Lowell to praise his "rather well read, and extremely well received" poems, which were presented at the National Arts Club. Warren also explained his current project, *Conversations on the Craft of Poetry,* for which he and Cleanth Brooks were collecting taped "interviews and long statements by several poets on technical questions, meter, etc. to be used in colleges." Warren was most charming in his effort to cajole Lowell's participation: "We'd like you very, very much. . . . Can you be persuaded? We devoutly hope so."[11] At the end of the note, Warren expresses his unyielding respect for Lowell's opinion of his work: "I'll be letting one [poem] totter on to your indulgent eye when my copies are available. At least, I hope that eye will be indulgent" (Clark, Hendricks, and Perkins, *Selected Letters* 4:287–88).

Far from an empty gesture of politeness, an examination of Warren's poems from this time period demonstrates that he admired and sometimes emulated his colleague, Lowell, just as Lowell had emulated Warren. After *Life Studies* was published, Warren wrote Lowell: "The pieces I like best" include "Beyond the Alps," "The Banker's Daughter," "Ford Madox Ford," "For Santayana," "Sailing Home," and "Memories of West Street" (Clark, Hendricks, and Perkins, *Selected Letters* 4:256). Warren's inclusion of Lowell's personal poem "Memories of West Street and Lepke" verifies that both authors understood the potential for the role of autobiographical material within art,[12] unlike Allen Tate, who disapprovingly assumed that "Lowell had written these poems while mad or on the verge of madness" (qtd. in Doreski 124). More than merely approving of where Lowell's poetry was headed, Warren proves that imitation is the sincerest form of flattery when he echoes Lowell's "Sailing Home from Rapallo" in his "Mortmain, 1. After Night Flight." Though it is a coincidence that Lowell's mother died in 1954, just one year before the death of Warren's father, the similar presentation of this autobiographical material does not seem accidental.

"Mortmain" is arguably the most personal poem in Warren's *You, Emperors, and Others,* so it is understandable why Warren would follow Lowell's impressive lead on how to handle such content; he did, after all, list "Sailing Home" as one of his favorite works from *Life Studies.* Both poems begin with narrators recounting the moment they reach the deathbeds of their parents. In Lowell's poem, the narrator arrives too late; his mother is already dead:

Your nurse could only speak Italian,
but after twenty minutes I could imagine your final week,
and tears ran down my cheeks. (1–3)

In Warren's poem, the narrator's father is unconscious:

In Time's concatenation and
Carnal conventicle, I,
Arriving, being flung through dark and
The abstract flight-grid of sky,
Saw rising from the sweated sheet and
Ruck of bedclothes ritualistically
Reordered by the paid hand
Of mercy—saw rising the hand. (1–8)

Both first-person narrators immediately refer to the hired help—Lowell's Italian nurse and Warren's "paid hand / Of mercy"—as a subtle expression of guilt for paying strangers to fulfill the role of caretaker for their parents. From there, the plots divide; Lowell focuses on the transport and burial of his mother's corpse, while Warren dwells on an actual memory of his father that he had related since: "Now unconscious, he occasionally moved. Once, as though by remarkable effort, his right arm slowly rose in the air, and the hand moved as though trying to grasp something" (qtd. in Blotner 296). Despite the divergent plotlines, similarities abound.

Most noticeably, Warren imitates Lowell's technique of invoking the elegiac tradition sparingly while relying more heavily on innovation. In his earlier work, Lowell often clung to traditional forms as a method for controlling and containing the emotion in his poems.[13] Despite the free verse, irregular stanza lengths, and absence of rhyme scheme in "Sailing Home," he still manages to control the emotion structurally, through the strategic juxtapositions of images. The tears mentioned in the first stanza are the only raw emotion Lowell permits in this poem. After the initial lines, each traditional grief-ridden image is juxtaposed with an image much lighter in tone, which effectively trivializes and subdues the emotional effect.

After Lowell's fourth line—"When I embarked from Italy with my Mother's body"—the reader expects an emotional outpouring from the narrator, especially considering the first stanza; instead, Lowell provides a colorful image: "the whole shoreline of the *Golfo di Genova* / was breaking into fiery flower" (4–6). The shock and grief that should accompany the image of "my Mother's body" is tempered by the vibrant and visually pleasing landscape. Though the contrast between death and nature's fecundity is a traditional convention of elegy, the juxtapositions are more jarring because of the immediate, personal subject matter Lowell invokes. He repeats this strategy throughout the poem:

> While the passengers were tanning
> on the Mediterranean in deck-chairs,
> our family cemetery in Dunbarton
> lay under the White Mountains
> in the sub-zero weather. (14–18)

Here the order is reversed. Lowell presents the reader with an image of travelers enjoying a carefree vacation, only to shock him with the cold, stark description of a cemetery. The poem ends with two more complex juxtapositions:

> In the grandiloquent lettering on Mother's coffin,
> *Lowell* had been misspelled LOVEL.
> The corpse
> was wrapped like *panettone* in Italian tinfoil. (35–38)

After Lowell describes all the pomp and circumstance surrounding his mother's family, "twenty or thirty Winslows and Starks. / Frost had given their names a diamond edge" (34), her married name is defiled and mocked with a misspelling etched permanently on her coffin. The calculated line break after "The corpse" creates a moment of suspense. After the highs and lows created by Lowell's juxtapositions, it is unclear how the poem will end. Lowell opts for an irreverent image cloaked heavily in irony as he compares his mother's dead body to an Italian dessert. Perhaps taking a cue from Lowell's irony, Warren's "newspaper headline-style" of "After Night Flight Son Reaches Bedside of Already Unconscious Father, Whose Right Hand Lifts in a Spasmodic Gesture, as Though Trying to Make Contact, 1955" alerts the reader to the fact that, like Lowell's, this poem will not be a typical elegy (Blotner 334).

Warren opts for a more traditional form—regular octaves and a consistent *abababaa* rhyme scheme, only occasionally disrupted by near-rhymes—to control the emotion of an intense experience for the narrator. Far from some of the stilted artifice of Warren's early work, the enjambment and speechlike rhythms control the pacing of this poem. After the narrator spots the rising hand, he succumbs to a very human spontaneous reaction:

> Christ, start again! What was it I,
> Standing there, travel-shaken, saw
>
> . . . .
> Rising? (9–10, 15)

In line with Jarrell's "Moving" and "Lady Bates" and Lowell's "My Last Afternoon with Uncle Devereux Winslow," Warren allows the narrative voice and content of the poem to determine the rhythm. Instead of determining line lengths according to a standard syllable or stress count, Warren inserts line breaks strategically to heighten the dramatic effect of the poem.

An example of the real-time revision effect, this poem also captures the spontaneous process of the mind. The exclamation mark after "Christ, start again!" creates a long pause before the narrator begins asking questions in an attempt to process the experience. T. R. Hummer acknowledges the symbolic weight of this line, arguing: "What is important about this moment is the impulse to *start again:* not ex nihilo, but in as full cognizance as possible of what has come before." Even in times of "profoundest crisis," the narrator must acknowledge the past ("Christ" 38). "Christ, start again!" may also be read as a rejection of the high style of Warren's earlier career. The following deliberate line breaks are highly effective for creating suspense and evoking speechlike rhythm: "What was it I, / Standing there, travel-shaken, saw /

Rising?" The break between *I* and *Standing there* highlights the narrator's attempt to parse dream from reality as he checks his "travel-shaken," weary brain for hallucinations. Similarly, the natural pause created between *saw* and *Rising?* seems precipitated by choking disbelief. It is as if the word *rising* is caught in the narrator's throat as he struggles to define the image before him.

Even though Warren does not imitate Lowell's free verse from "Sailing Home," he chooses to end four significant lines with *I*, drawing repeated emphasis to the poet's persona, a technique that intensifies the intimate tone and personal nature of the poem. Also like Lowell, Warren employs strategic juxtapositions that are more personal in nature than the standard conventions of an elegy. The intensity and grave nature of the situation builds for two and a half fervent octaves, until Warren breaks the tension with three lines of colloquial language:

> Lifts in last tension of tendon, but cannot
> Make contact—*oh, oop-si-daisy*, churns
> The sad heart, *oh, atta-boy, daddio's got*
> *One more shot in the locker, peas-porridge hot.* (21–24)

Although the sudden juxtaposition to these fond memories does not trivialize the situation, as Lowell's light and ironic images had done, it creates an analogous overall effect. Expectations for a sustained, somber, elegiac poem are purposely left unfulfilled as Warren substitutes a far more human, authentic, and tender portrayal of human response.

Another similarity to Lowell's flouting of the traditional elegy, the narrator's recollections of his father are far from distinguished. Warren immortalizes his father's childish colloquialisms, instead of some great remembered quotation, and he also selects several unsavory memories to recount, including "the failed exam" and "boyhood's first whore" (28, 30). In a final note of similarity that is characteristic of the rest of Lowell's and Warren's poetry, both poets are compelled to historicize their dead loved ones. For Lowell:

> The only "unhistoric" soul to come here
> was Father, now buried beneath his recent
> unweathered pink-veined slice of marble. (25–27)

Lowell's description of his father as "unhistoric"—a man who lacks the impressive and traceable ancestry of his wife—reveals a narrator who is considering his place among familial history, a practice that Warren championed in his poetry, fiction, and prose. This literary device is echoed in Warren's "After Night Flight":

> Like law,
> The hand rose cold from History
> To claw at a star in the black sky. (14–16)

Warren's narrator had already begun to consider his father a part of "History"; the rising hand acts to bring the past into the present for a moment of reconciliation. Hummer explains: "In his dying, the father is—predictably but nonetheless powerfully—identified with history, with guilt and debt and also with the human will" ("Christ" 38). The similarities are clear here.

Moving to the second noteworthy example of exchanged influence, Lowell's only play, *The Old Glory,* which premiered on November 1, 1964, is arguably the last of Lowell's works to draw all three authors together in like-mindedness. In this scenario, Warren serves as the influencer, Lowell the influenced, and Jarrell the steadfast supporter. In the same way that Lowell, through his renowned *Life Studies,* inadvertently stole Warren's credit as the first major poet to blend prose and poetry while drawing from autobiographical material, Lowell's success in the theater again overshadowed Warren's earlier attempts at drama. In particular, Lowell's *Old Glory* earned him far more recognition than Warren's *Brother to Dragons*—five Obie Awards, to be precise, including Best Off-Broadway Play (Lowell, "Conversation with Hamilton" 289).

Despite the fact that Lowell received all the praise, Lowell's *Old Glory*—a trilogy crafted from two of Nathaniel Hawthorne's stories, "Endecott and the Red Cross" and "My Kinsman, Major Molineux," and Herman Melville's novella *Benito Cereno*—is thematically and structurally reminiscent of Warren's work. Like Warren's defaming though truthful depiction of America's founding father, Thomas Jefferson, Lowell aims for his play to present a truer sense of American history than is even presented in the original works. Lowell is "careful to expose the wrongs of the dislodged oppressor. . . . [He] makes Delano shoot down the leader of the blacks and say, 'This is your future,'" a line that highlights racial inequities and sounds unmistakably Warrenesque (I. Hamilton 313). By forcing the guilty white characters into the light amid the racial issues underlying both works, the real-life passion Warren and Lowell shared for the civil rights movement surfaces in both literary works.

Robert Brustein's review of Lowell's *Old Glory*, a "cultural-poetic masterpiece," praises Lowell's unique assessment of the "American character at three different points in its historical development." Though perhaps not in a distinct three-part work like *Old Glory*, Warren had been examining the American character set against history since his earliest works of poetry and fiction. Furthermore, Brustein argues, "*the Old Glory*, certainly, is the first American play to utilize historical materials in a compelling theatrical manner" (79). Since Warren's *Dragons* was not originally performed onstage, Brustein may be technically correct. However, Warren scholars know that he presupposed Lowell not only with the theatrical format of *Dragons* but also in his historically based *All the King's Men* (1946), which premiered as a film version in 1949 and later as a play adaptation in 1960.

Jarrell's and Warren's responses to *Old Glory* are telling. The play, not surprisingly, earned Jarrell's overwhelming support and praise. First, Jarrell traveled to New York so that he would not miss the premiere; his wife further reported that he could not contain his enthusiastic reactions during the performance: "Jarrell crossed and uncrossed his legs in excitement, exclaiming in loud whispers, 'Oh, that's so clever!'" Then Jarrell continued spouting admiration to Lowell all evening, through the night, the next morning, and even "spent the hour before flight time in a telephone booth pouring a torrent of praise and suggestions into Lowell's ear" (M. Jarrell, *Randall Jarrell's Letters* 495–96). Once he returned home, Jarrell wrote a rave review in the form of a letter to the *New York Times*, including lines such as "The play is a masterpiece of imaginative knowledge" (I. Hamilton 315). Finally, he continued to write letters and speak to friends about the marvel of Lowell's work. Evidence that he was also gushing to Elizabeth Bishop, she wrote to Jarrell in February 1965: "All kinds of very different people have written me they liked Cal's *Benito Cereno*, too, and it is one thing I hate having missed" (Berg Collection, Elizabeth Bishop, 2 A.L.S.).

Warren, less exuberant though still genuinely appreciative of Lowell's play, wrote to Tate: "Saw Cal's *Cereno* last night. It is a triumph" (Clark, Hendricks, and Perkins, *Selected Letters* 4:421). Warren would not have minced words to Tate, so it is clear that he was, in fact, impressed by Lowell's work. One wonders, however, whether or not Lowell's similarities to his own *Brother to Dragons* were as apparent to him as they were to later critics. Lowell once wrote of Warren's play: "*Brother to Dragons* is a model and an opportunity. It can be imitated without plagiarism, and one hopes its matter and its method will become common property."[14] One may argue that is precisely what Lowell did to create *Old Glory*. Warren's play-like format in *Dragons,* which succeeds in blending dialogue, prose, and poetry in a sustained, eventful narrative, served as an example for Lowell, who had struggled with his previous long narrative "The Mills of the Kavanaughs." Pushing the argument further, Norma Procopiow asserts that when reading *Dragons,* "Lowell was searching for a model which successfully applied a documentary approach to a violent event in American history (an approach later utilized in *The Old Glory*)" (303–4). Not only did Warren's significant book inspire Lowell toward directly addressing sordid events of America's past, but it also pushed him "beyond the dramatic monologue to *Old Glory*" (Procopiow 11). This study aims not only to trace the influence Warren, Jarrell, and Lowell had on one another but also to define their roles more accurately in literary history; quite simply, Warren's influence deserves more credit for Lowell's accomplishments. It remains a question as to why Lowell was repeatedly praised for Warren's accomplishments, but one may surmise there were multiple factors at play. First and foremost, the importance of the personal and professional connection between Warren and Lowell has been heretofore undersold and underappreciated, so earlier critics may not have instinctually looked to Warren to measure his influence on Lowell. But one also wonders if Lowell's prominent and prestigious Massachusetts heritage kept the limelight shining more brightly on him than on his Kentucky-born counterpart.

Endings &
New Beginnings

1965: THE END OF AN ERA

By the mid-1960s, after almost thirty years of fruitful collaboration, Warren, Jarrell, and Lowell were to part ways. Jarrell's death in 1965 and Warren's opinion of Lowell's "last whole phase" as "self-exploitation and . . . pretty crazy" precluded a continuation of these robust personal and professional relationships (Farrell 298–300). Furthermore, with Warren at sixty years old, Jarrell at fifty-one, and Lowell at forty-eight, all three men were seasoned, renowned writers—not opposed to constructive criticism, though certainly more sure of their creative paths than in their early years as fledgling poets. From this point, Jarrell would publish his final, arguably most accomplished book of poetry, *The Lost World,* in 1965, before his death on October 14 of that year.[1] Lowell, though he would never earn the same level of praise as that bestowed upon him by his contemporaries for *Life Studies,* would go on to publish a handful of original books of poetry—including the more noteworthy *Notebook, 1967–68* (1969; revised and expanded in 1970), three sonnet books all published in 1973, and *Day by Day* (1977)—along with several works of translation. Warren, ultimately the most prolific of the group, would enjoy a resurgence, until his death in 1989, that included some of his best works, with over a half-dozen new books of poetry, including masterpieces such as *Audubon: A Vision* (1969) and *Rumor Verified: Poems, 1979–1980* (1981); a few insightful nonfiction works, such as *Jefferson Davis Gets His Citizenship Back* (1980); and even a couple of new novels, including *A Place to Come to* (1977). Quite a few literary critics have attempted to narrate and navigate the "late" careers of Lowell and Warren—though there is still room for further development—but for the purposes of this project, it is worth examining these writers' final collaborations and tracing the lingering impact of one another within these works.

JARRELL ACHIEVES "A REAL POINT OF DEPARTURE IN CONTEMPORARY REAL LIFE"

Contrary to the noticeable lack of critical attention he receives, Jarrell was and is a mighty force to be reckoned with in American literature. Stephen Burt's *Randall Jarrell and His Age* (2002) is a major work that aims to bring awareness to Jarrell's legacy, but he is still a sorely neglected literary figure overall. At age twenty-one, Jarrell's first essay for the *Southern Review* both extolled and lambasted Ellen Glasgow and Erskine Caldwell and other established writers.[2] Jarrell's scathing remarks and jabbing quips quickly became known and feared by his contemporaries, yet the distinctive insight and wisdom in his criticism also earned him an almost unparalleled respect within the literary community. This status helped him to earn notoriety among his literary circle but hurt his overall reputation as a poet as his creative works were often overshadowed. Even now, the tendency in Jarrell studies is to focus on a small slice of his career—his war poems, his literary criticism, or his prose works, for example. But it is important to identify Jarrell's deserving place as a major force in American poetry, not only as a prominent critic but also as a highly skilled poet who continues to influence younger writers today. His essential role in advancing the careers of Warren and Lowell has already been narrated, but it is crucial to appreciate Jarrell's own arrival at what would be his best work.

All three poets understood poetry to be both a healing salve and a potent force through which to enact change; however, they were realistic about the difficulties involved. In wise words often quoted, Jarrell observes: "When we look at the age in which we live—no matter what age it happens to be—it is hard for us not to be depressed by it. The taste of the age is, always, a bitter one" ("Taste of the Age" 16). Almost twenty years earlier, Jarrell declared that one must write about the world to make it "bearable" (M. Jarrell, *Randall Jarrell's Letters* 65). Amid growing grief over the ills of society and an increasing battle with depression, the last few years of Jarrell's life found him still doing just that. In the years leading up to *The Lost World*, his wife, Mary, reported how Jarrell was in a particularly gloomy disposition; right before *Sad Heart* was published, she observed, his sadness took hold "until he found a sentence of Luther's that seemed to ward it off: 'And even if the world should end tomorrow I still would plant my little apple-tree.' He quoted this to Cal [Lowell], and to classes, and put it in the front of his book *A Sad Heart at the Supermarket*" ("Group of Two" 289). Though the prophetic essays and wise criticism in *Sad Heart* prove to be influential and lasting in the world of American letters, the term *little apple-tree* seems more appropriate for Jarrell's final book of poetry, *The Lost World*.

In the same way that Warren reached his turning point in *Brother to Dragons* and *Promises* but found his voice in *Audubon*, Jarrell's *Lost World*, in following *The Woman at the Washington Zoo* (1960), marks his most admirable book of poems; it is highly unfortunate that it would also be his last. Lowell says it best: "In his last and best book, *The Lost World*, [Jarrell] used subjects and methods he had been developing and improving for almost twenty years" ("Randall Jarrell" 96). Indeed, *The Lost World* is a culmination of what Jarrell had been working toward since his initial quest for "what comes next" that began in the 1940s. Warren's "you-address" and Lowell's personal poetry continue to be hallmarks of this final work, yet the openness, vitality, and earthy quality—the "perverse savage" feature, in Lowell's words—of this work combine effectively to earn the title, Jarrell's "best book."

Private reviews are often more telling than public ones; thus, Lowell's letter to Elizabeth Bishop on February 25, 1965, grants a fuller sense of his honest reaction to Jarrell's work: "[Jarrell's] worst fault is the repetition of a style and subject. . . . Endless women, done with a slightly mannered directness, repeated verbal and syntactical tricks, and an often perverse and sadistic tenderness—but I am getting into clichés in describing. I like him better than any of us except you when he is good" (S. Hamilton 456). Indeed, one does get a sense of déjà vu after reading so many dramatic monologues from the point of view of unhappy, aging female narrators, though this was a topic that long-consumed Jarrell's poetic mind. When he interviewed Robert Frost in 1959, he had scribbled in his prepared notes: "Four or five of your very best narrative dramatic poems are about women in extreme circumstances, having a really hard . . . time. . . . Wish you'd talk some about how you came to write them in general, some about particular poems" (Berg Collection, 1959 interview with Robert Frost, Notes). In the actual interview, available at the Library of Congress, Jarrell spends over fifteen minutes questioning Frost on exactly this topic, most specifically in the context of "Home Burial."

One may argue that by the time of *Lost World*, Jarrell had discovered these answers for himself, such as in his powerful poem "Next Day":

> When I was young and miserable and pretty
> And poor, I'd wish
> What all girls wish: to have a husband,
> A house and children. Now that I'm old, my wish
> Is womanish:
> That the boy putting groceries in my car
>
> See me. It bewilders me he doesn't see me. (13–19)

Even with the repetition in subject and perspective, these poems come alive in a way that Jarrell's earlier poems do not. That insistent command "See me" would resonate for most aging women. After almost twenty years had passed, Jarrell finally took his own advice to "start from a real point of departure in contemporary real life" (M. Jarrell, *Randall Jarrell's Letters* 139). Lowell is correct: "when he is good," he is among the best. Along with the excellent title poem, almost the entire book—save perhaps "Woman" and "In Nature There Is Neither Right nor Left nor Wrong"—captures glimpses, if not entire poems' worth, of real life, vivid and engaging. Though Jarrell had been encouraging Warren and Lowell toward "authenticity" for over twenty years, this work embodies that quality most convincingly.

Several of these poems deserve close attention merely for their poetic achievement, but it is most fruitful for this study to point to the places in which Jarrell chose to emulate Warren and Lowell. As in *Washington Zoo*, Jarrell continued to develop Warren's technique of the you-address in order to engage his readers in meaningful acts of self-reflection. "In Galleries" is a particularly fine example of how, similar to Warren's work, the themes of Jarrell's prose are rendered into poetic form. In Jarrell's "The Taste of the Age," he observes: "Nothing is as dead as day-before-yesterday's newspaper. . . . Yet the novelist or poet or dramatist, when he moves a great audience, depends upon the deep feelings, the living knowledge, that the people of that audience share; if so much has become contingent, superficial, ephemeral, it is disastrous for him" (75). Essentially, Jarrell points to the power of archetypes—which slowly fades along with society's fading knowledge—upon which the artist must draw in order to move an audience. Jarrell glorifies not only the role of the novelist, poet, or dramatist but also the ability of audience members to comprehend the power of this ripple effect.

In the poem "In Galleries," Jarrell similarly exalts not only art but also those who facilitate and grasp the necessary appreciation for that art. Jarrell focuses on the stereotype of the often-ignored American gallery guard who "has no one to make him human" by noticing his presence (6). Jarrell then paints an Italian version of this unlikely hero in high regard: a champion of the arts, rare amid the current society's lack of appreciation for anything other than the "superficial" and "ephemeral." Jarrell describes:

> But in Italy, sometimes, a guard is different.
> He is poorer than a guard would be at home—
> How cheap his old uniform is, how dirty!
> He is a fountain of Italian:
>
> . . . .
> And whether or not you understand Italian,
> You understand he is human, and still hopes—
> And, smiling, repeating his *Bellisima!*
> You give him a dime's worth of aluminum.
>
> You may even see a guard who is dumb, . . .
> . . . .
> His gestures are full of faith in—of faith.
> When at last he takes a magnifying glass
> From the shiny pocket of his uniform
> And shows you that in the painting of a woman
> Who holds in her arms the death of the world
> The something on the man's arm is the woman's
> Tear, you and the man and the woman and the guard
> Are dumbly one. You say *Bellisima!*
> *Bellisima!* and give him his own rapt,
> Dumb, human smile, convinced he guards
> A miracle. Leaving, you hand the man
> A quarter's worth of nickel and aluminum. (16–19, 28–32, 36–49)

The word *you* is used thirteen times in this poem, a high ratio for Jarrell, and it is always presented in the further reaching, universalizing address of "you" that is characteristic of Warren's work. Appreciating art is what renders someone human; even the "dumb" guard has the ability to bring about a spiritually moving moment in which "you and the man and the woman and the guard / Are dumbly one." In a final reference to his views on American culture, he paints you as "*you* give him a dime" and "*you* hand the man / A quarter's worth of nickel and aluminum." Jarrell is, ultimately, saying to you, his audience, this is what you should value: the power of art that transcends language, faith, and culture. Art is what makes *us* one.[3]

In addition to Warren's influence, Jarrell draws heavily from Lowell's example in this last book. Much has already been written on how Jarrell emulates Lowell's deeply personal style, particularly in the title poem's sequence. Critics such as Robert Watson note, "For the first time he wrote extensively about his own life, a subject that had seldom entered his poems directly" (267). Some lines from "Children's Arms" reveal how different this poem is from Jarrell's typical dramatic monologue:

> My grandfather and I sit there in oneness
> As the Sunset bus, lit by the lavender
> And rose of sunrise, takes us to the dark
> Echoing cavern where Pop, a worker,
> Works for our living. (p. 285)

It is no wonder why Lowell reported to Bishop on May 8, 1963: "Randall has written an awfully good nineteen page terza rima poem on his childhood in Hollywood 'The Lost World'" (S. Hamilton 422). Lowell most likely acknowledged the similarities of Jarrell's integration of autobiographical material to his own.

Jarrell's lines from "Children's Arms" blend almost seamlessly with those of Lowell's in "My Last Afternoon with Uncle Devereux Winslow," a poem that Jarrell praised to Lowell in a letter: "I like the poem *very* much. The motion has changed and it is much clearer and easier" (M. Jarrell 427). In other words, in being "clearer and easier," it is more colloquial, conversational, and similar to regular speech. Lowell's lines read:

> Nowhere was anywhere after a summer
> at my Grandfather's farm . . .
>
> . . . .

One of my hands was cool on a pile
of black earth, the other warm
on a pile of lime. All about me
were the works of my Grandfather's hands. (6–7, 20–23)

Jarrell's poem, like Lowell's, celebrates his grandfather for being a "worker" and similarly honors this American work ethic amid the backdrop of nature's beauty. Lowell's Grandfather's farm seems almost interchangeable with Jarrell's "lavender / and rose of sunrise." Though Warren naturally had more warmth, earthiness, and life in his writing from the start, Jarrell had, at this point, finally began to capture the quality of vitality he had been striving toward. Watson says of Jarrell, which may also be said of the work of Warren and Lowell in this period, "Certainly 'The Lost World' is a poem that speaks directly to us in mid-twentieth century America, to our lives" (270).

In addition to the intimate first-person narration technique that Jarrell borrows from both Lowell and Warren, there are also several places in which Jarrell echoes Lowell's particular themes and diction. Lowell commented on this phenomenon to Bishop while privately reviewing Jarrell's work: "Most of the opening poems I think for the long 'Lost World' are good and I found *I was underlying a lot of lines in poems I didn't entirely like*" (S. Hamilton 456; emphasis added). Whether Lowell noticed it or not, he was also underlying a lot of lines in poems he did like, those poems of the "The Lost World" in particular. Jarrell frequently echoes language from "For the Union Dead," one of Lowell's poems that he held in highest regard. For example, Jarrell's last four lines of "Children's Arms" depict an image from the narrator's recollection of childhood:

We press our noses
To the glass and wish: the angel- and devilfish
Floating by on Vine, on Sunset, shut their eyes
And press their noses to the glass and wish. (p. 287)

These lines are almost identical, in tone, diction, and imagery, to the second stanza of Lowell's "For the Union Dead," in which the narrator, also recalling a childhood memory, relates his experience at the old South Boston Aquarium:

Once my nose crawled like a snail on the glass;
my hand tingled
to burst the bubbles
drifting from the noses of the cowed, compliant fish. (5–8)

Both narrators are frozen in eternity, noses pressed to glass, longing to interact with literal and figurative "fish." In Lowell's poem, after these lines, the
narrator breaks from his reverie and returns to present day, catching himself
reaching out while reliving that childhood memory. In response, he reports,
"My hand draws back" (9). Jarrell echoes this line in "Thinking of the Lost
World," as his narrator recalls: "Standing there empty-handed; I reach out to
it / Empty-handed, my hand comes back empty" (p. 338). Again, an attentive
reader naturally connects this image to the one already depicted by Lowell.

Jarrell also emulates the themes and language of "For the Union Dead" in
"The Old and the New Masters," perhaps one of Jarrell's poems that Lowell
"didn't entirely like." Lowell's apocalyptic "Union Dead" expresses grief over a
modern society that, instead of worshipping Christ and revering war heroes,
pays its utmost reverence to commercialism:

The ditch is nearer.
There are no statues for the last war here;
on Boylston Street, a commercial photograph
shows Hiroshima boiling

over a Mosler Safe, the "Rock of Ages"
that survived the blast. Space is nearer. (53–58)

In a similar fashion, Jarrell first describes "the old masters" for whom,
"When someone suffers, no one else eats" (1–2). This is a community of
the faithful who suffer together—"The taste of vinegar . . . on every tongue"
(19)—and who believe

everything
That was or will be in the world is fixed
On its small, helpless, human center
[Jesus Christ]. (47–49)

Though Jarrell, unlike Lowell, is not particularly known for his religiosity, he—like Lowell—was concerned by the shift of the "new masters" of American society who strayed far from the grounding center of Christ. In the end, Jarrell's observation echoes that of Lowell's:

> For the dogs playing at the feet of Christ,
> The earth is a planet among galaxies.
> Later Christ disappears, the dogs disappear: in abstract
> Understanding, without adoration, the last master puts
> Colors on canvas, a picture of the universe
> In which a bright spot somewhere in the corner
> Is the small radioactive planet men called Earth. (55–61)

Similar to Lowell's "Union Dead," Jarrell's apocalyptic vision paints the earth as doomed for men who "come to see / What is important [and] see that it is not important" (51–52).

A final example that demonstrates the link between Lowell and Jarrell is Jarrell's subtle likeness in "X-Ray Waiting Room in the Hospital" to Lowell's "Waking in the Blue." Beneath the lines of these poems is a biographical connection between the two poets. Lowell's first acute manic episode was in 1949. After that first trip to the hospital, he was in and out of hospitals and sanatoriums for the rest of his life. Jarrell, on the other hand, only began to suffer seriously from depression in 1963. After Jarrell cut his wrist in April 1965, he, too, began the cycle of medication and hospitalization. Lowell wrote to console him:

> I must say that I am heart-broken to hear that you have been sick. Your courage, brilliance and generosity should have saved you from this, but I suppose all good qualities are unavailing. I have been through this sort of thing so often myself that I suppose there's little in your experience that I haven't had over and over. What's worst, I think, is the groveling, low as dirt purgatorial feelings with which one emerges. If you have such feelings, let me promise you that they are temporary. . . . Please let me tell you how much I admire you and your work and thank you for the many times when you have given me the strength to continue. Let me know if there's anything I can do. And *courage,* old Friend! (S. Hamilton 458)

This touching, sincere letter embodies their commiseration over common struggles and also demonstrates how they drew closer to one another at the end of Jarrell's life.

Returning to the poetry, Jarrell's "X-Ray Waiting Room" appears to be a nod to Lowell's "Waking in the Blue." Unlike Lowell, who openly admits, "(This is the house for the 'mentally ill')" (10), Jarrell transforms the purpose of his narrator's hospital visit into a "myelogram" for his spine. Despite this thin veil to cover the truth of his personal life, Jarrell establishes a tie to Lowell's poem immediately:

> I am dressed in my big shoes and wrinkled socks
> And one of the light blue, much-laundered smocks (1–2)

Though Jarrell is ostensibly complaining about inadequacies of "modern" health care, it is difficult not to read more deeply into lines such as "All of us miss our own underwear / And the old days." The great leap from undergarments to a desperate longing in general for past times hints to the fact that the "misery" Jarrell describes is derived from much more than a blue smock. It is that blue smock, however, that readers of Lowell connect instinctively to "Waking in the Blue." Lowell's narrator complains that the "Azure day / makes my agonized blue window bleaker" (5–6). These men were equally connected to one another in the "blue-ness" of their hospital visits and even more so in the greater misery of the world that haunted Jarrell to his death that year.

JARRELL'S DEATH

After suffering from bouts of depression since 1963, Jarrell had a moment of acute despair in April 1965, when he cut his wrist deeply by putting his hand through a glass window (S. Hamilton 463). Warren responded to this incident with a letter full of characteristic genuine praise and sincere expression of friendship: "I have been wanting to write you, simply to say that your friends—the friends in this house—are unhappy to think of your being unhappy. . . . The other night Bill Meredith stopped by with us, and among poems read aloud were some of yours, and how beautifully they came off. And I don't suppose it would hurt your feelings to know your last book [*The*

Lost World], as all agreed, is splendid" (Clark, Hendricks, and Perkins, *Selected Letters* 4:437–38). His mind always partly on poetry, the tie that bound their friendship, Warren included a copy of "the longish poem" he had been working on, which was most likely the "Tale of Time" sequence (438). In one of his last letters, Jarrell replied to Warren, praising that poem, expressing gratitude, and stating, "As I read it everything in it was extraordinarily real to me" (M. Jarrell 515). Despite the depression that was most likely haunting Jarrell at that very moment, he still made the effort to encourage Warren on their shared endeavor to create *real* poetry, authentic and full of life.

When Jarrell was struck and killed by an oncoming car just one month later—the question of accidental death or suicide still a mystery—both Lowell and Warren were devastated. After Jarrell's death, Lowell wrote letters to Bishop in which he contemplated his friend's state of mind and the details of his death. In the end, Lowell concluded, "Oh but he was an absolutely gifted, and noble man, poisoned and killed, though I can't prove it, by our tasteless, superficial, brutal culture" (S. Hamilton 465–66). Lowell felt especially tied to Jarrell in the end through their lamentations on American culture. Throughout the rest of his life, Lowell spared no opportunity to express an outpouring of appreciation for Jarrell and his invaluable presence in the literary world.

Warren, also deeply aggrieved by the loss of his friend, took a slightly different, though characteristic, approach to handling Jarrell's death. Unlike Lowell, who mourned by writing lengthy, emotional letters to friends, Warren turned his sorrow into action. More than anyone else, Warren took charge in planning Jarrell's memorial, from the larger points to the smaller details of logistics. He wrote to Jarrell's widow: "Three people would speak for some 15 minutes, and a number of others some 5 or 6 minutes, the whole program lasting a little under an hour and a half. This would be followed by a reception, or something of the sort. We—the people who are making the arrangements—are very anxious to have you come. Would you be willing? . . . Please know that [this letter] represents something of the affection and admiration in which Randall was held by many, many people. I have always regarded him as a bright and particular spot in my own life, and, as you know, have held him as a prized and special friend" (Clark, Hendricks, and Perkins, *Selected Letters* 4:445).

Warren penned similar letters to John Crowe Ransom and Allen Tate and also took a lead role alongside Lowell as coeditor in the tribute book, *Randall Jarrell, 1914–1965*. Despite all of Warren's hard work on this book,

Warren expressed some misgivings to Michael di Capua in August 1967: "I wish I had been able to do more for the book. . . . It wasn't until too late that I realized that, being the first of Randall's literary friends, knowing him very well from those early years, I should have done a little memoir, quoting liberally from the letters. . . . That would have given something on the pre-Kenyon period" (Berg Collection, Robert Penn Warren, T.L.S., Mrs. Jarrell's MS Notes). Lowell and Warren equally mourned the loss of this significant figure in their lives—their mentor, colleague, and dear friend. A line from Jarrell's "The Intellectual in America" is a fitting conclusion to pay tribute to his life: "The man who will make us see what we haven't seen, feel what we haven't felt, understand what we haven't understood—he *is* our best friend" (15). Not only does this quotation describe the relationships among Warren, Jarrell, and Lowell, each equally bringing one another constantly to new levels of understanding, but it also serves as an appropriate description for the role Jarrell played, and continues to play, in the lives of his readers.

The reactions by the rest of his contemporaries foreshadowed the legacy Jarrell would leave for American literature—that is, mostly as brilliant literary critic. In a tribute to Jarrell, Robert Watson revealed a combination of trepidation and admiration for Jarrell that was common among his colleagues: "Writing about Randall Jarrell, I can only think how much better he would have written this essay than I. I imagine him looking over my shoulder and sighing, You call *that* prose" ("Last Years" 257). Even Lowell, who had benefited from Jarrell's comprehensive critiques, joked to Elizabeth Bishop: "I think of [Jarrell] as a fencer who has defeated and scarred all his opponents . . . Randall stands leaning on his foil, . . . unchallenged, invulnerable, deadly" (S. Hamilton 247). Despite the high level of respect Jarrell enjoyed from those closest to him, he never, in life nor after death, received the recognition his talent earned. In a published homage to Jarrell, Lowell points to Jarrell's literary greatness and the additional public acclaim he felt his friend so rightly deserved: "In his own life, he had much public acclaim and more private. The public, at least, fell cruelly short of what he deserved. Now that he is gone, I see clearly that the spark from heaven really struck and irradiated the lines and being of my dear old friend—his noble, difficult and beautiful soul" ("Randall Jarrell" 98). Jarrell's difficult and beautiful soul made him an equally difficult and beautiful poet, though it is arguably the complexity of the man and the artist that make him difficult to classify, both personally and professionally.

Lowell observed that Jarrell "blows hot and cold on one," a fitting portrayal of the writer's personality (S. Hamilton 247). Jarrell famously described the poetry of Oscar Williams as giving "the impression of having been written on a typewriter by a typewriter," and Lowell reportedly found Jarrell's talk on "The Obscurity of the Poet" (1950) to be so "rude" that it caused the only temporary break in their lifelong friendship (Mariani 193). On the other hand, Jarrell is also known for his tender portrayals of women and children in poetry; his charismatic and attentive teaching, particularly during his extended tenure at the Woman's College of the University of North Carolina at Greensboro; and for the unselfish attention he lavished upon the work of his friends. Lowell captures a sense of Jarrell's overwhelming generosity: "Randall was the only man I have ever met who could make other writers feel that their work was more important to him than his own" ("Randall Jarrell" 106). Perhaps Jarrell truly did believe the creative work of Lowell and Warren was more important than his own, for the legacies of these poets owe much to the careful attention of their invaluable friend's advice.

In terms of Jarrell's legacy, however, it is arguable that his talent was lost in the shuffle of the early-drawn categories of American literature in the twentieth century. According to canonical literary history, one would not learn Jarrell's name by rote as linked to a particular movement or school, such as Ransom the formalist, Tate the high modernist, Warren the southern poet, or Lowell the "confessional" writer. Jarrell's creative practice never resulted in a quick and easy label. Though Jarrell did not consider himself a "southern poet," scholars are beginning to group him as such. More than his commonalities with Warren, the fact that he came to have a strong influence on the next generation of southern authors supports his placement in this camp. As quintessential southern writers, such as James Dickey and Eleanor Ross Taylor, began to name Jarrell among their greatest influences, hindsight presents Jarrell—along with Warren and the transplant "southerner" Lowell—as an influential writer who encouraged southern poets to move toward a more personal, less formal poetic style that emphasizes the exploration of selfhood.

After Jarrell's death, Warren and Lowell continued to publish poetry for many years, steadily maturing into styles that were ever more distinctly their own. Warren was vocal among his close circle about his distaste for Lowell's late phase. In a characteristically straightforward letter to Tate in 1973,

Warren cemented his souring take on Lowell's work while simultaneously commenting on his own style:

> You refer to "confessional poetry." This may be of that genre. It is rather straight. But ordinarily, there's a great deal of fictionalizing and indirection in poetry, even when it takes off a factual base. . . . There is, however, a lot of straight stuff in BTD [Brother to Dragons], for better or worse. This reminds me of Cal. I have just read his last three books [Near the Ocean; Notebook, 1967-1968; and History], if that is what I can be said to have been doing. I find them, in fact, just this side of unreadable. Plain dull. When something prospers a little, it gets swallowed up in the general morass. If a change of medication, as I have been told by B[ill] Meredith . . . started this notebook stuff, they had better go back to the old bottle. (Clark, Hendricks, and Perkins, Selected Letters 5:339)

Warren's words confirm several things for the aims of this study. First, Warren, like Lowell, immediately recognized the inadequacies of the term *confessional*, arguing that the "fictionalizing and indirection in poetry" prevents even factually based material from being truly "confessional." Second, Warren admits that the "straight stuff" in *Brother to Dragons*, which arguably inspired Lowell's personal poetry in *Life Studies*, also reminds him of Lowell. Third, this letter reveals that *For the Union Dead* is the last book of Lowell's poetry that earned Warren's approval. And so, in the wake of Jarrell's tragic death came the end of these mutually gratifying literary relationships but the beginning of new endeavors for Lowell and Warren.

THE PENDULUM SWINGS BACK: LOWELL'S RETURN TO SONNETS

After 1965, Lowell produced six books of original poetry and three books of translations before his natural death on September 12, 1977. These works, like those of Warren in his later years, deserve a separate study in order to trace Lowell's ongoing experimentation with style and content, but here the focus will remain on the ways his later work shows the influence of Warren and Jarrell. Considering the death of Jarrell and the firmly voiced dissatisfaction Warren felt for Lowell's *Near the Ocean* (1967) and beyond, there is no reason to trace these writers' personal relationships further. Moreover,

Lowell's and Warren's distinctly unique writing styles of the seventies—and the eighties for Warren—no longer appear to greatly affect or inspire change in one another's work. However, Warren and Lowell admittedly continued to draw from earlier lessons learned from one another and from Jarrell, and the lingering impact of these relationships is evident. It is also fascinating to observe the vivacity with which these two authors continued to usher in the "new American poetry," thereby influencing the next generation of poets with their abundant and significant final works.

Steven Gould Axelrod, among other critics, acknowledges that *Near the Ocean* marks "a new phase of [Lowell's] life and career" (*Robert Lowell* 176). This book, which serves as the height of Lowell's explicitly political poetry, was published shortly after he publicly rejected a White House invitation because of his views on Vietnam. Lowell admits, "This brought more publicity than poems, and I felt miscast, felt burned to write on the great theme, private though almost 'global'" ("Conversation with Ian Hamilton" 270). In an effort to find a form that suited his content, his book invokes aesthetic forms ranging from Marvel's eight-line stanza to free verse, mostly in an attempt to vocalize his concerns for America, such as in "Fourth of July":

> Blue twinges of mortality
> remind us the theocracy
> drove in its stakes here to command
> the infinite, and gave this land
> a ministry that would have made
> short work of Christ, the Son of God,
> and then exchanged His crucifix,
> hardly our sign, for politics. (25–32)

The politically charged content and the references to religion serve as a pattern for this work, a prophetic exploration of America's current state.

After *Ocean*, Lowell's *Notebook, 1967–68* takes on a more spontaneous and ostensibly unfinished style, as the title implies. Though we know what Warren privately thought about this work, his letter to Lowell from October 12, 1969, regarding *Notebook* is telling: "The book you sent [*Notebook*] has been much appreciated. . . . It has a new quality, however. . . . Your work, in general, has been formed under such pressures and intensities, with every poem hard, sharply outlined, assertive. This book seems, on the contrary, to flow in and out of life, to emerge from shadow and slip back into it, to extend itself without any thing more than a heightening from life. . . . All with magnificent ease. . . . Here the reader has the sense of poetry not made and offered him, but of witnessing poetry growing—not poems already made" (Clark, Hendricks, and Perkins, *Selected Letters* 5:77–78). A knowing audience will recall Warren's letter to Tate and read between the lines that Lowell's "new quality," which lacks "pressures and intensities," was not necessarily pleasing to Warren. Yet in his praise, Warren still echoes what all three authors admired in Robert Frost and in each other's transitional poems; ultimately, Warren applauds Lowell's ability to capture real life and the spontaneous process of the poet's mind as well as the dramatic flashes of imagery and the nontraditional range of his well-crafted art. The organic quality of the *Notebook* that Warren praises overflows into *History, For Lizzie and Harriet*, and *The Dolphin*. By drawing deeply from his strained relationships with his ex-wife, daughter, and third wife, Lowell captures—as Warren notes in his October 12 letter—"language rising inevitably from experience rather than language framed to make a poem" (Clark, Hendricks, and Perkins, *Selected Letters* 5:27).

Lowell's last book, *Day by Day*, resembles Warren's latest works in its emphasis on old age and nostalgia for the past, perhaps a somewhat inevitable direction for aging writers. It is touching how often Lowell refers to "the boys in my old gang" in his late works, even choosing to write one poem for Warren and three poems on Jarrell ("Homecoming" 2). For example, Lowell reminisces about Warren at Louisiana State University in 1940:

> Robert Penn Warren talked three hours
> on Machiavelli . . . the tyrannicide
> of princes, Cesare Borgia, Huey Long,
> citing fifty English and Italian sources—
> . . . .
> . . . .
> Red, you could make friends with anyone,
> criminals, or even showy writer giants
> you slaughtered in a review . . .
>
> Your reminiscences have more color than life—
> but because, unlike you, I'm neither novelist

nor critic, I choose your poetry:
Terror, Pursuit, Brother to Dragons, Or Else.
. . . .

an old master still engaging the dazzled disciple. (7–10, 16–18, 20–23, 36)

In remembering Warren, Lowell chooses to celebrate his own role as "dazzled disciple," awed by Warren's emphasis on history while teaching, his gregarious nature, and his poetry—*Brother to Dragons,* not surprisingly, included on his short list, given its influence on Lowell's *Life Studies* and *Old Glory.*

The poems on Jarrell are more pained since they were inspired by Jarrell's unexpected death, but Lowell still captures glimpses of what their close friendship was:

I grizzle the embers of our onetime life,
our first intoxicating disenchantments,
dipping our hands once, not twice into the newness . . .
coming back to Kenyon on the Ohio local. ("Randall Jarrell 2" 1–4)

They come this path, old friends, old buffs of death.
Tonight it's Randall, his spark still fire though humble,
his gnawed wrist cradled like *Kitten.* "What kept you so long,
racing the cooling grindstone of your ambition?
You didn't write, you *re*wrote. . . . But tell me,
Cal, why did we live? Why do we die?" ("Randall Jarrell" 9–14)

These lines embody not only the lasting significance of their formative years together but also the intensity of their friendship, fueled by candid discussions on poetry and metaphysics. It is arguable that out of these three authors, Lowell was the most deeply affected by his relationships with Warren and Jarrell—both for the development of his poetic talent and in the way he relied personally upon their friendships. Ultimately, Lowell, a man famous for his personal proclivity for extremes, found a necessary balance among Warren and Jarrell.

• • •

A POETIC RENAISSANCE: WARREN'S LATE GREAT PERIOD

The path that Warren set out upon alongside Jarrell and Lowell in the late 1940s freed him from many of the conventions from his apprenticeship under Ransom and Tate and encouraged him to create authentic portrayals of the world that spring to life in dramatic flashes. Though the guidance and constructive criticism of Jarrell and Lowell were invaluable for Warren's growth and maturation as a poet—especially leading up to the debut of his new style in *Brother to Dragons* and *Promises*—from 1965 forward, Warren was chiefly responsible for honing a gripping narrative voice that was all his own. Unlike Lowell's late works, which receive abundantly more negative criticism than praise, the last twenty-five years of Warren's life resulted in remarkable poetry—not only the best poetry in his personal oeuvre but arguably some of the best poetry written by any writer of his time. Despite the absence of influence from his once constant companions, Warren carries the techniques and strategies they discovered together into the creation of his late works while allowing for some fruitful experimentation with aesthetic forms.

As noted, by the close of the 1960s, both Warren and Lowell turned their attention even more toward history. After Lowell's *Notebook, 1967–68* was published, he wrote to Alfred Kazin that he had become "'more firmly hooked to fact and records' and furthermore that though the historian 'didn't quite *make* history' it was equally true that most lived history was 'dull, petty, hardly worth preserving, until the great historian' entered the mass of facts to shape them" (qtd. in Mariani 373). Though Lowell, like Warren, was never interested in becoming purely a "great historian," both poets were compelled, especially during this time period, to set an artistic hand to the task of rendering history into a form worth preserving. Joseph Blotner notes the continuity of Warren's historical theme in *Incarnations* (1968), arguing that Warren "longs to know his place in [the world], to make sense of the continuum of history, and to know how to live in time" (378). The title *Incarnations* tips the reader to its unique emphasis on man's particular struggle with the mortal coil; rather than "The Incarnation," the embodiment of God in the human form of Jesus, this book explores multiple incarnations of man, who is literally embodied in burdensome flesh. Some poems do refer characteristically to specific people, events, or myths in history. "What Day Is," for example, alludes to the Phoenicians, Celts, Romans, Monks, Moors, and the English. Furthermore, "Myth on Mediterranean Beach:

Aphrodite as Logos" presents a paradoxical depiction (or a "Botticellian parody") of Aphrodite as an "old hunchback in bikini" with a "gee-string" to "garland the private parts" (54, 12, 19). For the most part, however, the flavor of this book is uniquely sensual, visceral, and centered on the faceless individual.

It is noteworthy that *Incarnations* includes a poem entitled "Paul Valéry Stood on the Cliff and Confronted the Furious Energies of Nature" because, though Warren initially learned the techniques associated with French Symbolists from Allen Tate in the 1920s, he did not present their characteristic intermingling of the senses so skillfully until this book. Even Warren's earliest work presented a more corporeal depiction of the world than many of his contemporaries, but *Incarnations* marks his point of mastery in creating evocative imagery such as:

> The air
> Is motionless, and the fig,
> Motionless in that imperial and blunt
> Languor of glut, swells, and inward
> The fibers relax like a sigh in that
> Hot darkness, go soft, the air
> Is gold.
>
> When you
> Split the fig, you will see
> Lifting from the coarse and purple seed, its
> Flesh like flame, purer
> Than blood. ("Where the Slow Fig's Purple Sloth" 11–22)

Or much of "Keep That Morphine Moving, Cap":

> And where he sits, while deep inside,
> Inside his gut, inside his gut,
> The pumpkin grows and grows, and only
> In such a posture humped, can he
> Hold tight his gut, and half believe,
> Like you or me, like you or me,
> That the truth will not be true. (27–33)

Essentially, Warren worked through his final growing pains in *Incarnations* as he achieved expertise in sensual imagery and practiced pushing even harder on flexible aesthetic forms, all while maintaining a complex level of philosophical ponderings on man's place in history.

All pieces fall into place for Warren's next work, *Audubon: A Vision*, from 1969, arguably one of the greatest American poems of the twentieth century. This long poem fruitfully achieves the goals set by the influential trio of Warren, Jarrell, and Lowell while simultaneously marking the beginning of Warren's late great period in poetry. The poem's success has drawn more critical attention than almost all of his other works, with the exception of *All the King's Men.*[4] Though much can be made of this highly original poem, it is most essential to demonstrate how this seminal work represents the culmination of Warren's ripening period and the inauguration of his poetic golden era—replete with the lingering influence of Jarrell and Lowell—in which all his midcentury stylistic changes achieve unity and cohesion.

In an interview with Peter Stitt, Warren revealed that though he originally conceived the germ for *Audubon* while researching *World Enough and Time* in the 1940s, he "couldn't find the frame for it, the narrative line," and was forced to "set it aside" for twenty years (244). Considering the absence of measured meter, the lack of rhyme scheme, and the abundance of irregular stanza and line lengths in *Audubon*, it is clear why Warren was only able to return to this poem after undergoing major stylistic changes—most significantly, his loosening of forms and divergence from traditional formalism. Also reflecting the goals Warren shared with Jarrell and Lowell, Warren told Richard B. Sale in an interview that his aim was to capture an authentic portrayal of life in this poem: "It's about Audubon's life as a kind of focus for a lot of things about humans. *I hope it's the way life is.* It's about his heroic solution of his problems and the problem of being a man" (119; emphasis added).

By centering the poem on the historical figure Jean Jacques Audubon, a naturalist and ornithologist, Warren employs a historical backdrop in order to consider the American individual's place in history—a method that characterizes much of his late poetry. Warren confirms: "The poem is about a man and his fate—all along, Audubon resisted his fate and thought it was evil—a man is supposed to support his family, and so forth. But now he accepts his fate" (Stitt 244). The harrowing tale of Audubon, who nearly faces death at the hands of a filthy countrywoman and her equally offensive sons, gives way to peace and acceptance for the narrator when he realizes that

> he was,
> In the end, himself and not what
> He had known he ought to be. The blessedness! ("The Sign Whereby He
>   Knew" [A] 3–5)

This theme of coming to know oneself and consequently accepting one's fate is often repeated throughout Warren's late great period.

In addition to the larger structural format and content of the poem, the secondary elements of *Audubon* equally reveal Warren's entrance into a mature stage of mastery over even the finer points of aesthetics. For example, the sensual imagery that Warren perfected in *Incarnations* intensifies crucial moments in *Audubon*, such as when the reader is first introduced to Jean Jacques contemplating "his passion"; the narrator

> Saw,
> Eastward and over the cypress swamp, the dawn,
> Redder than meat, break;
> And the large bird,
> Long neck outthrust, wings crooked to scull air, moved
> In a slow calligraphy, crank, flat, and black against
> The color of God's blood spilt, as though
> Pulled by a string. ("I. Was Not the Lost Dauphin" [A] 5–12)

Or when Audubon forces himself into action after witnessing the strange beauty of the old woman who is hanged with dignity "And is what she is." The narrator is frozen in time, in contemplation, until he realizes that he must leave the scene before he will

> Hear the infinitesimal stridor of the frozen rope
> As wind shifts its burden, or when
> The weight of the crow first comes to rest on a rigid shoulder. ("II. The
>   Dream He Never Knew the End Of" [M] 18–20)

Just as such skillful imagery heightens these sections of *Audubon*, Warren's unique approach to integrating autobiographical material serves to bring satisfying closure to the poem and raises its significance to the universal level.

Similar to the technique used in *Brother to Dragons,* Warren inserts his own persona to narrate the last section of *Audubon.* More refined and subtle than the loquacious, didactic R.P.W. character in *Dragons,* Warren's voice serves as a reminder of the connection Audubon's character has to the rest of humanity. In lines reminiscent of both Jarrell and Lowell, Warren introduces himself as one who, like Audubon, was early fascinated with birds:

Long ago, in Kentucky, I, a boy, stood
By a dirt road, in first dark, and heard
The great geese hoot northward.

He then ends with the frequently quoted lines:

Tell me a story.

In this century, and moment, of mania,
Tell me a story.
Make it a story of great distances, and starlight.

The name of the story will be Time,
But you must not pronounce its name.

Tell me a story of deep delight. ("VII. Tell Me a Story" [A] 1–3, [B] 1–7)

Warren's words etch deeply the message that in these tumultuous times of "mania" in America, a tale about a man who accepts his fate can, indeed, be "a story of deep delight." Without the shaping forces of Jarrell and Lowell, *Audubon* would have been a very different poem in the 1940s—it is safe to say, a far inferior poem to the masterpiece at hand.

After the milestone work of *Audubon,* Warren took a short hiatus from poetry to focus on his role as influential literary critic with works such as *Homage to Theodore Dreiser* (1971) and *American Literature: The Makers and the Making* (1973). He also turned his attention even more critically to U.S. current events and their impact on American society, a trend also identifiable in the late years of Jarrell's and Lowell's lives. In 1974, Warren gave two lectures on Thomas Jefferson as part of the National Endowment for the Humanities Program that were later transformed into his book *Democracy and Poetry* (1975). At this time, Richard Nixon was still in the White House denying involvement in the Watergate scandal. As America questioned its government, Warren's timely response called attention to the damaging effects of poor national leadership. The Jefferson lectures prompt the question: "How are the arts to fare, then, in an America that has moved this far from the leadership afforded by a figure like Jefferson himself?" Not immune from judgment, however, the forefathers are also criticized for their idealistic vision of democracy. This sentiment, of course, is in line with Warren's (and Jarrell's and Lowell's) increasing concern with presenting history truthfully. Paul Mariani, who explores this same concept while writing as Lowell's biographer, explains that for Warren, the "decay of the concept of self" is a result of the "unfolding of our democratic experiment over the past two centuries" ("Robert Penn Warren" 212–13). For Warren, part of how "the arts are to fare" relies on the artist's ability to alert Americans to these issues.

Continuing with his call to action for society, Warren's influential 1977 essay "The Use of the Past" takes advantage of the bicentennial as an opportunity to comment on the self-imposed selective blindness that most Americans have for history—a complaint he shared with Jarrell and Lowell. Warren quips, "Americans, by and large, have had little use for the past except for purposes of interior decorating, personal vanity, or pietistic and self-congratulatory celebrations." This observation leads Warren to encourage Americans to see the bicentennial not as merely a date for prideful and shallow national sentiment but as an occasion for reflecting on the past. He questions: "Are we ready to learn from our past that . . . there is such a thing as 'the irony of history'? For what was once our future has now become our past—and that is the deepest irony of all" ("Use of the Past" 31, 36). "The Use of the Past" is essentially the fully formed argument of the underlying assumptions in poems such as "Two Studies in Idealism" or prose works such as *The Legacy of the Civil War* and *Who Speaks for the Negro?* Its concepts also serve as regular themes within Warren's late poetic works.

Though a preoccupation with history is a constant thread in Warren's poetry, prose, and nonfiction throughout his career, the structure and stylistics of his later poetry afford him the opportunity to use historical backdrops even more effectively in order to consider the individual's place in modern America. It is telling that Warren needed a twenty-year gestation period to discover the appropriate frame for *Audubon*. In a sense, once that floodgate was opened, his poetry of the 1970s and 1980s flowed freely in an expression of the meditations on history and identity, and the relationship between the two, that consumed his thoughts. Warren believed that "[poetry] may trigger the energy necessary to effect a change, in ourselves and in the world in which we live. Poetry might thus serve to renew the democratic impulse, even in post-Vietnam, post-Watergate America" (Clark, *American Vision* 126). As evidence of this desired trigger effect, within *Or Else: Poem/Poems, 1968–1974* (1974) through *Altitudes and Extensions, 1980–1984* (1985), readers are not merely instructed to acknowledge their past but, instead, are drawn in through poetic devices to participate in Warren's vision for an aware America. In particular, Warren's mature poetic style—with its loose forms, evocative imagery, and informal diction—allows him to create a conversational, open colloquy with his readers, encouraging them to "return . . . to a scrutiny of our own experience of our own world" in order to discover selfhood and therefore understand how to fit into America (*Democracy and Poetry* 41).

T. R. Hummer notes that "the most completely characteristic fact about Warren's poetry from *Promises* onward is its unwillingness to rest in any achieved style. Warren's poetry *is* a dialectic of change" ("Christ" 39). Particularly for this reason, a brief overview of Warren's poetry from the 1970s and 1980s does not do justice to the richly textured and individually unique bodies of work. While Hummer is correct to assert that Warren experimented with elements of aesthetic form and content until his death, much like Lowell, there are some underlying consistencies from that fully developed, mature poetic voice in *Audubon*. By continuing to engage readers with innovative techniques, Warren presents additional narrators who face their fate by reckoning with the past.

For Warren, an understanding of the self comes from obtaining knowledge of all parts of an individual's past—not only personal and familial but also regional and national. Before demonstrating how these ideas are at work within these books of poetry, it is important to make a distinction between Warren's definitions of *history* and *the past*. L. Hugh Moore Jr. once observed that defining Warren's philosophy of history "represents perhaps the greatest challenge for the critic attempting to study Warren's thought" (64). While it does pose significant challenges, Warren makes clear enough distinctions between history and the past. In the most general of terms, the word *history* refers to events that have been filtered through the self, while *the past* is a broader, more objective term for the composite list of all events that have occurred in time. Other critics have observed this delineation of terms; for example, Hugh Ruppersburg notes, "History for Warren is always perceived, experienced, and acted out by the individual" (21). Similarly, Moore claims that Warren uses the term *history* "in relation to the individual's personal past and his family heritage" (15). On the other hand, the past may be seen as something more fixed, something that can provide relative meaning to the present and the future. Knowledge of the past is necessary for understanding where and how we fit into the greater scope of our personal, regional, and national progress. Warren's poetic works render *history* and *the past* indefinitely connected. One may clearly see this theory at work in all of Warren's late poetry, from *Or Else* through *Altitudes and Extensions*, as the narrators are often in the process of coming to terms with the past and subsequently filtering this knowledge through the self to inform their sense of personal history.

An example of how an understanding of selfhood is derived from knowledge of all parts of an individual's past can be seen in *Or Else*'s poem "*Interjection #1: The Need for Re-evaluation.*" The poet literally "interjects" into another poem in order to pose the insistent question and subsequent command:

> *Is this really me?* Of course not, for Time
> Is only a mirror in the fun-house.
> . . . .
> You must re-evaluate the whole question. (1–4)

As in Warren's earlier works, he contemplates the concept of identity, but here his inclusive *you* provokes readers to reevaluate *their* whole question of the self. The same may be said for "Ah, Anima!" in *Now and Then: Poems, 1976-1978* (1978), in which the narrator implores: "Can you locate yourself / On the great chart of history?" (10–11); or in "How to Tell a Love Story," which plainly states:

> As sweet as a babe's and with no history—but, Christ,
> If there is no history there is no story.
> And no Time, no world. (7–9)

Over and over, Warren champions the necessity for understanding the past, and therefore one's personal history, in these modern ages. "Dreaming in Daylight," in *Being Here: Poetry, 1977–1980* (1980), also captures this sentiment:

> Is going on inside you, but with no name. Do you
> Know your own name? Do you feel that
>
> You barely escape the last flicker of foam
> Just behind, up the beach of
>
> History—indeed, that you are
> The last glint of consciousness before
>
> You are caught by the grind, bulge, and beat of
> *What has been?* Indeed, by
>
> The heaving ocean of pastness? (13–21)

Once again, identity—or knowing your own name—is contingent upon an awareness of what has been.

A logical correlation with Warren's emphasis on knowing one's past is his augmented desire to present a truthful version of history. Just as Lowell had become "more firmly hooked to fact and records" in 1969, Warren moved toward presenting a less abstract and idealistic, more concrete and realistic version of history in his later works (Mariani 373). In 1979, Warren even printed an edited version of his long poem *Brother to Dragons*, originally published in 1953, in order to make it more historically accurate. It is worth noting that Lowell's original review of Warren's poem found fault precisely with the historical elements of the work.

Lowell argued: "Warren's spirit of history has a rough time: occasionally it maunders in a void, sometimes it sounds like the spirit of Seneca's rhetoric, again it just enjoys the show. The difficulties are great" ("Robert Penn Warren's *Brother to Dragons*" 69). Lowell's criticism must have registered in some part with Warren because straightening the line of history is one of the major changes made to Warren's new volume. By introducing Meriwether

Lewis earlier and allowing Thomas Jefferson to see his own involvement in the "surrogate son's tragic suicide," Warren emphasizes the "awareness of human culpability rather than perfectibility" (Blotner 448). In this revised edition, Warren's characters acknowledge and take more responsibility for the past, therefore demonstrating the moral awareness that Warren advocated for Americans.

Considering the fact that Warren became increasingly insistent about reckoning with the past—whether as a result of aging or mounting concern for his country or a combination of both—it is worth examining the embodiment of this philosophy in his last works in relation to his mature poetic style. Readers need not look any further than the first page of *Rumor Verified: Poems, 1979–1980* to see how prominently Warren's philosophy of the past informs this late period. Warren was highly familiar with Dante's *Divine Comedy*, after spending each day at lunch reading Dante with Lowell at LSU, so it is significant that he selects the last lines of the last canto of *The Inferno* for the epigraph of *Rumor Verified*. In canto 34, from which the epigraph is derived, Dante and Virgil are in the Fourth Ring of the Ninth Circle of hell, the deepest point and, most significantly, the representative pinnacle of mankind's hierarchy of sins.

Dante and Virgil, finally at the end of their long journey, come across a three-headed Lucifer chewing on the three most evil traitors in history, Judas Iscariot, Brutus, and Cassius. Directly after witnessing this vile form of evil, Virgil tells Dante, "'tis time that we depart, / for we have seen the whole" (canto 34, 68–69). With Dante clinging to his back, Virgil climbs the hairy body of Lucifer to reach the center of the earth, and then both follow the path through the hemisphere to escape from hell. Once they emerge, Warren's chosen lines from Dante are presented:

> i' vidi de le cose belle
> Che porta il ciel, per un pertugio tondo,
> E quindi uscimmo a riveder le stele.

They translate to "I beheld through a round aperture / Some of the beauteous things that Heaven doth bear; / Thence we came forth to rebehold the stars" (canto 34, 136–39). These lines not only reflect Warren's philosophy of the past, they also encapsulate a pattern established in *Or Else* that continues through the remainder of his work.

In Dante's *Inferno,* the narrator is exposed to humanity's immorality as he encounters the minor and major sinners in history and those in between. Only after Dante has witnessed this realistic portrayal of the past, horrors included, is he able to emerge from hell, return to the world, and behold the stars with new vision. While the narrators of Warren's poems do not end up in heaven, they are often awakened to a more enlightened understanding of themselves and of the world after confronting the past. Moore explains that for Warren "knowledge even of the evil history, of horrible events like the gory butchering of a slave, has value. Such horrible facts, first, help the individual confront his own sinful nature. And, second, optimistic illusions perish in the fire of history, for the facts of the past will correct any such delusions" (14). In Warren's late poems, just as in canto 34 of Dante's *Inferno,* "such horrible facts" as "Black face, eyes white-bulging, mouth shaped like an *O*" and "the gargle of blood on bronze blade" force the narrator to "confront his own sinful nature" and/or that of his country ("Looking Northward, Aegeanward," *Rumor Verified* 27).⁵ Reminiscent of the journey of Dante and Virgil, a reader of Warren's late poetry figuratively accompanies the narrator through his confrontation with the past and the self.

Throughout this poetic period, dreamlike delusions are often shattered and replaced by stark, realistic images once the narrator has "awakened." As the title poem of *Rumor Verified* tells us, the "rumor verified" is "that you are simply a man, with a man's dead reckoning, nothing more" (34). Warren illustrates the destruction of "optimistic illusions" by the "fire of history" through rich, symbolic imagery in his poems. For example, the first poem of the prologue, "Chthonian Revelation: A Myth," contains a narrator who appears to be leaving a dream and entering a new reality, looking "back / Just once through the dwindling aperture" (22–23). The "dwindling aperture" harks back to Dante, as does some of the imagery and word choice within these late works. However, while Dante gazes at heaven through the aperture, this narrator looks back to a life that seemed real but is now recognized as illusion (Runyon 92).⁶ In these later poems, the narrator often experiences a moment of awakening after reckoning with the past, only to realize that his former self had no identity since it was formed in a world of illusion; as for this narrator, it is merely "a dream half-remembered."

In "Going West," as in the prologue, the narrator's abstract view of the past is replaced with a concrete, aware vision for the future. This poem may serve as a model for how Warren uses historical backdrops to employ his larger philosophy that Americans must know and understand the past in order to develop their sense of self. "Going West" confirms Warren's overarching message found in the poetry, fiction, and nonfiction alike: "We live in the world, and our understanding of it is of crucial importance to us. Only by trying to know our role in the world can we, in the end, come to know ourselves" ("Use of the Past" 42).

Warren has argued that the westward expansion and the resulting brutality to Native Americans was a frightening consequence of when Americans were blinded by their self-righteous quest to fulfill the Manifest Destiny. He saw this move westward as a false liberation, an irresponsible attempt to escape the historical implications for the future. In "The Use of the Past," Warren concedes that America's "mission to make all things new" resulted in "an unquenchable optimism" and laments that along with this rebirth came the belief that Americans were "a Chosen People" who felt that "God's will and their own were miraculously identical" (32). It is precisely this kind of blindness that Warren's late poems strive to bring into the light.

In a 1984 interview, Warren refers to the poem "Going West" as "the bloody story of the West . . . one of the most murderous stories we can think of" (qtd. in Ruppersburg 113). This poem exemplifies Warren's attempt for poetry to "[fulfill] its function of bringing us face to face with our nature and our fate" ("Use of the Past" 31). A seemingly pleasant road trip westward takes an unexpected twist when a man is faced with his nation's sordid past. Quite literally, "Going West" is a poem with a narrator "driving toward" his illusion of the Promised West, only to be faced "directly" with the literal blood and guts of a pheasant and the figurative blood and guts of America's past. Warren points to the false, dreamlike illusion of the West and the shocking destruction of this ideal while drawing the audience into the poem in an attempt to encourage personal self-reflection. The poetic devices of Warren's mature style that function to create this interactive experience in "Going West"—such as the significant integration of *you* to address the reader; tense changes; vivid imagery; notably loosened structure choices involving varied line and stanza lengths and speechlike rhythms created by timely line breaks, enjambment, spacing, and other pacing techniques—can all be found achieving similar ends throughout his late poetry. To quote his "Pure and Impure Poetry," Warren explains: "A good poem involves the participation of the reader; it must . . . make the reader into 'an active creative being'" (25).

"Going West" carries a similar message to Warren's "wake-up call" in his prose from this period, but the poetry creates a more powerful participatory experience for readers. The first section of twelve lines describes the dream-like ride into the West. The poem begins:

Westward the Great Plains are lifting, as you
Can tell from the slight additional pressure
The accelerator requires. (1–3)

Warren believed that "resistance" was a necessary element for successful poetry. His play with language and pacing in this poem, and especially in these three lines, represents the "tension between the rhythm of the poem and the rhythm of speech" that Warren credits for enhancing poetry ("Pure and Impure Poetry" 24). Along with the pressure on the gas pedal, the reader also experiences some extra strain while chugging through the dense, non-poetic language of "the slight additional pressure the accelerator requires."

Moving on, the sun, as with much of the natural imagery in *Rumor Verified,* is personified as possessing a certain wisdom;[7] most likely, Warren is pointing to the truth that natural elements—sun, water, earth—have an advantage over humans in knowing all of the past since the beginning of time. Here "The sun, / Man to man, stares you straight in the eye" (3–4), in a nonverbal challenge to the narrator's vision. The presence of the engaging "you" also challenges readers' vision and makes them question their understanding of the past. As the car presses along, the solid imagery of "wheat stubble" melts away into increasingly less tangible, less defined descriptions of "nothing but range land" and the "Blur of burnt goldness" (6, 7, 9). The shift in imagery here signals "tension between the particular and the general, the concrete and the abstract," that Warren praised for bringing texture and richness to poetry ("Pure and Impure Poetry" 24). It also reaffirms the trend in Warren's imagery that began alongside Jarrell and Lowell: reality is associated with palpable details, while illusions are aligned with abstract images.

Next there is a long, lazy line to lure readers into a lifeless dream state, rife with nonsensical combinations of words, reminiscent of that state between awake and dreaming: "With tire song lulling like love, gaze riding white ribbon, forward / You plunge" (8–9). The lack of an end-stop in that long line makes us linger even longer on the primary stressed word, *plunge* that finally ends the sentence in line 9. Those two simple words *You plunge*

in line 9 slow the reader down to a complete stop before shooting forth once
again into a

> Blur of burnt goldness
> Past eye-edge on each
> Side back-whirling, you arrow
> Into the heart of hypnosis. (9–12)

The significant shift from the long, lazy line to a series of three short, abrupt
lines with alliteration, near rhymes, and wordplay of *eye, edge,* and *each*
gives readers a sense of the experience of "back-whirling" and "hypnosis"
as a state of mild confusion and excitement. This energetic description of
"arrow[ing] into the heart of hypnosis" may hearken back to the blind "sense
of being freed from the past" that Warren warns Americans against ("Use of
the Past" 32).

The next line, which demands attention by standing on its own, reveals
Warren's commentary on this young man's dreamlike drive west: "This is one
way to write the history of America" (13). Since Warren's views on the false
escape and illusion of the west are evident, readers may rest assured that this
is not the way *he* would wish to write America's history, with eyes half-shut,
blinded by the sun, and hypnotized by the winding road and bogus promises
of new beginnings. As the narrator soon discovers, man may only live undis-
turbed in this mind-set with his eyes half-closed, because as soon as his eyes
are forced open, he cannot return to the blissful ignorance of that hypnotic
dream.[8] The tense next shifts to reveal that those first twelve lines are the re-
telling of a memory and Warren presents a current working through of the
narrator's thought process as he realizes the impact this event had on him.
The all-inclusive *you* switches to *I* as readers join the narrator's personal
self-reflection and his experience of gaining understanding of the nation's
past. The narrator remembers being lured even deeper into that hypnotic
state:

> I had to slap
> The back of my neck to stay awake,
> Eyes westward in challenge to sun-gaze, lids
> Slitted for sight. (15–18)

His eyes (his vision) have decreased to mere "slits" as he boldly continues into the false dream of the West. This may be seen as a metaphor for the Americans who blindly pushed westward, unencumbered by the death and destruction they were causing for the Native Americans on the way.

The next few lines,

> The land,
> Beyond miles of distance, fled
> Backward to whatever had been,

capture Warren's frustration with Americans who attempted to escape the reality of time by running west into untouched land, "as though space were time" (18–21). James Grimshaw explains: "Warren suggests that time *does* exist and that it is the responsibility of those who pass through it to use it wisely, learning from the past and leaving for following generations the lessons gained from time" (*Understanding* 15). And so, Warren describes the West's free space as simulating the effects of a time machine, flying "backward to whatever had been" (20). This attempt was, of course, ultimately irresponsible and ineffective. There is a hard break after this line, followed by a space, another tense change back to the present time of the accident, and then three lines, three dreamy questions, standing by themselves as a stanza:

> Now do I see the first blue shadow of foothills?
> Or is that a cloud line?
> When will snow, like a vision, lift? (22–24)

The narrator is tricked into false excitement by "shadows," "clouds," and "visions." The questions reveal a naive, confused narrator hopeful for the prize of the West, until—splat—the narrator is forced to face the true reality of the illusory dream.

The narrator describes his moment of realization:

> I do not see . . .
> . . . the wing burst. See only
> The bloody explosion, right in my face. (25–30)

Suddenly the blurry, dreamlike imagery is replaced by vivid, shocking details of impact and blood. The next line reveals that it is nothing more than
a "fool pheasant" that flew into his windshield (31), but the narrator's reaction proves that he understands this event on a much deeper level. So,
as he sees the land "all washed in blood, in feathers, in gut-scrawl," he is
coming to terms with the fact that the very dream he was chasing in this
westward drive is the same illusion that lured frontiersmen and led to the
"intoxicated," blinded, falsely justified mass murder of Native Americans.
The poetic description of the land, "forward, forever," reveals the thought
process of the narrator. This experience has "forever" changed the way he
will view the West; his illusion has exploded, just like the bird's body on his
windshield. With an understanding of the past, however, comes new vision
and preparedness for the future.

The narrator is forced to drive off the road, literally and figuratively:

Hands clamping the wheel with a death grip
To hold straight while brakes scream, I,
With no breath, at the blood stare. The ditch
Is shallow enough when the car, in the end, rolls in. (32–35)

All movement in the poem comes to a "screaming" halt, and the readers are
forced to stop along with the narrator to "stare" at the blood on the page
and contemplate its significance. As Warren argues: "The tensions in the
poetry are what force the reader to be involved and actually make this act of
self reflection" ("Use of the Past" 34). This moment, when movement ceases
altogether, is one of those moments of tension that invite readers' personal
self-reflection. Later, once the car is moving westward again, the narrator
uses "handfuls of dry dirt" and "water at a gas station" to remove the "fried
blood" from his windshield (42–43). Masked by the illusion of progress,
Americans were able to wash away the blood of the Native Americans with
their modern, divine justification of destined growth and expansion.

For the narrator, the experience of directly coming to terms with the
truth of the West contributes to an understanding of the past and, therefore,
of himself. The tense shifts again to a second reflection on that event; the
line stands alone: "Even now, long afterward, the dream" (44). The narrator
contemplates the moment when he was wakened from the dream, from the
illusion of the idealized West. The poem ends with a three-line reflection:

I have seen blood explode, blotting out sun, blotting
Out land, white ribbon of road, the imagined
Vision of snowcaps. (45–47)

As the narrator realizes that the white, pure, "vision of snowcaps" in the West is nothing more than an illusion, nothing more than "the illusions of our national infancy—the illusion of our innocence, virtue, and omnipotence," his dream is replaced by the bloodred reality of the past ("Use of the Past" 34).

The new understanding of America's past birthed a fuller development and awareness of self for the narrator in this poem. While readers do not see whether or not this new awareness changes the way the narrator acts in history, the fact that he is still reflecting back on this incident years later at least proves the deep impact that it had on his thought process and on his understanding of the past. Many of Warren's late poems are characterized by a similar invitation for readers to join the narrator's reckoning. Whether the narrator is coming to terms with man's insignificance on the larger scale of history, coping with the alienation and dehumanization that result from the Industrial Revolution, or realizing the profound ramifications of the atomic bomb, Warren's poetry encourages personal self-reflection for the reader that will result in an awareness and knowledge of how to fit into this modern world—that is, of course, to not only identify one's place in history but also to actively influence history for the best.

As in "Going West," there is a strong push for cutting through illusions to gain a realistic picture of the past within most of the poetry and prose of this time period. In line with Warren's thinking behind the more historically accurate revised version of *Brother to Dragons, Jefferson Davis Gets His Citizenship Back* (1980) explains the relationship between "current conditions and their genesis in past events" and promotes the idea of one's "moral duty . . . to confront responsibility for the problems of modern day" (Ruppersburg 129). These "problems" include everything from the civil rights issue to the potential threat of nuclear war that faced modern American society. Once again, Warren argues that obtaining a realistic understanding of the past is the first step toward developing a constructive conception for positive change in these matters and for America's future. A similar philosophy shapes *Chief Joseph of the Nez Perce* (1982), in which Warren, quite literally, teaches his readers a history lesson about the federal government's seizure of American Indian land.

Ruppersburg outlines the didactic function of *Chief Joseph:* "It places the Nez Perce war in the larger context of post–Civil War materialism; corrects the historical record; and suggests that the forces which led to the war remain evident in America today" (76). From the three epigraphs on the introduction page, readers immediately sense that Warren will expose all sides of this historical event, from Sherman's ignorant opinion that "the more I see of these Indians, the more convinced I am that they will all have to be killed or be maintained as a species of paupers" to the open-minded yet somewhat naive voice of Thomas Jefferson and, finally, to the haunting words of Chief Sealth. Warren frequently inserts real history—from battlefield markers to interviews to *American Sculpture: A Catalogue of the Collection of the Metropolitan Museum of Art*—in order to emphasize the truthful elements in the tale of Chief Joseph. Warren often employs these bits in order to juxtapose popular American history, often lies and exaggeration, with the unflattering truth about the bloody battle fought and lost by the victimized Native Americans.

In part 9, the more abstract tale of honor, pain, and sacred land switches abruptly to the concrete details of "O'Hare airport," "the Honda," and "shouts of friends" as Warren's persona enters the poem in present time (9). Through Warren's autobiographical meditation, an echo of *Audubon*'s end, readers are challenged to enter their own epistemological journey. Warren wonders:

> if when the traffic light
> Rings green, some stranger may pause and thus miss
> His own mob's rush to go where the light
> Says go, and pausing, may look,
> Not into a deepening shade of canyon,
> Nor, head now up, toward ice peak in moonlight white,
> But, standing paralyzed in his momentary eternity, into
> His own heart look while he asks
> From what undefinable distance, years, and direction,
> Eyes of fathers are suddenly fixed on him. To know. (155–64)

Clearly, "some stranger" is meant to apply to all readers, as Warren provokes them to challenge their own understanding of the American past and to awaken their desire *to know.*

Altitudes and Extensions, 1980–1984, Warren's collection of new poems in his last book of poetry, *New and Selected Poems, 1923–1985* (1985), creates a similar interactive experience for the reader through the poetic devices of his mature style. "New Dawn," part 3 of this nine-part volume, reflects the furthest departure from his earliest poetic phase. Long gone are the classicist tendencies and meticulously constructed meter; here Warren invokes the loosest of forms to engage his audience. In 1983, as Warren's role as spokesman for national affairs reached its peak, John Hersey asked Warren for a poem to serve as a preface to a deluxe edition of his book *Hiroshima.* Warren consented and produced "New Dawn," a series of poems that trace everything from the *Enola Gay's* departure to the bomb's explosion over Hiroshima.[9] In the same way that "Going West" responds to the brutality committed against Native Americans, "New Dawn" responds to the epochal event of the atomic bomb. This segmented poem is characterized by an unusual straightforwardness combined with the inclusion of a chart, a numbered list, and plentiful dialogue, somewhat of an amplified version of Warren's technique in *Chief Joseph.* The narrative voice is disembodied in this section, as if Warren wants the horror of the event to speak for itself, yet he still aims to make readers reflect on this major event in America's past.

In "Self and Non-Self," Warren provides an imaginary account of Paul Tibbets directly after dropping the bomb when he "sees / The slow, gray coiling of clouds" and "For an instant, / He shuts his eyes" (1–2, 6–7). At this point, the poem shifts to imperative commands:

Shut
Your own eyes, and in timelessness you are
Alone with yourself. You are
Not certain of identity.
Has that non-self lived forever? (8–12)

In line with all of Warren's late poems examined thus far, this poem contains a narrator in a moment of realization as he reckons with a significant piece of the past while questioning his identity.

The strategic line breaks leave the reader breathless at the end of each line, highly anticipating what will come next, and the direct orders in this poem force readers to envision this moment in America's history and experience this reflection along with Tibbets. The poem ends, "There / Is the world" (13–14), and these words ring out as a wake-up call for not only Tibbets but also for Warren's readers. The phrase *There is the world* doubles as an appropriate synopsis for what Warren, Jarrell, and Lowell achieved in their post–World War II poetry. There is the world, presented authentically, infused with life, yet artfully crafted by these artists' brilliant minds. To quote once more from Warren's "The Use of the Past": "If literature does anything for us, it stirs up in us a sense of existential yearning. . . . The truth we want to come to is the truth of ourselves, of our common humanity, available in the projected self of art" (48). Essentially, with every stylistic progression—whether while under the tutelage of Ransom and Tate or alongside Jarrell and Lowell or while drawing from his own core—Warren came to fulfill literature's intended purpose with ever greater skill. When Warren died, on September 15, 1989, he left an unparalleled legacy that will continue to stir up a sense of existential yearning for years to come.

NOTES

1. Fugitive Roots & Blossoming Friendships

1. The details of Warren's life have been skillfully compiled in Joseph Blotner's invaluable biography of Warren.

2. Biographical information drawn from M. Jarrell, *Randall Jarrell's Letters;* Bryant; and Pritchard, *Randall Jarrell.*

3. Biographical information drawn from Fein; I. Hamilton; Mariani; and S. Hamilton.

4. Quotation regarding Ransom in Blotner 55; also referenced in Doreski 21; and Beck, *Fugitive Legacy* 99. Quotation regarding Tate in Blotner 41; also referenced in Doreski.

5. Charlotte Beck argues that Jarrell's dedication to Tate was a "gesture of mixed gratitude and defiance" (*Fugitive Legacy* 83, 84).

6. Key works on the Fugitives include Brinkmeyer, *Fourth Ghost;* Hook; Beck, *Fugitive Legacy;* Kreyling, *Inventing Southern Literature;* Blotner; Doreski; Conkin; Gray; Cowan; and Bradbury, *Fugitives.*

7. When Warren entered Vanderbilt in the fall of 1921, he became deeply entrenched in this invigorating hive of intellectuals. He later recalls his "great good fortune" to attend Vanderbilt University: "For this was the time of the Fugitives at Vanderbilt, a group of poets and arguers—including John Crowe Ransom, Donald Davidson, Allen Tate, Merrill Moore—and I imagine that more of my education came from those sessions than from the classroom" (Warren, "Self Interview" 2). Warren, an undergraduate at the time, submitted his first poem to the *Fugitive* in 1923, and served as Ransom's assistant editor for all four issues in 1925 (Conkin 19; Blotner 56).

8. "Kentucky Mountain Farm": "I. Rebuke of the Rocks," line 2; "II. At the Hour of the Breaking of the Rocks," lines 10–11; "VII. The Return," line 4.

9. They were openly married in September 1930.

10. *John Brown: The Making of a Martyr* (1929).

11. Jarrell was, however, a stepfather to second wife Mary von Schrader's daughters.

12. *Five Young American Poets* is a book of poetry that includes George Marion O'Donnell, John Berryman, Mary Barnard, W. R. Moses, and Jarrell's *The Rage for the Lost Penny.* Ransom's review is entitled "Constellation of Five Young Poets" (1941).

13. Mary Jarrell was Randall's second wife and a highly influential factor in his life and work.

14. Peter Taylor notably underwent the same intensive Ransom-Tate tutelage as our authors,

and—more important—he was a lifelong friend to Warren, Jarrell, and Lowell alike. They were so close, in fact, that it was Taylor, along with Lowell and Warren, who coedited *Randall Jarrell, 1914–1965,* a tribute book compiled upon Jarrell's early death. An expanded version of this study might even warrant the addition of Taylor as a fourth name in the title; however, this book focuses on poetry, whereas Taylor is known for his novels, plays, and short stories.

15. For example, when he arrived on Allen Tate's doorstep, he was already experimenting with William Carlos Williams's simple free verse.

16. Quotation in *Fugitive Legacy,* 111; also argued in Mariani 119.

17. They were married on April 2, 1940.

18. Quotation from Blotner 192; referenced in Beck, *Fugitive Legacy* 109; and Mariani 92.

19. Quotation originally from the Bible: Matthew 24:28. Dante refers to this parable in *Purgatorio,* canto 9, "Dante's Dream of the Eagle."

20. Dante's original poem reads: "i' vidi de le cose belle / Che Portia il ciel, per un pertugio tondo, / E quindi uscimmo a riveder le stele." *Inferno,* canto 34.

21. "Terror" was originally published in *Poetry* (February 1941) and later in *Eleven Poems on the Same Theme* (April 1942).

22. Though Lowell remained attentive to Warren's work until his death in 1977, Jarrell's death in 1965 simultaneously marked the point of Warren's declining interest in Lowell's later poetry.

23. Warren's adolescent years were plagued by anxiety and emotional distress, leading eventually to an attempted suicide in May 1924. Perhaps Warren had more sympathy for Lowell's situation than previous critics have acknowledged.

2. Creating a New Aesthetic, Together

1. Jarrell published a novel, *Pictures from an Institution,* in 1954, which received tepid reviews, along with some children's books.

2. "The End of the Line" was published on February 21, 1942, in the *Nation.* This article is an elaboration on his short piece "A Note on Poetry," originally published in *Five Young American Poets* in 1940.

3. Though some of these characteristics are frequently found in high modernism, they are employed to achieve different ends. In high modernism, the loosening of forms and irregularity in rhythm, line lengths, and rhyme schemes are often utilized to create a purposeful disharmony or discordance, often in an effort to reflect the chaos inherent in the subject matter (e.g., T. S. Eliot's *The Waste Land*). For Warren, Jarrell, and Lowell, however, these techniques were used in order to create a more informal, conversational, personal mode.

4. The lecture "Levels and Opposites: Structure in Poetry" was presented in 1942. The essay was first published in the *Georgia Review* 50.4, copyright 1966 by Mary Jarrell.

5. Lowell wrote on September 7, 1943: "The war has entered on an unforeseen phase; one that can by no possible extension of the meaning of the words be called defensive. By demanding unconditional surrender we reveal our complete confidence in the outcome, and declare that we are prepared to wage a war without quarter or principles, to the permanent destruction of Germany and Japan" (S. Hamilton 39).

6. The poem "Memories of West Street and Lepke" reads:

These are the tranquilized *Fifties,*
and I am forty. Ought I to regret my seedtime?
I was a fire-breathing Catholic C.O.,
and made my manic statement,
telling off the state and president, and then
sat waiting sentence in the bull pen. (12–17)

7. The *Sewanee Review* was under Tate's control from 1944 to 1946.

8. Known for honest criticism on the work of other writers but also for loyalty to his friends, Jarrell most likely would have felt embarrassed to address such personal matters in a review of his dear friend Warren's work.

9. Joseph Blotner posits that "the causes for the long drought were several," involving everything from a preoccupation with fiction to a difficult work schedule as well as several facets of his personal life, though I would emphasize that in this time he was also searching for a new style for his poetry (211). John Burt adds that this ten-year dry spell was a "dark time" partly "because these were the years of the dissolution of his turbulent first marriage. But it was also, Warren repeatedly says, a period during which he was unable to complete a poem, short or long" (J. Burt, "Afterword" 480).

10. "The Ballad of Billie Potts," "Variation: Ode to Fear," and the five-part sequence "Mexico is a Foreign Country: Five Studies in Naturalism."

11. Jarrell also favored "The Quaker Graveyard in Nantucket," calling it Lowell's "very best big poem" (M. Jarrell 137).

3. Robert Frost: A Unifying Figure to Guide Change

1. It is interesting to note that Lowell already favored the "later work" of Warren.

2. All three dealt with marriages and the ends of marriages. Lowell divorced Jean Stafford in 1946 and married Elizabeth Hardwick in 1949; Warren divorced Emma "Cinina" Brescia in 1951 and married Eleanor Clark in 1952; and Jarrell divorced Mackie Langham in 1951 and married Mary von Schrader in 1952. All three writers, at one point or another, struggled with physical or mental health issues, though most notably Lowell, who suffered from manic depression. Jarrell became a father by way of Mary's two daughters.

3. Chief Joseph was a real-life Nez Perce chief who, after being threatened to accept an undesirable renegotiated treaty by the U.S. federal government, led his followers in a heroic attempt to escape to Canada.

4. Though Jarrell was not a drinker, except for "the occasional German white wine," it never stopped him from socializing at parties among literary friends (Pritchard 142).

5. The lecture, presented in May, was later published in *Michigan Alumnus Quarterly Review* in December 1947.

6. The theme of Frost's "darkness" is one that stuck with Jarrell. The Berg Collection of English and American Literature holds five pages, front and back, of handwritten notes by Randall Jarrell on what he should ask Robert Frost when he interviewed him in 1959. The notes, covered in marginalia and peppered with page numbers and specific references, often return to this concept. For example, he scribbles: "How does it make you feel to have some poems a thousand

times better known than others just as good? To have your relatively sunny poems so much better known than relatively shady ones—the dayside of your poetry so much better known than the night side?"

7. The hemlock evergreen shrub mentioned in this poem is not the same plant as the one that was the source of the poison Socrates drank, yet there is still plentiful associations in popular culture about the poisonous nature of hemlock.

4. The Turning Point at Midcentury

1. "Randall Jarrell's Wild Dogmatism" was originally published in the *New York Times Book Review* on October 7, 1951.

2. Though Red is a fairly common nickname due to its association with redheads, it is worth noting that Lowell invokes Warren's moniker in "Mills of the Kavanaugh" for the character Red Kavanaugh, and Jarrell repeats it here.

3. Warren and Lowell also took lengthy hiatuses from poetry around the point of their style shifts. Warren went ten years between "The Ballad of Billie Potts" (1943) and *Brother to Dragons* (1953), and Lowell went eight years between *The Mills of the Kavanaughs* (1951) and *Life Studies* (1959).

4. By this point, many critics have worked to explain and contextualize Warren's controversial contribution of "The Briar Patch" to *I'll Take My Stand*, including Byrne; Suarez; Kreyling, *South That Wasn't There;* Szczesiul; Blotner; Ruppersburg; and Conkin; among others. While this is still a lively debate and regularly brings Warren's name to the forefront of literary study, its direct relevance to the topic of this book is minimal. To provide some historical context, however, it is worthwhile to quote Natasha Trethewey in her final lecture as U.S. poet laureate, "'The World of Action and Liability': On Saying What Happens" (2014): "Warren's social criticism, his rhetoric, certainly had the power to influence the thinking of others, but I argue that the quarrel with himself, his poetry, is a grander model for displaying the process of ideological evolution and thus even more influential; it allows us to see ourselves in the mirror of his reckoning." Ultimately, Warren's "quarrel with himself" over issues of race follows the same pattern as the additional political issues he addresses head-on in his poetry from the 1950s onward. Trethewey's invocation of the word *reckoning,* a word often used by Warren in his later poetry, is perfectly apt.

5. R.W.B. Lewis, James A. Grimshaw Jr. (126), and Hilton Kramer (11), to name a few.

6. After Jarrell's death, Lowell again praised *Pictures,* despite "its fictional oddities," for being "a unique and serious joke-book" (qtd. in Angus 266).

7. *The Seven-League Crutches* (1951) and *Life Studies* (1959), respectively.

5. Reconsidering *Life Studies* & Lowell's Career

1. Reference is to the theories espoused in Harold Bloom's *Anxiety of Influence.*

2. Frank Bidart was a close friend of Lowell's and is one of the editors of Lowell's *Collected Poems.*

3. Axelrod, *Robert Lowell;* Longenbach; Travisano, "Confessional Paradigm Revisited," *Midcentury Quartet;* and Sisack.

4. Paul Mariani notes that in 1954, Lowell started writing an "'autobiographical monster,' only to learn that writing prose is hell" (235).

5. "91 Revere Street" was first published in a 1956 issue of the *Partisan Review* and later published in its entirety as part 2 of *Life Studies*.

6. Lowell is referring to a section in "How Poems Come About."

7. Lowell, "Robert Penn Warren's *Brother to Dragons*," 73.

8. Though he later rejoined the Episcopal Church in 1955, many describe him as agnostic in his later life, further distancing himself from his Puritan heritage.

9. In November 1960, Jarrell wrote to Lowell: "Thanks so much for your letter about the book [*The Woman at the Washington Zoo*]. . . . Did you see a piece of mine in *Daedalus* named 'A Sad Heart at the Supermarket'? It rather goes with your *Atlantic Monthly* poem ['For the Union Dead']. I liked it" (M. Jarrell, *Randall Jarrell's Letters* 446).

10. Mussolini in "Beyond the Alps" and Dwight D. Eisenhower in "Inauguration Day: January 1953," e.g.

11. Critics including Marius Bewley, Paul Mariani, Jerome Mazzaro, David Perkins, and Selim Sarwar have all acknowledged this point.

12. William James was also a significant figure for Robert Penn Warren's work. See John Burt's *Robert Penn Warren and American Idealism* (1988) for further reading—particularly his second chapter, "Neutral Territory: Pragmatism."

6. The 1960s: "The Times They Are A-Changin'"

1. For more information about Jarrell's Marxist leanings, see Travisano 135–36; Mariani 98–99; and Bryant 7.

2. Other examples in which Jarrell employs the you-address include "The Face," "The Contrary Poet," "A Rhapsody on Irish Themes," "A Conversation with the Devil," "The Black Swan," and "Afterwards."

3. These translations fit naturally into Jarrell's body of work since they contain parallel themes of childhood, isolation, and loneliness. The female narrator in Jarrell's title poem even bears a remarkable similarity to the weary, desperate narrator in his translation of Rilke's "The Grown-Up."

4. Some examples include, but are not limited to, "To the Reader," "Voyage to Cythera," "The Drunken Boat," and "Hitlerian Spring."

5. Mary Jarrell reported: "To cover fifty years of American poetry in a one-hour speech, Jarrell singled out fifty-seven poets to mention. Who got the most space was significant, and who placed at the finish line was significant. In his conclusion, Jarrell gave Wilbur 230 words, Shapiro 250, and Lowell 700" (*Randall Jarrell's Letters* 457).

6. Bly's harsh critique continues: "Most of the poems in *For the Union Dead* are bad poems. . . . [The book] has a peculiarly stale and cold air, instantly recognizable. It is the air of too many literary conversations, an exhausting involvement with the Establishment. . . . Lowell's ideas are banal and journalistic" (74). One cannot ignore that the last part of Bly's statement strikingly resembles the criticism Jarrell received for his later work, which is also often considered somewhat "banal and journalistic." Considering the mutual influence on one another's work, it is not a surprise that the praise and criticism alike would invite similarities.

7. Warren expresses this concept even more clearly in a later poem, "Bad Year, Bad War: A New Year's Card, 1969" (1969):

> For conscience
> . . . .
> Is, of innocence, the final criterion, and the fact that now we
> Are troubled, and candidly admit it, simply proves
> . . . .
> That in the past we, being then untroubled,
> Were innocent. Dear God, we pray
> . . . .
> To be restored to that purity of heart
> That sanctifies the shedding of blood. (20–26)

8. Joseph Blotner explains Warren's reasoning in *Robert Penn Warren: A Biography:* "The war gave the South the Great Alibi and gave the North the Treasury of Virtue. . . . 'By the Great Alibi pellagra, hookworm, and illiteracy are all explained.' . . . The Southerner 'turns defeat into victory, defects into virtues.' For the Northerner, the Treasury of Virtue is 'a consciously undertaken crusade so full of righteousness that there is enough overplus stored in Heaven' to constitute 'a plenary indulgence, for all sins past, present, and future, freely given by the hand of history'" (344). Hints of this philosophy are inherent within Warren's poem "Two Studies in Idealism: Short Survey of American, and Human, History."

9. He also confronted his early racist views in poems such as "Old Nigger on One-Mule Car Encountered Late at Night When Driving Home from Party in the Back Country," in which the narrator discovers common humanity with a black man he had once dismissively and mistakenly named a "fool-nigger."

10. This quotation is from a character in *Under Western Eyes,* by Joseph Conrad.

11. Lowell did in fact agree to participate in the project.

12. Warren also wrote to Lowell: "Speaking of poetry, you mentioned in a letter that Snodgrass is a friend of yours. Did I ever tell you how damned good I thought his book [*Heart's Needle*]? . . . In confidence, I'll recall that he was my #1, with the winner [Donald Justice] my #2" (Clark, Hendricks, and Perkins, *Selected Letters* 4:289). Clearly, Warren had an appreciation for the more personal poetry that was gaining popularity at the time.

13. Demonstrated in the explication of Lowell's "Her Dead Brother" earlier.

14. Lowell, "Robert Penn Warren's *Brother to Dragons*," 68.

7. Endings & New Beginnings

1. Jarrell's posthumous publications include *The Complete Poems* (1969, by Mrs. Randall Jarrell), *The Third Book of Criticism* (1969), and two translations, *The Three Sisters* (1969) and *Faust, Part 1* (1976).

2. Fall 1935.

3. Jarrell's utilizes the "you-address" in a similar fashion in "Well Water," "The Lost Children," "Hope," "The One Who Was Different," and "Field and Forest," to name a few.

4. Some examples include Clements; Duane; Jarman; Justus; D. Smith; and Strandberg, "Robert Penn Warren."

5. "Old Nigger on One-Mule Cart Encountered Late at Night When Driving Home from Party in the Back Country," *Can I See Arcturus from Where I Stand*, 1, 24.

6. Runyon suggests, "Only at the end of 'Chthonian Revelation,' in the very last word, does what Dante saw become what Warren's protagonists see, through the arch (of sea cave and swimming stroke) that is the equivalent here of his pertugio, a framed, glorified, fragment of heaven" (92).

7. Other examples include the "time-polished facet" of the "sand-grain," in "Law of Attrition" (42, 44); "stones wise with suffering" and "the sea" that can "tell us of the blind depth of groan out yonder," in "If" (21, 34); and the "stream" with "murmurous wisdom there uttered," in "What Voice at Moth-Hour" (6).

8. An echo of "Bad Year, Bad War: A New Year's Card, 1969" (1969).

9. In *Warren after Audubon*, Millichap argues that "because 'New Dawn' was written for much different purposes, it somewhat disturbs the order and effect of *Altitudes and Extensions*" (155). Though this section may not fully adhere to Millichap's prevailing themes of age-work, life review, and transcendence, it perfectly exemplifies how Warren succeeds in shaping U.S. history into a highly interactive experience for readers through unique aesthetic forms.

WORKS CITED

Abrams, M. H. *Natural Supernaturalism*. New York: Norton, 1971.

Alighieri, Dante. *Divine Comedy*. Translated by Mark Musa. Indiana Critical Edition. Bloomington: Indiana University Press, 1995.

Altieri, Charles. "From Symbolist Thought to Immanence: The Ground of Postmodern American Poetics." *boundary 2* 1.3 (Spring 1973): 605–42.

Alvarez, A. "Robert Lowell in Conversation." In *Robert Lowell: Interviews and Memoirs*, edited by Jeffrey Meyers, 79–83. Ann Arbor: University of Michigan Press, 1988.

———. "A Talk with Robert Lowell." *Encounter* 24.2 (February 1965): 40–45.

Angus, Sylvia. "Randall Jarrell, Novelist: A Reconsideration." In *Critical Essays on Randall Jarrell*, edited by Suzanne Ferguson, 266–71. Boston: G. K. Hall & Co., 1983.

Axelrod, Steven Gould. "Lowell's *The Dolphin* as a 'Book of Life.'" *Contemporary Literature* 18.4 (Fall 1977): 458–74.

———. *Robert Lowell: Life and Art*. Princeton: Princeton University Press, 1978.

Bauer, Carlene. *Frances and Bernard*. New York: Houghton Mifflin Harcourt, 2012.

Bawer, Bruce. *The Middle Generation: The Lives and Poetry of Delmore Schwartz, Randall Jarrell, John Berryman, and Robert Lowell*. Hamden, Conn.: Archon Books, 1986.

Beck, Charlotte H. *The Fugitive Legacy: A Critical History*. Baton Rouge: Louisiana State University Press, 2001.

———. "Randall Jarrell and Robert Penn Warren: Fugitive Fugitives." *Southern Literary Journal* 17.1 (Fall 1984): 82–91.

Berryman, John. "On Poetry and the Age." In *Randall Jarrell, 1914–1965*, edited by Robert Lowell, Peter Taylor, and Robert Penn Warren, 10–13. New York: Farrar, Straus and Giroux, 1967.

Bewley, Marius. "The Complete Fate." In *Robert Lowell: A Portrait of the Artist in His Time*, edited by Michael London and Robert Boyers, 5–13. New York: David Lewis Publishers, 1970.

Bidart, Frank. "On 'Confessional Poetry.'" In *Robert Lowell: Collected Poems,* edited by Frank Bidart and David Gewanter, 997–1001. New York: Farrar, Straus and Giroux, 2003.

Bloom, Harold. *The Anxiety of Influence: A Theory of Poetry.* New York: Oxford University Press, 1997.

Blotner, Joseph. *Robert Penn Warren: A Biography.* New York: Random House, 1997.

Bly, Robert. "Robert Lowell's *For the Union Dead.*" In *Robert Lowell: A Portrait of the Artist in His Time,* edited by Michael London and Robert Boyers, 73–76. New York: David Lewis Publishers, 1970.

Bradbury, John M. *The Fugitives: A Critical Account.* Chapel Hill: University of North Carolina Press, 1958.

———. "Warren as Poet." In *Robert Penn Warren's* Brother to Dragons: *A Discussion,* edited by James A. Grimshaw Jr., 70–79. Baton Rouge: Louisiana State University Press, 1983.

Breslin, James E. B. *From Modern to Contemporary: American Poetry, 1945–1965.* Chicago: University of Chicago Press, 1984.

Brinkmeyer, Robert H., Jr. *The Fourth Ghost: White Southern Writers and European Fascism, 1930–1950.* Baton Rouge: Louisiana State University Press, 2009.

———. "The Southern Literary Renaissance." In *A Companion to the Literature and Culture of the American South,* edited by Richard Gray and Owen Robinson, 148–65. Malden, Mass.: Blackwell Publishing, 2004.

Brooks, Cleanth. *William Faulkner: The Yoknapatawpha Country.* 1963. Reprint, Baton Rouge: Louisiana State University Press, 1991.

———. *William Faulkner: Toward Yoknapatawpha and Beyond.* New Haven: Yale University Press, 1978.

Brooks, Cleanth, and Robert Penn Warren. "How Poems Come About: Intention and Meaning." In *Understanding Poetry,* 514–50. 3rd ed. New York: Holt, Rinehart and Winston, 1960.

———. "Robert Lowell: An Interview by Cleanth Brooks and Robert Penn Warren." In *Robert Lowell: Interviews and Memoirs,* edited by Jeffrey Meyers, 34–47. Ann Arbor: University of Michigan Press, 1988.

Brustein, Robert. "*The Old Glory.*" In *Robert Lowell: A Portrait of the Artist in His Time,* edited by Michael London and Robert Boyers, 77–79. New York: David Lewis Publisher, 1970.

Bryant, J. A., Jr. *Understanding Randall Jarrell.* Columbia: University of South Carolina Press, 1986.

Burt, John. "Afterword" to *Brother to Dragons: A Tale in Verse and Voices,* by Robert Penn Warren. MS.

———. *Robert Penn Warren and American Idealism.* New Haven: Yale University Press, 1988.

Burt, Stephen. *Randall Jarrell and His Age*. New York: Columbia University Press, 2002.

Byrne, Clare. "When Is an Agrarian Not an Agrarian? A Reading of Robert Penn Warren's 'The Briar Patch.'" *Robert Penn Warren Studies* 10 (2016), art. 2. https://digitalcommons.wku.edu/rpwstudies/vol10/iss1/2.

Clark, William Bedford. *The American Vision of Robert Penn Warren*. Lexington: University Press of Kentucky, 1991.

———. "A Meditation on Folk-History: The Dramatic Structure of Robert Penn Warren's 'The Ballad of Billie Potts.'" *American Literature* 49.4 (January 1978): 635–45.

———, ed. *Selected Letters of Robert Penn Warren*, vol. 1: *The Apprentice Years, 1924–1934*. Baton Rouge: Louisiana State University Press, 2000.

———, ed. *Selected Letters of Robert Penn Warren*, vol. 2: *The* Southern Review *Years, 1935–1942*. Baton Rouge: Louisiana State University Press, 2001.

Clark, William Bedford, Randy Hendricks, and James A. Perkins, eds. *Selected Letters of Robert Penn Warren*, vol. 4: *New Beginnings and New Directions, 1953–1968*. Baton Rouge: Louisiana State University Press, 2008.

———, eds. *Selected Letters of Robert Penn Warren*, vol. 5: *Backward Glances and New Visions, 1969–1979*. Baton Rouge: Louisiana State University Press, 2011.

Clements, A. L. "Sacramental Vision: The Poetry of Robert Penn Warren." *South Atlantic Bulletin* 43.4 (November 1978): 47–65.

Conkin, Paul K. *The Southern Agrarians*. Knoxville: University of Tennessee Press, 1988.

Cowan, Louise. *The Fugitive Group: A Literary History*. Baton Rouge: Louisiana State University Press, 1959.

Dickey, James. "Randall Jarrell." In *Randall Jarrell, 1914–1965*, edited by Robert Lowell, Peter Taylor, and Robert Penn Warren, 33–48. New York: Farrar, Straus and Giroux, 1967.

Dooley, Dennis M. "The Persona R.P.W. in Warren's *Brother to Dragons*." In *Robert Penn Warren's* Brother to Dragons: *A Discussion*, edited by James A. Grimshaw, 101–11. Baton Rouge: Louisiana State University Press, 1983.

Doreski, William. *The Years of Our Friendship: Robert Lowell and Allen Tate*. Jackson: University Press of Mississippi, 1990.

Doreski, William, and Robert Lowell. "'One Gallant Rush': The Writing of Robert Lowell's 'For the Union Dead.'" *New England Quarterly* 67.1 (March 1994): 30–45.

Duane, Daniel. "Of Herons, Hags and History: Rethinking Robert Penn Warren's *Audubon: A Vision*." *Southern Literary Journal* 27 (Fall 1994): 25–35.

Ellman, Richard, and Robert O'Clair, eds. *The Norton Anthology of Modern Poetry*. 2nd ed. New York: Norton, 1988.

Farrell, David. "Reminiscences: A Conversation with Robert Penn Warren." In *Talking with Robert Penn Warren,* edited by Floyd C. Watkins, John T. Hiers, and Mary Louise Weaks, 284–300. Athens: University of Georgia Press, 1990.

Faulkner, William. "Nobel Prize Acceptance Speech, 1950." In *Nobel Lectures, Literature, 1901–1967,* edited by Horst Frenz, 439–47. Amsterdam: Elsevier, 1969.

Fein, Richard J. *Robert Lowell.* New York: Twayne Publishers, 1970.

Ferguson, Suzanne. *Jarrell, Bishop, Lowell & Co.: Middle-Generation Poets in Context.* Knoxville: University of Tennessee Press, 2003.

——, ed. *Critical Essays on Randall Jarrell.* Boston: G. K. Hall & Co., 1983.

Fowler, Russell. "Randall Jarrell's 'Eland': A Key Motive and Technique in His Poetry." In *Critical Essays on Randall Jarrell,* edited by Suzanne Ferguson, 176–90. Boston: G. K. Hall & Co., 1983.

Frenz, Horst, ed. *Nobel Lectures: Literature, 1901–1967.* Amsterdam: Elsevier, 1969.

Gelpi, Albert. "The Reign of the Kingfisher: Robert Lowell's Prophetic Poetry." In *Robert Lowell: Essays on the Poetry,* edited by Steven Gould Axelrod and Helen Deese, 70–79. New York: Cambridge University Press, 1986.

Gilbert, Sandra M. "Mephistophilis in Maine: Rereading 'Skunk Hour.'" In *Robert Lowell: Essays on the Poetry,* edited by Steven Gould Axelrod and Helen Deese, 70–79. New York: Cambridge University Press, 1986.

Giroux, Robert, ed. *Robert Lowell: Collected Prose.* New York: Farrar, Straus and Giroux, 1987.

Graziano, Frank, ed. *Homage to Robert Penn Warren.* Durango, Colo.: Logbridge-Rhodes, 1981.

Grimshaw, James A., Jr. *Understanding Robert Penn Warren.* Columbia: University of South Carolina Press, 2001.

——, ed. *Robert Penn Warren's* Brother to Dragons: *A Discussion.* Baton Rouge: Louisiana State University Press, 1983.

Guerin, Wilfred L., Earle Labor, Lee Morgan, Jeanne C. Reesman, and John R. Willingham, eds. *A Handbook of Critical Approaches to Literature.* 4th ed. New York: Oxford University Press, 1999.

Hamilton, Ian. *Robert Lowell: A Biography.* New York: Random House, 1982.

Hamilton, Saskia, ed. *The Letters of Robert Lowell.* New York: Farrar, Straus and Giroux, 2005.

Hathcock, Nelson. "Standardizing Catastrophe: Randall Jarrell and the Bomb." In *Jarrell, Bishop, Lowell, & Co.: Middle-Generation Poets in Context,* edited by Suzanne Ferguson, 113–25. Knoxville: University of Tennessee Press, 2003.

Hendricks, Randy J. "Warren's Wandering Son." *South Atlantic Review* 59.2 (May 1994): 75–93.

Holder, Alan. "Going Back, Going Down, Breaking: *Day by Day.*" In *Robert Lowell: Essays on the Poetry,* edited by Steven Gould Axelrod and Helen Deese, 156–79. New York: Cambridge University Press, 1986.

Hook, Andrew. "Fugitives and Agrarians." In *A Companion to the Literature and Culture of the American South,* edited by Richard Gray and Owen Robinson, 32–44. Malden, Mass.: Blackwell, 2004.

Hummer, T. R. "Christ, Start Again: Robert Penn Warren, a Poet of the South?" In *The Legacy of Robert Penn Warren,* edited by David Madden, 32–44. Baton Rouge: Louisiana State University Press, 2000.

Jarman, Mark. "A Story of Deep Delight: The Life of Robert Penn Warren." *Hudson Review* 50.3 (Fall 1997): 435–43.

Jarrell, Mary. "The Group of Two." In *Randall Jarrell, 1914–1965,* edited by Robert Lowell, Peter Taylor, and Robert Penn Warren, 274–98. New York: Farrar, Straus and Giroux, 1967.

———, ed. *Randall Jarrell's Letters: An Autobiographical and Literary Selection.* 1985. Reprint, Charlottesville: University of Virginia Press, 2002.

Jarrell, Randall. *Blood for a Stranger.* New York: Harcourt, Brace and Co., 1942.

———. *The Complete Poems.* New York: Farrar, Straus and Giroux, 1969.

———. "The End of the Line." *Kipling, Auden & Co.: Essays and Reviews, 1935–1964,* 76–83. New York: Farrar, Straus and Giroux, 1980.

———. "From the Kingdom of Necessity." In *Robert Lowell: A Portrait of the Artist in His Time,* edited by Michael London and Robert Boyers, 19–27. New York: David Lewis Publisher, 1970.

———. "The Intellectual in America." *A Sad Heart at the Supermarket,* 3–15. Atheneum, N.Y.: Murray Printing Co., 1967.

———. "An Introduction to the Selected Poems of William Carlos Williams." *Poetry and the Age,* 237–49. Expanded ed. Gainesville: University Press of Florida, 2001.

———. *Kipling, Auden & Co.: Essays and Reviews, 1935–1964.* New York: Farrar, Straus and Giroux, 1980.

———. "Levels and Opposites: Structure in Poetry." *Georgia Review* 55.4–56.1 (Winter 2001–Spring 2002): 389–404.

———. "A Note on Poetry." *Kipling, Auden & Co.: Essays and Reviews, 1935–1964,* 47–51. New York: Farrar, Straus and Giroux, 1980.

———. "The Obscurity of the Poet." In *Randall Jarrell: No Other Book, Selected Essays,* edited by Brad Leithauser, 3–18. HarperCollins, 1999.

———. "On the Underside of the Stone." *Kipling, Auden & Co.: Essays and Reviews, 1935–1964,* 176–77. New York: Farrar, Straus and Giroux, 1980.

———. "The Other Frost." *Poetry and The Age,* 28–36. New York: Knopf, 1953.

———. *Pictures from an Institution.* Chicago: University of Chicago Press, 1954.

———. *Poetry and the Age.* Expanded ed. Gainesville: University Press of Florida, 2001.

———. "Poetry in War and Peace." *Kipling, Auden & Co.: Essays and Reviews, 1935–1964,* 127–34. New York: Farrar, Straus and Giroux, 1980.

———. "Poets." *Poetry and the Age,* 220–36. New York: Knopf, 1953.

———. "Reflections on Wallace Stevens." *Poetry and the Age*, 133–48. Expanded ed. Gainesville: University Press of Florida, 2001.

———. "A Sad Heart at the Supermarket." *A Sad Heart at the Supermarket*, 64–89. Atheneum, N.Y.: Murray Printing Co., 1967.

———. *A Sad Heart at the Supermarket*. Atheneum, N.Y.: Murray Printing Co., 1967.

———. "Some Lines from Whitman." *Poetry and the Age*, 112–32. Expanded ed. Gainesville: University Press of Florida, 2001.

———. "The Taste of the Age." *A Sad Heart at the Supermarket*, 16–42. Atheneum, N.Y.: Murray Printing Co., 1967.

———. "Three Books." *Poetry and the Age*, 250–65. New York: Knopf, 1953.

———. "The Woman at the Washington Zoo." In *Understanding Poetry*, edited by Cleanth Brooks and Robert Penn Warren, 538–48 3rd ed. New York: Farrar, Straus and Giroux, 1960.

Justus, James H. *The Achievement of Robert Penn Warren*. Baton Rouge: Louisiana State University Press, 1981.

Kirsch, Adam. *The Wounded Surgeon: Confessions and Transformations in Six American Poets*. New York: Norton, 2005.

Kramer, Hilton. "Robert Penn Warren and His Poetry: An Introduction." In *Homage to Robert Penn Warren*, edited by Frank Graziano, 9–16. Durango, Colo.: Logbridge-Rhodes, 1981.

Kramer, Lawrence. "Freud and the Skunks: Genre and Language in *Life Studies*." In *Robert Lowell: Essays on the Poetry*, edited by Steven Gould Axelrod and Helen Deese, 80–98. New York: Cambridge University Press, 1986.

Krell, David Farrell. *Of Memory, Reminiscence, and Writing on the Verge*. Bloomington: Indiana University Press, 1990.

Kreyling, Michael. *Inventing Southern Literature*. Jackson: University Press of Mississippi, 1998.

———. *The South That Wasn't There: Postsouthern Memory and History*. Baton Rouge: Louisiana State University Press, 2010.

Labrie, Ross. *The Catholic Imagination in American Literature*. Columbia: University of Missouri Press, 1997.

Leibowitz, Herbert. "Robert Lowell: Ancestral Voices." In *Robert Lowell: A Portrait of the Artist in His Time*, edited by Michael London and Robert Boyers, 199–221. New York: David Lewis Publisher, 1970.

Leithauser, Brad, ed. *Randall Jarrell: No Other Book, Selected Essays*. Michael di Capua Books, HarperCollins, 1999.

Logan, William. "Introduction." *Poetry and the Age*, by Randall Jarrell, xi–xx. Expanded ed. Gainesville: University Press of Florida, 2001.

London, Michael, and Robert Boyers, eds. *Robert Lowell: A Portrait of the Artist in His Time*. New York: David Lewis Publisher, 1970.

Longenbach, James. *Modern Poetry after Modernism*. New York: Oxford University Press, 1997.

Lowell, Robert. "After Enjoying Six or Seven Essays on Me." In *Robert Lowell: Collected Poems*, edited by Frank Bidart and David Gewanter, 989–93. New York: Farrar, Straus and Giroux, 2003.

———. "A Conversation with Ian Hamilton." In *Robert Lowell: Collected Prose*, edited by Robert Giroux, 267–90. New York: Farrar, Straus and Giroux, 1987.

———. "Dr. Williams." In *Robert Lowell: Collected Prose*, edited by Robert Giroux, 37–44. New York: Farrar, Straus and Giroux, 1987.

———. "Elizabeth Bishop's *North & South*." In *Robert Lowell: Collected Prose*, edited by Robert Giroux, 76–80. New York: Farrar, Straus and Giroux, 1987.

———. "Introduction to *Imitations*." In *Robert Lowell: Collected Poems*, edited by Frank Bidart and David Gewanter, 195–96. New York: Farrar, Straus and Giroux, 2003.

———. "John Crowe Ransom, 1888–1974." In *Robert Lowell: Collected Prose*, edited by Robert Giroux, 17–28. New York: Farrar, Straus and Giroux, 1987.

———. *The Mills of the Kavanaughs*. In *Robert Lowell: Collected Poems*, edited by Frank Bidart and David Gewanter, 71–107. New York: Farrar, Straus and Giroux, 2003.

———. "On *Imitations*." In *Robert Lowell: Collected Prose*, edited by Robert Giroux, 232–34. New York: Farrar, Straus and Giroux, 1987.

———. "On 'Skunk Hour.'" In *Robert Lowell: Collected Prose*, edited by Robert Giroux, 230–31. New York: Farrar, Straus and Giroux, 1987.

———. "On the Gettysburg Address." In *Robert Lowell: Collected Prose*, edited by Robert Giroux, 165–66. New York: Farrar, Straus and Giroux, 1987.

———. "On Translating Phèdre." In *Robert Lowell: Collected Prose*, edited by Robert Giroux, 230–31. New York: Farrar, Straus and Giroux, 1987.

———. "Randall Jarrell, 1914–1965." In *Robert Lowell: Collected Prose*, edited by Robert Giroux, 90–98. New York: Farrar, Straus and Giroux, 1987.

———. "Randall Jarrell's Wild Dogmatism." In *Critical Essays on Randall Jarrell*, edited by Suzanne Ferguson, 27–28. Boston: G. K. Hall & Co., 1983.

———. *Robert Lowell: Collected Poems*. Edited by Frank Bidart and David Gewanter. New York: Farrar, Straus and Giroux, 2003.

———. "Robert Penn Warren's *Brother to Dragons*." In *Robert Lowell: Collected Prose*, edited by Robert Giroux, 66–73. New York: Farrar, Straus and Giroux, 1987.

———. "To President Lyndon Johnson." In *Robert Lowell: Collected Prose*, edited by Robert Giroux, 370–71. New York: Farrar, Straus and Giroux, 1987.

———. "Visiting the Tates." In *Robert Lowell: Collected Prose*, edited by Robert Giroux, 58–60. New York: Farrar, Straus and Giroux, 1987.

Lowell, Robert, Peter Taylor, and Robert Penn Warren, eds. *Randall Jarrell, 1914–1965*. New York: Farrar, Straus and Giroux, 1967.

Madden, David, ed. *The Legacy of Robert Penn Warren.* Baton Rouge: Louisiana State University Press, 2000.

Mailer, Norman. "From *The Steps of the Pentagon.*" In *Robert Lowell: A Portrait of the Artist in His Time,* edited by Michael London and Robert Boyers, 199–221. New York: David Lewis Publisher, 1970.

Malone, Michael P. "Beyond the Last Frontier: Toward a New Approach to Western American History." *Western Historical Quarterly* 20.4 (November 1989): 409–27.

Mariani, Paul. *Lost Puritan: A Life of Robert Lowell.* New York: Norton, 1994.

Mazzaro, Jerome. *The Poetic Themes of Robert Lowell.* Ann Arbor: University of Michigan Press, 1965.

McCormick, John. "Falling Asleep over Grillparzer: An Interview with Robert Lowell." In *Robert Lowell: Interviews and Memoirs,* edited by Jeffrey Meyers, 23–32. Ann Arbor: University of Michigan Press, 1988.

Meyers, Jeffrey. *Manic Power: Robert Lowell and His Circle.* New York: Arbor House, 1987.

———, ed. *Robert Lowell: Interviews and Memoirs.* Ann Arbor: University of Michigan Press, 1988.

Michelson, Bruce. "Randall Jarrell and Robert Lowell: The Making of 'Lord Weary's Castle.'" *Contemporary Literature* 26.4 (Winter 1985): 402–25.

Miller, Mark D. "Faith in Good Works: The Salvation of Robert Penn Warren." *Mississippi Quarterly* 48.1 (Winter 1994–95): 57–71.

Millichap, Joseph R. *Robert Penn Warren after Audubon.* Baton Rouge: Louisiana State University Press, 2009.

Monroe, Keith. "Principle and Practice in the Criticism of Randall Jarrell." In *Critical Essays on Randall Jarrell,* edited by Suzanne Ferguson, 256–65. Boston: G. K. Hall & Co., 1983.

Moore, L. Hugh, Jr. *Robert Penn Warren and History: "The Big Myth We Live."* The Hague: Mouton, 1970.

Nelles, William. "Saving the State in Lowell's 'For the Union Dead.'" *American Literature* 55.4 (December 1983): 639–42.

New Oxford Annotated Bible. Edited by Michael D. Coogan. Oxford: Oxford University Press, 2007.

North, Michael. "The Public Monument and Public Poetry: Stevens, Berryman, and Lowell." *Contemporary Literature* 21.2 (Spring 1980): 267–85.

Olson, Charles. "Projective Verse." In *Twentieth-Century American Poetics: Poets on the Art of Poetry,* edited by Dana Gioia, David Mason, and Meg Schoerke, 174–81. New York: McGraw-Hill, 2004.

Ostriker, Alicia. "Beyond Confession: The Poetics of Postmodern Witness." In *After Confession: Poetry as Autobiography,* edited by Kate Sontag and David Graham, 317–32. St. Paul, Minn.: Graywolf Press, 2001.

Parini, Jay, ed. *The Columbia Anthology of American Poetry.* New York: Columbia University Press, 1995.

Partridge, Elise. "'But We Must Notice': Lowell's Harvard Classes on Berryman, Bishop, and Jarrell." In *Jarrell, Bishop, Lowell, & Co.: Middle-Generation Poets in Context,* edited by Suzanne Ferguson, 303–12. Knoxville: University of Tennessee Press, 2003.

Perkins, David. *A History of Modern Poetry: Modernism and After.* Cambridge: Harvard University Press, 1987.

Pritchard, William H. *Randall Jarrell: A Literary Life.* New York: Farrar, Straus and Giroux, 1990.

———. "Randall Jarrell: Poet-Critic." In *Critical Essays on Randall Jarrell,* edited by Suzanne Ferguson, 120–39. Boston: G. K. Hall & Co., 1983.

Procopiow, Norma. *Robert Lowell: The Poet and His Critics.* Chicago: American Library Association, 1984.

Quinn, Sister M. Bernetta. "Randall Jarrell: Landscapes of Life and *Life.*" In *Critical Essays on Randall Jarrell,* edited by Suzanne Ferguson, 203–27. Boston: G. K. Hall & Co., 1983.

———. "Warren and Jarrell: The Remembered Child." *Southern Literary Journal* 8.2 (Spring 1976): 24–40.

Ransom, John Crowe. "Constellation of Five Young Poets." In *Critical Essays on Randall Jarrell,* edited by Suzanne Ferguson, 15–16. Boston: G. K. Hall & Co., 1983.

———. "The Rugged Way of Genius." In *Randall Jarrell, 1914–1965,* edited by Robert Lowell, Peter Taylor, and Robert Penn Warren, 155–81. New York: Farrar, Straus and Giroux, 1967.

———. "Waste Lands." In *T. S. Eliot: The Critical Heritage,* edited by Grant, Michael, 172–79. London: TJ Press, Padstow, Cornwall, 1982.

Robert Lowell Papers, 1861–1976. Houghton Library. Papers, 1861–1976 (inclusive), 1935–70 (bulk). MS Am 1905 (2074). Houghton Library, Harvard University, Cambridge.

Romano, Joan A. "'For the Union Dead.'" In *Masterplots II: Christian Literature,* edited by John K. Roth, 650–53. Pasadena, Calif.: Salem Press, 2008.

Rosenthal, M. L. "Poetry as Confession." In *Robert Lowell: A Portrait of the Artist in His Time,* edited by Michael London and Robert Boyers, 44–57. New York: David Lewis Publisher, 1970.

Rudman, Mark. *Robert Lowell: An Introduction to the Poetry.* New York: Columbia University Press, 1983.

Runyon, Randolph Paul. *The Braided Dream: Robert Penn Warren's Late Poetry.* Lexington: University Press of Kentucky, 1990.

Ruppersburg, Hugh. *Robert Penn Warren and the American Imagination.* Athens: University of Georgia Press, 1990.

Sale, Richard B. "An Interview in New Haven with Robert Penn Warren." In *Critical Essays on Robert Penn Warren*, edited by William Bedford Clark, 81–110. Boston: G. K. Hall & Co., 1981.

Sarwar, Selim. "Robert Lowell: Scripting the Mid-Century Eschatology." *Journal of Modern Literature* 25.2 (Winter 2001–2): 114–30.

Szczesiul, Anthony. *Racial Politics and Robert Penn Warren's Poetry*. Gainseville: University Press of Florida, 2002.

Seidel, Frederick. "The Art of Poetry: Robert Lowell." In *Robert Lowell: Interviews and Memoirs*, edited by Jeffrey Meyers, 48–73. Ann Arbor: University of Michigan Press, 1988.

———. "An Interview with Robert Lowell." In *Robert Lowell, A Portrait of the Artist in His Time*, edited by Michael London and Robert Boyers, 261–91. New York: David Lewis Publisher, 1970.

Shapiro, Karl. "In the Forests of the Little People." In *Critical Essays on Randall Jarrell*, edited by Suzanne Ferguson, 30–31. Boston: G. K. Hall & Co., 1983.

Shifflett, Joan Romano. "'Reckoning' with America's Past: Robert Penn Warren's Later Poetry." In *RWP: An Annual of Robert Penn Warren Studies*, edited by Mark D. Miller, 63–82. Bowling Green: Western Kentucky University Press, 2012.

Simpson, Lewis P. "The Ferocity of Self: History and Consciousness in Southern Literature." *South Central Review* 1.1/2 (Spring–Summer 1984): 67–84.

Sisack, Christian. "Lowell's 'Confessional' Subjectivities and Compulsory Confessional Moments." In *Jarrell, Bishop, Lowell, & Co.: Middle- Generation Poets in Context*, edited by Suzanne Ferguson, 269–86. Knoxville: University of Tennessee Press, 2003.

Smith, Dave. "Warren's Ventriloquist: J. J. Audubon." In *The Legacy of Robert Penn Warren*, edited by David Madden, 111–29. Baton Rouge: Louisiana State University Press, 2000.

Smith, Ernest J. "'Approaching Our Maturity': The Dialectic of Engagement and Withdrawal in the Political Poetry of Berryman and Lowell." In *Jarrell, Bishop, Lowell, & Co.: Middle-Generation Poets in Context*, edited by Suzanne Ferguson, 287–302. Knoxville: University of Tennessee Press, 2003.

Stitt, Peter. "An Interview with Robert Penn Warren." In *Talking with Robert Penn Warren*, edited by Floyd C. Watkins, John T. Hiers, and Mary Louise Weaks, 233–46. Athens: University of Georgia Press, 1990.

Strandberg, Victor H. *A Colder Fire: The Poetry of Robert Penn Warren*. Lexington: University of Kentucky Press, 1965.

———. "Robert Penn Warren and the 'New Paradigm': A Case Study of the Birds." In *The Legacy of Robert Penn Warren*, edited by David Madden, 155–74. Baton Rouge: Louisiana State University Press, 2000.

———. "Warren's Osmosis." In *Critical Essays on Robert Penn Warren*, edited by William Bedford Clark, 122–36. Boston: G. K. Hall & Co., 1981.

Suarez, Ernest. "Writing the South." In *The Cambridge History of American Poetry*, edited by Alfred Bendixen and Stephen Burt, 795–822. New York: Cambridge University Press, 2015.

Tate, Allen. *The Forlorn Demon: Didactic and Critical Essays*. Chicago: Regnery, 1953.

———. "Introduction to *Land of Unlikeness*." In *Robert Lowell: Collected Poems*, edited by Frank Bidart and David Gewanter, 859–60. New York: Farrar, Straus and Giroux, 2003.

———. *The Man of Letters in the Modern World: Selected Essays, 1928–1955*. New York: Meridian Books, 1955.

Thurston, Michael. "Robert Lowell's Monumental Vision: History, Form, and the Cultural Work of Postwar American Lyric." *American Literary History* 12.½ (Spring–Summer 2000): 79–112.

Travisano, Thomas. *Midcentury Quartet: Bishop, Lowell, Jarrell, Berryman, and the Making of a Postmodern Aesthetic*. Charlottesville: University Press of Virginia, 1999.

Trethewey, Natasha. "'The World of Action and Liability': On Saying What Happens." U.S. Poet Laureate Address, May 14, 2014, Library of Congress, Washington, D.C.

Twelve Southerners. *I'll Take My Stand: The South and the Agrarian Tradition*. 1st ed. New York: Harper and Brothers, 1930.

Vendler, Helen. "The Complete Poems." In *Randall Jarrell, 1914–1965*, edited by Robert Lowell, Peter Taylor, and Robert Penn Warren, 37–41. New York: Farrar, Straus and Giroux, 1967.

Warren, Robert Penn. *Brother to Dragons: A Tale in Verse and Voices*. New York: Random House, 1953.

———. *Brother to Dragons: A Tale in Verse and Voices, A New Version*. Baton Rouge: Louisiana State University Press, 1979.

———. *The Collected Poems of Robert Penn Warren*. Edited by John Burt. Baton Rouge: Louisiana State University Press, 1998.

———. *Democracy and Poetry*. Cambridge: Harvard University Press, 1975.

———. "Ernest Hemingway." *New and Selected Essays*, 163–96. New York: Random House, 1989.

———. "Foreword." *Who Speaks for the Negro?* New York: Random House, 1965.

———. *The Legacy of the Civil War*. New York: Random House, 1961.

———. *New and Selected Essays*. New York: Random House, 1989.

———. "Notes on the Poetry of John Crowe Ransom at His Eightieth Birthday." *New and Selected Essays*, 303–32. New York: Random House, 1989.

———. "A Poem of Pure Imagination: An Experiment in Reading." *New and Selected Essays*, 336–423. New York: Random House, 1989.

———. "Pure and Impure Poetry." *New and Selected Essays*, 3–28. New York: Random House, 1989.

———. "A Self Interview." In *Talking with Robert Penn Warren,* edited by Floyd C. Watkins, John T. Hiers, and Mary Louise Weaks, 1–3. Athens: University of Georgia Press, 1990.

———. "The Themes of Robert Frost." *New and Selected Essays,* 285–301. New York: Random House, 1989.

———. "University Tribute." *Alumni News* (University of Greensboro) (1966): 19.

———. "The Use of the Past." *New and Selected Essays,* 29–54. New York: Random House, 1989.

———. *Who Speaks for the Negro?* New York: Random House, 1965.

Watson, Robert. "Randall Jarrell: The Last Years." In *Randall Jarrell, 1914–1965,* edited by Robert Lowell, Peter Taylor, and Robert Penn Warren, 257–73. New York: Farrar, Straus and Giroux, 1967.

Williams, William Carlos. "The Poem as a Field of Action." In *Twentieth-Century American Poetics, Poets on the Art of Poetry,* edited by Dana Gioia, David Mason, and Meg Schoerke, 51–57. New York: McGraw-Hill, 2004.

Wimsatt, W. K., and Monroe C. Beardsley. "The Intentional Fallacy." In *The Critical Tradition: Classic Texts and Contemporary Trends,* edited by David H. Richter, 749–56. 2nd ed. New York: Bedford / St. Martin's, 1998.

Woodward, C. Vann. *The Burden of Southern History.* 3rd ed. Baton Rouge: Louisiana State University Press, 1993.

Wormser, Baron. "Robert Lowell's 'For the Union Dead' and 'Political Poetry.'" *Manhattan Review* 12.2 (Fall–Winter 2006–7): 108–17.

INDEX